RECURRENT GENOCIDAL NIGHTMARES

The Hidden Side of Euro-African Encounters, 1450-1950

Tatah Mentan

I0084285

Langaa Research & Publishing CIG
Mankon, Bamenda

Publisher:

Langaa RPCIG

Langaa Research & Publishing Common Initiative Group
P.O. Box 902 Mankon
Bamenda
North West Region
Cameroon
Langaagrp@gmail.com
www.langaa-rpcig.net

Distributed in and outside N. America by African Books Collective
orders@africanbookscollective.com
www.africanbookscollective.com

ISBN-10: 9956-550-57-4

ISBN-13: 978-9956-550-57-9

© Tatah Mentan 2019

All rights reserved.

No part of this book may be reproduced or transmitted in any form or by any
means, mechanical or electronic, including photocopying and recording, or be
stored in any information storage or retrieval system, without written permission
from the publisher

Dedication

To

Victims of Genocide, Politicide, Ecocide, Dmocide, Politicide and

Linguicide in Africa and Beyond.

Table of Contents

Acknowledgement

This book is intended primarily for students of historical sociology, scholars and policy makers grappling with human atrocities in historical perspective. I am heavily indebted to Ashley Riley Sousa, History Department, Yale University: "'They will be hunted down like wild beasts and destroyed!': A Comparative Study of Genocide in California and Tasmania," Journal of Genocide Research 6:2 (June 2004), pp.193-209; Arendt, H. (1964) *Eichmann in Jerusalem: A Report on the Banality of Evil*. New York: Viking; Benjamin Madley, "From Africa to Auschwitz" (European History Quarterly, 35:3 (2005), pp. 429-64); Genocide and Literature: The Herero-/Nama-Uprising in German colonial literature, by Jörg Wassink, M.A. (2004); Lemkin, R. (1944) *Axis Rule in Occupied Europe*. Washington DC: Carnegie Endowment for International Peace. Their works invaluably inspired this study.

Chapter One

Introduction:
Understanding the Unthinkable

On Thursday April 20, 2017, the 678th Peace and Security Council of the African Union Meeting on preventing ideology of genocide in Africa issued a Communique recalling (**Annexture I**):

> ... the horror of the 1994 genocide against the Tutsi in Rwanda and reiterates its commitment to prevent the recurrence of similar mass atrocities, hate crime and ideologies of genocides throughout the African continent. In this context, Council underlines the imperative of early and appropriate responses to credible early warning signs of situations that, if not addressed in a timely and effective manner, could lead to potential genocides. In the same context, Council also underlines the importance of use of clear analysis and proper terminology in order to avoid falling into the problem of denials.

Genocide is not new to Africa. Unlike most twentieth-century cases of premeditated mass killing, the African slave trade was not undertaken by a single political force or military entity during the course of a few months or years. The transatlantic slave trade lasted for 400 years, from the 1450s to the 1860s, as a series of exchanges of captives reaching from the interior of sub-Saharan Africa to final purchasers in the Americas. It has been estimated that in the Atlantic slave trade, up to 12 million Africans were loaded and transported across the ocean under dreadful conditions. About 2 million victims died on the Atlantic voyage (the dreaded "Middle Passage") and in the first year in the Americas.

"Mass Genocides in Mighty Africa"[1] was a screaming headline of a news story in 1994. Genocide by definition is the deliberate killing of a large group of people, usually those of an ethic group or religion. There are many examples of genocides throughout history but when someone says genocide most people think of two immediately, those

---

[1] http://www.history.com/topics/rwandan-genocide

1

being the Holocaust and the Rwandan Genocide. These are two examples of horrible deeds done by disgusting people who put others down due to religion or for subtle differences like appearance and colour. The holocaust is much more popular than the Rwandan genocide however thee Rwandan genocide is a very horrific event. It was the slaughter of over 800,000 Tutsi by the hands of their enemy the Hutu. The hatred between the two groups started to heat up when the Belgian colonists came to their country and deemed Tutsi's superior to the Hutu based on irrelevant measurements.

100 days of hell: Rwanda's 1994

Skulls of victims of the Ntarama massacre during the 1994 genocide are lined in the Genocide Memorial Site church of Ntarama, in Nyamata 27 February 2004. In the Bugesera province, where the small town of Nyamata is located, the 1994 Rwandan genocide was particularly brutal. Among the 59.000 Tutsis who lived in the province, 50.000 were killed during the genocide, and among them 10.000 were slain in the church. AFP PHOTO/GIANLUIGI GUERCIA (Photo credit should read GIANLUIGI GUERCIA/AFP/Getty Images).

3 May 1994: Refugees wait for relief food from the Red Cross near the border between Rwanda and Tanzania Reuters

5 May 1994: Displaced Rwandans collect water from a polluted lake near a refugee camp in Benako, Tanzania Gerard Julien/AFP

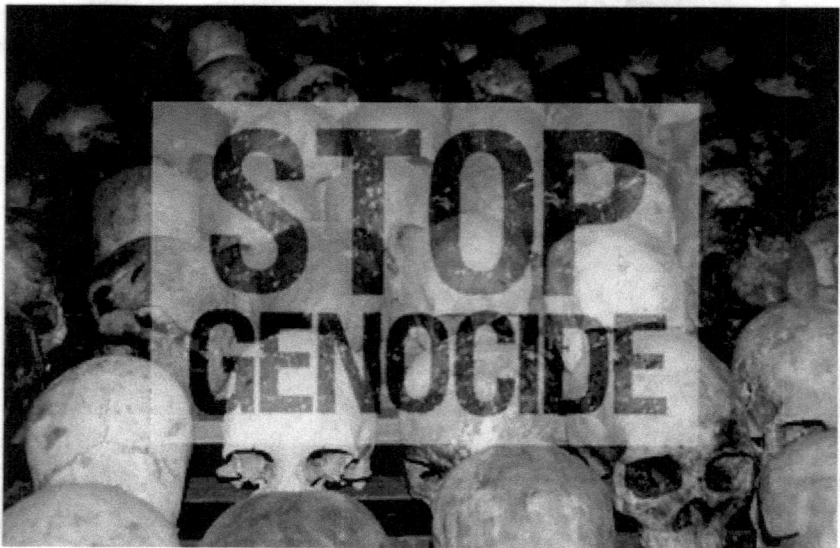

On January 29, 2016, Gregory Stanton wrote in the Mail and Guardian, South Africa, that:

> From Armenia and the Nazi Holocaust to the Soviet Gulag, the Chinese Cultural Revolution, Biafra, Cambodia, Rwanda and Darfur, people have been slaughtered in their millions simply because of race,

religion or social class. Now we have the International Criminal Court and, for the past decade, genocide has been less common.

"But, today in Africa, I see worrying signs of its return. The discovery of mass graves in Burundi this month is not just a sign that people have been murdered. It is also a garland of shame around the African Union, which did nothing when the warnings sounded for months that mass killing was about to recur."

"In Nigeria, Boko Haram has murdered thousands. In Libya, the Islamic State is establishing strongholds. The government of Sudan has killed more than three million of its own people, and continues a genocide in Darfur, the Blue Nile and South Kordofan. But African governments allow Sudan's dictator to travel with impunity."

"South Sudan is gripped by a civil war between the Dinka and the Nuer, and could see thousands more lives sacrificed on the altar of political power. How do we make sure there's not a return to the horror of Rwanda or Biafra"?

There is ongoing genocide in Cameroon. People are being murdered in their thousands, others burnt to death in their sleep, while other are maimed with impunity. Looting, torture, and raping are merely referred to as maintaining "law and order", defending the "territorial integrity of the state", "carnage", and "targeted killing."

But, the United Nations and the African Union avoid taking forceful, preventive action by calling the massacres, "crimes against humanity." The term that demands action – genocide – has been narrowed by international lawyers to cases of wholesale murder like the Holocaust, Cambodia, Guatemala, Rwanda or Darfur.

When Popes Become Penitents: Slavery, Colonialism & the Holocaust

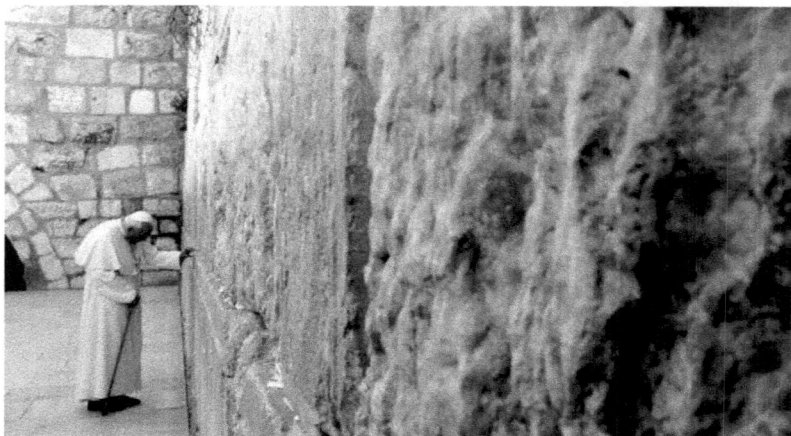

On March 26, 2000, Pope John Paul II visited the Western Wall in the Old City of Jerusalem asking for Christian forgiveness. (Credit: Jerome Delay/AP Photo)

In 1993, John Paul continued to address the church's behaviour in past centuries by issuing an apology for the church's role in the African slave trade. Similarly to Francis' 2015 apology to indigenous people in the Americas regarding the Catholic Church's role in colonialism, this gesture addressed something that happened long ago but continues to negatively affect communities today.

Rwandan genocide: Pope Francis asks forgiveness for Church failings

Papal apologies for the Catholic Church's behaviour are a relatively recent phenomenon. Pope John Paul II, who held the title between 1979 and 2005, was the first to issue them. His successor, Benedict XVI, timidly followed that precedent; but it is Pope Francis who has turned the symbolic apology into something of a masterstroke, helping to shift the church's atonement from a focus on historical wrongs to accepting moral responsibility for more current events.

Rwanda's President Paul Kagame greets Pope Francis during a private meeting at the Vatican March 20, 2017. Photo courtesy of REUTERS/Tony Gentile

At a meeting with Rwandan President Paul Kagame, Pope Francis said on Monday (March 20) that priests and Roman Catholic faithful had taken part in the slaughter of some 800,000 people from the ethnic Tutsi minority as well as moderates from the Hutu majority.

"(The pope) implored anew God's forgiveness for the sins and failings of the Church and its members, among whom priests, and religious men and women who succumbed to hatred and violence," the Vatican said in a statement.

An official Rwandan statement repeated the government's long-standing accusation of Catholic complicity in the massacres: "Today, genocide denial and trivialization continue to flourish in certain groups within the Church and genocide suspects have been shielded from justice within Catholic institutions," said a government statement.

Christian Struggles with Biblical Accounts of Genocide and "Holy War"

How do we explain God's command to slaughter the Canaanites in the Old Testament? Though a Christian, I have serious issues with the doctrine of scriptural infallibility, especially where the Old Testament is concerned. I am particularly disturbed by the accounts of divinely authorized genocide and "Holy War" recorded in Numbers, Deuteronomy, and Joshua. When the Israelites captured Jericho, the Bible says that "they utterly destroyed all that was in the city, both man and woman, young and old, ox and sheep and donkey, with the edge of the sword" (Joshua 6:20-21). How could a gracious, loving God sanction this kind of slaughter? And how does all this fit in with the New Testament's message of love, compassion, and forgiveness for enemies?

At first glance, it *does* seem almost impossible to reconcile a passage like Joshua 6:20-21 with Jesus' teachings about love for enemies, turning the other cheek, and laying down the sword. This issue isn't easy to resolve. But it *can* be done if we are willing to dig a little deeper. Let's take a closer look. Jesus preached a God of love and forgiveness. No doubt about that. But we have to remember that

8

there was another side to His teaching. He never shied away from confronting His hearers with the terrible reality of God's righteousness. Judgment and wrath were common themes with Him. As a matter of fact, He had more to say about hellfire and damnation than almost any other biblical concept. Matthew 13:41-42 is a good example: "The Son of Man will send out His angels, and they will gather out of His kingdom all things that offend, and those who practice lawlessness, and will cast them into the furnace of fire. There will be weeping and gnashing of teeth." Clearly, the God of Jesus is a God who does not tolerate sin and who is capable of executing fierce judgment upon the wicked.

This, generally speaking, is how Christian theologians have interpreted the Old Testament "ban" (Hebrew *cherem*). This term refers to God's strict commandment to grant the heathen no quarter, to take neither prisoners nor spoil, but to destroy everything found in the cities of their enemies. Repulsive as it sounds to us today, this ruthless brand of warfare was not technically "genocide." Not in the modern sense of the term. According to most biblical scholars, it was actually an expression of God's *judgment* upon the Canaanites.

To say this another way, it was neither Joshua nor Moses but *the Lord Himself* who put the idolatrous nations of the Promised Land to the sword. This is perfectly legitimate from a strictly theological point of view. After all, God is the One who gives life. Accordingly, He also has the authority to take it away. His sentence was simply carried out by the agency of His chosen people, Israel. To quote one commentator, "The Canaanite civilization was so totally corrupt that coexisting with them would have been a serious threat to the survival and spiritual welfare of the Hebrew nation. Israel here is God's instrument of judgment against those who refuse to honour Him."

In the New Testament, we move into an era in which this type of judgment becomes unthinkable. Why? Jesus tells us in John 18:36: "My kingdom is not of this world. If My kingdom were of this world, My servants would fight, so that I should not be delivered to the Jews; but now My kingdom is not from here" (John 18:36).

The implication is plain. God no longer executes His judgment by means of the weapons of worldly soldiers. Instead, He punishes His enemies with the "sword of the Spirit", which is His Word (Ephesians 6:17). That judgment will receive its final and ultimate expression when the true Bearer of the sword, Jesus Himself, the King of Kings and Lord of Lords, returns to "strike the nations." At that time He will "tread the winepress of the fierceness and wrath of Almighty God" (see Revelation 19:11-16). Meanwhile, His followers are instructed to conduct themselves with love, humility, and forbearance toward unbelievers. As Christians, we are called to "live peaceably with all men", and to "give place to wrath: for it is written, 'Vengeance is mine, I will repay', says the Lord" (Romans 12:18, 19).

What all this demonstrates is that Christians have held diverse views towards violence and non-violence through time. Currently and historically there have been four views and practices within Christianity toward violence and war: non-resistance, Christian pacifism, Just war theory, and the Crusade-Holy or preventive war (*Clouse, 1986:12-22*). Many readers of the Bible are troubled by passages in the Hebrew Bible/Old Testament that portray God behaving violently and commanding others to do likewise.

Historical hindsight instructs us that in the fourth century, Christianity became the official religion of the Roman Empire, and the Church came increasingly to dominate the Western world. As it did so, it put theory into practice and Jews began to lose the civil rights that had been theirs under Roman law. They were not allowed to hold public office (Synod of Claremont, 535 C.E.); they were forbidden to have Christian servants or slaves (538), which effectively excluded them from agriculture; their books were burned (681); they were taxed to support the Church (1078); they were forced to wear a badge on their clothing (1215); they were forced into ghettos (1267); and they were denied university degrees (1434). In addition to these official decrees of Church synods and councils, there were unofficial persecutions, in which many Jews lost their lives; forced "conversions"; and mass expulsions from one country after another. Antisemitism became a common feature of all of Western culture and history, and it did so frequently using the continuing theological anti-Judaism of the Christian church. When Hitler said that he was only putting into effect what the Church had always taught, he was quite correct, until his decision to kill every Jew in Europe.

In the light of the Holocaust, the churches have begun to reverse their ancient tradition of anti-Judaism. Beginning with the Second Vatican Council, the Roman Catholic Church has repudiated its charge of deicide and acknowledged the continuing validity of God's covenant with the Jewish people. With increasing clarity, Church statements, both Protestant and Catholic, European and American, have denounced Antisemitism and repudiated the tradition of contempt for Jews and Judaism. Whether the Church at the grass roots level will succeed in making this about face remains to be seen. For six million Jews, the turn has come much too late, but for the future of the Jewish people, this reversal of "the teaching of contempt" may be of no small consequence, for it begins to get at the primary root of Antisemitism. That root, however, is deeply embedded in the theology of the Church and eliminating it will be no easy matter. It will require of the Church a new reading of its own sacred texts and a new understanding of its own identity. Until that happens at the level of the ordinary Christian, the theological roots of Antisemitism will not be dead.

Throughout its history, organized Christianity has therefore been ambiguous, to say the least. It's been wielded as a sword in the hands of empires; used to legitimize wars, genocide, and a murderous exploitation of the commons as well as the neighbour it urges us to love as ourselves. And in the modern era, it's been a potent political tool by parties, political strategists, and politicians themselves.

And Today?

The twenty-first century faces four grave challenges: an increasing scarcity of water, food, and fuel; increasing population growth, particularly in the developing world and in those very areas of greatest resource scarcity; the increasing spread of ever-more-lethal weapons ; and a growing population of angry, poor, disenfranchised and radicalized youth who feel they have nothing to lose through violence. These challenges suggest that genocide may become even more frequent

The term "genocide" did not exist before 1944. It is a very specific term, referring to violent crimes committed against groups with the intent to destroy the existence of the group. This book therefore aims at describing the state of recurrent genocidal nightmares in Africa, its historicisation, and causation, placing genocide cases into their historical context, and genocide in the world capitalist system today.

Proclaimed democratic and free market states in Africa have contributed to the murderous dynamic quite as much as authoritarian/totalitarian regimes and states with command or *dirigiste* economies. This existential situation compels us to broadly concur with structuralist and materialist interpretations of genocide. The reason is that in reality, all explanations eschew monocausality and embrace varying contexts and contingencies, just as even the most contingent or, again, the most structural explanations cannot account for anything without some reference to ideology and human agency. **Is** capitalism **not** genocide? What else would you call a policy whereby trillions of dollars are spent to bail out the banking system, trillions of dollars are spent on war, and people are deliberately starved by a combination of financial policy and food cartel machinations? It is a decidedly anti-human policy, intended to restore what the London-centred international financial oligarchy sees as the natural order of things: itself on top, and everyone else expendable. The greatest asset any society has is the power of reason of individual human minds, for it is from those minds that the scientific and technological discoveries are made which increase the productive power of human labour. Societies which nurture this process succeed, and societies which do not, fail. A nation-state organized around these concepts is the most powerful, and most modern, form of political structure possible. All I seek in this book is to open up the debate about the relationship between individual acts of genocide and the wider political economy and norms of the African historical worlds in which they occur, whether or not those worlds are coextensive with the actual globe.

For instance, the aim of globalization is to ensure the domination over the planet of the Anglo-Dutch Liberal system. That is to be accomplished by the bankers and the Four Horsemen of the Apocalypse, using methods of which the evil Lord Bertrand Russell said, they might be unpleasant, but what of it. Or, as Dick Cheney might put it: So what? Their goal is a dramatic reduction in global population, through a combination of famine, disease, war, and financial warfare. This effectively destroys a nation's ability to develop into a sovereign nation capable of resisting imperial designs.

12

Examples abound. Wars are very efficient ways of killing large numbers of people, as we have seen in several African countries, Cambodia under the Khmer Rouge, the former Yugoslavia, and in western Asia, to name just a few.

What, indeed, is genocide?

Genocide, the intentional destruction of a specific group, is an important subject for scholars of state crimes, yet it remains underexplored within the discipline. In light of the increasing pervasiveness of genocide in the twentieth century, it is perhaps surprising that genocide studies have tended to be the remit of historians and theologians. Social scientists rarely turned their attention to the study of this particular type of criminality until the 1970s (Fein, 1979; Horowitz, 1982:3; Bauman, 1989:3, Fein 1993:5; Fein, 2002:75). Hirsch (1995: 75) suggests that even today sociological attention to this topic has at best grown from almost nonexistent to scarcely existent.

There is no indication as to where or when the first genocide occurred, the evidence from antiquity being contradictory, ambiguous or missing. Kuper (1981) argued the word is new, the crime ancient, making reference to horrifying genocidal massacres in the eighth and seventh centuries BC in the Assyrian empire in addition to accounts of the many genocidal conflicts in the Bible and in the chronicles of Greek and Roman historians.

In a 1941 BBC radio broadcast, the British Prime Minister, Winston Churchill, described the actions of the Nazis in Europe as a crime without a name (Elder, 2005: 470). Two years later, Raphael Lemkin, the Polish Jewish specialist in international law, created the neologism of genocide to express the use or a user of deliberate, systematic measures such as killing, bodily or mental injury, unliveable conditions, and prevention of births, calculated to bring about the extermination of a racial, political, or cultural group or to destroy the language, religion, or culture of a group (Elder, 2005: 469). In developing this new term, Lemkin combined the Greek word genos (race, tribe) and the Latin word cide (killing). Lemkin became the founding figure of the United Nations Genocide Convention (UNGC).

13

Why Does Genocide Matter?

This is a fair question. Genocide and the forces that conduct and benefit from it, often wear many masks and disguises. Often genocide is conducted under such banners and rationales as: "missionary zeal and evangelism"; "making the world safe for democracy"; "alliance and treaty responsibilities"; "cultural diffusion"; "natural and inexorable processes of globalization of market forces and cultures"; "Manifest Destiny"; "Lebensraum"; "Haaretz Israel"; "traditional ethnic rivalries"; and other masks, disguises and rationales are possible. Behind these masks, and underneath these surface rationales, certain economic and non-economic interests, imperatives, power structures, institutions, etc. can be shown to be common to almost all forms and cases of genocide—past and present—especially if one defines genocide, as it is defined in international law, in Article II of the 1948 UN Convention on the Punishment and Prevention of the Crime of Genocide.

Some of the common denominators, and real motives and reasons underlying various genocides, as revealed in the internal documents and utterances of those conducting genocide, include: quests for relatively secure and cheap supplies of land, labour, capital and natural resources; imperatives to smash traditional non-market institutions and value systems seen to be potentially antagonistic to market-based interests, imperatives, institutions and value systems; quests for expanding and secure markets and market shares; necessary consequences of social systems engineering campaigns; quests for imperial hegemony; antagonistic and clashing ideologies and paradigms; crushing "external enemies" to forge "domestic unity"; etc.

For example, the number of people killed in Darfur, Sudan, so far is modest in global terms: estimates range from 200,000 to more than 500,000. In contrast, four million people have died since 1998 because of the fighting in Congo, the most lethal conflict since World War II. In addition, malaria annually kills one million to three million people—meaning that three years' deaths in Darfur are within the margin of error of the annual global toll from malaria. So, yes, you can make an argument that Darfur is simply one of many tragedies and that it would be more cost-effective to save lives by tackling diarrhoea, measles and malaria.

But, I don't buy that argument at all. We have a moral compass within us, and its needle is moved not only by human suffering but also by human evil. That's what makes genocide special—not just the number of deaths but the government policy behind them. And that in turn is why stopping genocide should be an even higher priority than saving lives from AIDS or malaria. Even the Holocaust amounted to only 10 percent of World War II casualties and cost far fewer lives than the AIDS epidemic. But the Holocaust evokes special revulsion because it wasn't just tragic but also monstrous, and that's why we read Anne Frank and Elie Wiesel. Teenage girls still die all the time, and little boys still starve and lose their parents—but when this arises from genocide, the horror resonates with all humans.

Or it should. But for whatever reason, Sudan's decision to kill people on the basis of tribe and skin colour has aroused mostly yawns around the globe. Now Sudan is raising the stakes by starting a new military offensive in Darfur—and by eliminating witnesses. The government charged Paul Salopek, an ace Chicago Tribune correspondent, with espionage in an effort to keep foreign reporters away (on Saturday it released him after a month in prison). And even African Union peacekeepers may be forced out of Darfur by the end of this month. Twelve aid workers have been killed since May — more than in the previous three years. These killings are forcing aid groups to pull back, and the U.N. warns that if the humanitarian operation collapses, the result will be "hundreds of thousands of deaths." If all foreign witnesses are pushed out, the calamity is barely imaginable.

We urgently need U.N. peacekeepers, even over Sudan's objections. If Sudan sees them coming, it will hurriedly consent. Should the U.S. also impose a no-fly zone from Chad and work with France to keep Chad and the Central African Republic from collapsing into this maelstrom? President Bush showed an important flash of leadership on Darfur, but fell quiet again. He could appoint a special envoy for Darfur and use his bully pulpit to put genocide on the international agenda —for starters, by employing his speech to the U.N. General Assembly to remind the world of the children being tossed onto bonfires in Sudan. He could also announce that the U.S. will choose candidates to support for U.N. secretary general based in part on their positions on the genocide. The same could be done for the "targeted killing" of people from the former United Nations Trust Territory called Southern Cameroons (Ambazonia).

Genocide Matters

An Oxford Handbook of Genocide Studies is easily justified. 'Genocide' is unfortunately ubiquitous, all too often literally in the attempted destruction of human groups, but also rhetorically in the form of a word that is at once universally known and widely invoked—perhaps because it is frequently misunderstood. From its introduction to the international public sphere with the United Nations General Assembly resolution on genocide in 1946, the term was seized upon by all sides to name the criminality of their persecution.

This criminality of genocide makes it impossible to imagine what Raphael Lemkin would be thinking and doing if he were alive today. He dedicated his life to stopping mass violence against people based on their identities and to holding those who were responsible accountable for their crimes. As a young man, he studied past slaughters, including pogroms against Jews, and he immersed himself in understanding the mass murder of the Armenians by the Turkish state, the failure to stop it, and to punish those who were responsible for it. In the midst of his efforts to draw attention to these issues, he lost 49 family members, including his parents, in the Holocaust. They died in the Warsaw ghetto, in concentration camps, and in the death marches. Lemkin was responsible for coining the word genocide, which was used at the Nuremberg Trials. It became the basis of the newly established United Nations December 9, 1948, Convention on the Prevention and Punishment of Genocide. But in the wake of the Convention, genocide continues to happen—from Rwanda to Bosnia to Cambodia. In recent months, Syria and Iraq have been added to that list.

Lemkin himself was convinced that genocide had always been a part of the human experience, and the UN Convention on the Prevention and Punishment of Genocide explicitly refers to its transhistorical character. What certainly have changed over time are the social cleavages on which genocide-like violence is perpetrated. It is in the enumeration of potential victim groups on select grounds of communal identity that the specifically mid-twentieth century context of the Genocide Convention is exposed, whatever the historical allusions of the document. To what extent we can use the Convention's terms concerning 'ethnic', 'national', and 'religious' groups (not to mention 'racial' [sic] groups) for different times in human history is open to a contestation that varies in intensity depending upon the period in question.

The decision to exterminate a group of people is the extreme end of a continuum that lies beyond proclamations that they cannot live, worship, or love as they see fit and beyond decisions to ghettosize them or force them out of your country. In his landmark work on the Holocaust, Raul Hilberg writes of this continuum in the destruction of the European Jews: "The missionaries of Christianity had said in effect: You have no right to live among us as Jews. The secular rulers who followed had proclaimed: You have no right to live among us. The German Nazis at last decreed: You have no right to live."

In the twentieth century, this form of destruction would come to be called "genocide," but it is not a modern phenomenon. The human reality of genocide predated its semantic taxonomy. As Leo Kuper, one of the pioneers in genocide studies, said, "The word is new, the concept is ancient." From the Hittites to the Greeks to the Romans to the Mongols to the Albigensian Crusades to the witch hunts in Europe to colonial destructions of indigenous peoples throughout the world, human history has been replete with cases of mass destruction. In modern times, however, we have gotten very good—in a morally inverted sense of the word—at committing genocide. Aptly dubbed the "Age of Genocide," the past century saw a massive scale of systematic and intentional mass murder coupled with an unprecedented efficiency of the mechanisms and techniques of mass destruction. Genocidal death rates worldwide—7,700 per 100,000—were an eight-fold increase over the previous 69 centuries. On the historical heels of the physical and cultural genocide of North American indigenous peoples during the nineteenth century, the twentieth century writhed from the near- complete annihilation of the Hereros by the Germans in Southwest Africa in 1904; to the brutal assault on the Armenian population by the Turks between 1915 and 1932; to the implementation of Soviet manmade famine against the Ukrainian Kulaks in 1932–1933 that left several million peasants starving to death; to the extermination of two-thirds of Europe's Jews during the Holocaust of 1939–1945; to the massacre of approximately half a million people in Indonesia in 1965–1966; to genocide or mass killings in Bangladesh (1971), Burundi (1972), Cambodia (1975–1979), East Timor (1975–1979), Argentina (1976–1983), Guatemala (1980s–1990s), Sri Lanka (1983–2009), Iraq (1987–1988), the former Yugoslavia (1992–1995), and Rwanda (1994).

Although this list is not exhaustive, it certainly suggests the universality of the potential—perhaps even the ubiquity of the reality—for genocide. It is clear that genocide cannot be confined to one culture, place, or time in modern history. Even the most restrictive of definitions estimates that at least 60 million men, women, and children were victims of genocide and mass killing in the past century alone. On the upper end, political scientist Rudolph Rummel argues that close to 170 million civilians were done to death by their own governments in the twentieth century. Even for those who survive, genocide is a collective trauma, a redefining destruction that shatters their assumptive world and transforms societies for generations.

Unfortunately, the first decades of the twenty-first century have brought little light to the darkness as a variety of international watch lists suggest that close to 20 countries are currently "at risk" for genocide. As former U.S. Secretary of State Hillary Clinton suggested, the "wood is stacked" in those countries and we cannot passively wait for the "match to be struck." Because once the firestorm of genocide is at full blaze, history shows us that death comes in conflagrations of hundreds of thousands and the options for responding are difficult and costly. To borrow the words of Kofi Annan, former Secretary-General of the United Nations, genocide and other large- scale attacks on civilians are "problems without passports." That is, they are global problems that transcend not only countries and regions, but the capabilities and resources of any one nation or sector. In many regards, genocide can take rightful claim as the most pressing human rights problem of the twenty-first century.

This blog is grounded in the belief that the world as it is now is not the world, as it has to be. As ubiquitous as genocide seems, it is a human problem and, as such, has a human solution. This is not a quixotic utopian statement about human perfectibility. It simply is a statement that we can, at least in large part, undo a problem that we have created. Genocide is not a problem that came to us from another world or was ingrained in our behavioural genetic repertoire. At its root, genocide happens because we choose to see a people rather than individual people and then we choose to kill those people in large numbers and over an extended period of time. In the midst of that bad news, the good news is that we can make another choice; we can find constructive, rather than destructive, ways to live with our diverse social identities.

Given contending ideologies, cleavages, and logics of genocide, does it therefore make sense to delineate 'modern' from 'premodern' genocide in the same way one might crudely delineate modern from premodern society? The answer depends upon how one understands the protean concept 'modernity'. An understanding that leans particularly upon modernity's material (economic and technical) aspects would of course allow that the development of surveillance, bureaucracy, central state strength, weaponry, etc., would create greater facility to pursue and murder 'enemies', and would equally allow that the increasing contact between different peoples and the more intensive and extensive exploitation of resources might provoke more and increasingly intense intergroup conflicts, but distinctions along these lines between modern and premodern are of dimension rather than fundamental principle.

Why should we study genocide in Africa?

a. Exploring the history of genocide in Africa can provide insights into the origins of social behaviours which lead up to mass murder: i.e.: prejudices; stereotypes; racisms; religious hatreds; ethnic hatreds and discriminations which, if tolerated as acceptable within a group can, in certain situations, lead up to and result in genocide.

b. To attempt to understand why genocide is perpetrated: Genocide has been perpetrated at least as long as humans have been recording history. It remains a social pathology which continues to claim victims to the present day. To explore "why" genocide has occurred can elucidate the conditions of economy, political groups and social customs which could have contributed to the polarization of different groups within a region. One can further determine the roles that natural resources, despotism, ideology or retribution play in forming the catalysts of mass destruction of groups.

c. A course of study in genocide can initiate a deeper understanding of human rights and their violations around the world: This course of study can also initiate understanding of personal responsibilities and the dangers of remaining silent; apathetic or indifferent to the suffering or witnessing of violence to others.

d. Study of the history of genocide can be understood within the context of international law and how it has evolved in the past centuries: Study of the development of international criminal law and human rights can further the growth of international institutions dedicated to prevention and punishment of these crimes against humanity.

e. Prevention through education: Every human being has the potential to violate another person. Grappling with "why" genocide occurs enables insightful perspective, and comparative analysis of prejudicial behaviours around the world and how the individual participates either as a perpetrator; bystander or victim.

Genocide and the Nation-State—Agency

The history of the world has always been punctuated by cycles of violence, regardless of time, region or race. Genocide, which is one of the worst forms of violence, has always led to horrific socio-economic and environmental impacts. The last decade of the 20th century was the most turbulent Rwanda has ever experienced in its history. The country was ravaged by civil war, genocide, mass migrations, economic crisis, diseases, return of refugees and environmental destruction. Rwandan families were affected by and are still dealing with impacts such as death, disease, disability, poverty, loss of dignity and imprisonment.

Historically, genocide always takes place in wartime. It followed revolutions in which the limits of the old social order were shattered. Indeed, genocides were committed against ethno-religious minorities which while socially and economically progressive were looked down upon by those in power, super nationalism and racism as well as religious fundamentalism played major roles in instituting genocide, and dictatorial parties were in charge of the governments, and the minorities were thus seen as major impediments in reaching some mystical goal of racial, religious, or national purity.

But, what is it about the nation-state that makes it such a lethal polity? Levene recognizes that the empires were racist, hierarchical and often practiced retributive genocide when challenged, but they were inclusive if subject nations, peoples and cities towed the line. They were not inherently genocidal. Extermination or the effacement of otherness was not a constituent part of their nature. The problem of the nation-state, which begins with the martial French Republican state of the 1790s, actually has sources a thousand years earlier in a European peculiarity. Here is the surprising cultural dimension of Levene's argument; the uniquely European origins of the nation-state. They lie in the unique combination of political power and religious legitimation in the European reaction to the disintegration of the Roman Empire and formation of Western Europe in the Middle Ages (2005, 1: 121). With Christianity as the official religion of small feudal entities, the inevitable conflicts were met with declarations of war on schismatics and heretics, who were scapegoated in a phobic way. This phobic reaction, a pattern and term Levene uses in relation to totalitarian regimes like the Nazis, starts here. This constellation of religion and politics exhibited the:

> power of a thought system that, now duly institutionalized as the official religion of the West, adapted itself perfectly well to the new political reality of small or medium-sized aristocratic-led feudal kingdoms, principalities or city-states which gradually emerged out of the debris of empire, or in the Germanic lands, beyond its historical borders. If in this we have a thumbnail sketch of the historic emergence of the "West," we also have the conditions for the tensions between liberty and uniformity (2005, 2: 125).

The European system of small states emphasized uniformity, a tendency exacerbated in reformation with imposition of national confessions in official church authorities. A corollary was, as

21

mentioned above, a tendency to phobic reactions to threats: there was well-organized plot, religious minorities were seen as dangerous, wicked foreign bodies (2005, 2: 125). There would have been more extermination of schismatic movements had they not been protected by neighbouring powers.

Given that the master narrative for Levene, then, is the rise of the West—meaning the rise of the nation state model—the historical turning point is not 1492—the spread of European power abroad in blue water empires, as scholars like David Stannard and other proponents on the colonial genocide thesis maintain—but the French Revolution, with its militarized nationalism and nation state model borne out of defensive wars. For it was here that the first modern genocide occurred, the counter-insurgency against royalist rebels who, in the new dispensation, were regarded as evil opponents of reason and progress embodied in the new nation. This new ideology knew no internal limits against the extirpation of such opponents, nor was there a chance of conversion, which Christian Europe at least offered heretics and non-Christians. It was a totalizing agenda of people making from above, engendering the new religion patriotism, and ultimately mass politics that elites found difficult to contain 100 years later, as German historians sceptical of the Enlightenment, Gerhard Ritter and Friedrich Meinecke, also pointed out.

The imperative for uniformity so characteristic of pre-modern Europe was thus secularized in the nineteenth century. The social glue of religion was replaced by utopian concepts like race or class. Agreeing with critics of modernity like Bauman and Foucault, Levene agrees that liberal colonial and totalitarian leaders shared the utopian ideal to "reformulate the social organism, or body politic in a quite unprecedented fashion" (2005, 2: 113). Here was a state directed model of rapid and militant modernization that was adopted by peoples who wanted to establish and protect their sovereignty. Imperial Germany became the European state embodying it by the end of the nineteenth century, and of course Nazi Germany decades later, which was the most radical modernizer in its drive for population uniformity and internal coherence.

Genocide, then, is explained not by recourse to cultural or political contingencies endogenous to specific nation states, although the cultural perception of their elites remains important, but by the pressure that a competitive, indeed Darwinistic, system of state economies places on national leaderships to establish and maintain sovereign viability. In some cases, usually among the second tier late-comer states (postcolonial) to the club established by Westerners, desperate shortcuts had been taken to accelerate and institutional modernization: by exterminating a native people who live in an area desired for economic exploitation, or by exterminating a minority associated with an external enemy that is held responsible for endangering the nation in a security crisis, or holding back the country's independent development by effectively representing the interests of a competitor. Thus, under stable conditions, the empires of Eurasian tectonic plate could accommodate considerable national/ethnic diversity, but not when placed under geopolitical pressure by the West. Nor when it favoured minorities like the Armenians, who then, in Turkish eyes, became disloyal, indeed, dangerous subjects (2: 223-25).

A target of Levene is also the argument like those of David Stannard, Sven Lindqvist, Jürgen Zimmerer and myself who point to the continuity and links between colonial genocides and twentieth century ones. Levene writes:

> By arguing in effect that genocide's crystallization lies in the various post-1492 European colonialism and imperialism, they do not entirely satisfy as to what the exact relationship is between these events and the significantly greater incidence of twentieth-century mass murders whose hallmarks more closely resemble that of our specific phenomena, and whose context is often only marginal colonial, non-colonial or definitely post-colonial (2005, 1: 174).

And he argues that while the late colonial and imperial surge of violence between 1890 and 1914 was indeed perpetrated by the Empires, the context marked a specific phase in world history: the pressure placed on Chinese, Russian, and Ottoman Empires by the West to compete, to be more efficient, provoked indigenous uprisings. They themselves put down rebellions: Germans and British in Africa, for instance. It was a phase in the rise of the West, whose model of the sovereign nation state was globalized after World

War II. Colonialism was still indentured to developmental agenda. So not colonialism but the nation-state is the master concept or key driver of genocide because Britain could not survive without dumping its own internally cleansed people to its imperial fringes: the Scots, the Irish, its proletariat.

These are the preconditions of genocide. What makes them more likely is a confluence of factors: when modernizing elites perceive that their attempts to secure the political and economic sovereignty of their nation state are hampered by national minorities, such as Armenians in the Ottoman Empire or Jews in Imperial Germany, who are regarded as proxies of foreign enemies, and—this is important—were held responsible for the failure of previous attempts at sovereignty, for instance, the perceived Armenian disloyalty in the late nineteenth century, and perceived Jewish and leftist betrayal of the army between 1917-1920 by weakening the home-front and driving socialist and Bolshevik revolutions. In fact, these minorities were held responsible for national decline over various time frames. The Tutsis may have been overthrown in Rwanda in the early 1960s, but ever since then they harried the new regime, even massacring Hutu in neighbouring Burundi. Never again would the national elites permit such minorities to undermine national security and progress again by representing foreign influence, he argues. But that is not all. These elites fantasized about a "powerful and resplendent past" so much that they contrasted with a "diminished and enfeebled present." Such ideologies served as a compensatory ideology for enervated and traumatized national elites or would-be elites in the present, driving them to vain attempts— genocidal shortcuts—at breaking through to sovereignty. Those minorities held responsible for the troubled present were in mortal danger (2005, 1: 187-99).

On this basis, he can show that it exerts exogenous (external) pressure on local, regional, and national economic subsystems because they are forced to compete for their own survival by protecting their markets and penetrating those of their rivals. The most vicious struggles occur between semi-peripheral states that aim to join the most powerful core group (the West and later, Japan) as they simultaneous attempt to prevent sliding into the oblivion of the peripheral ones. Their activity keeps the system in perpetual disequilibrium, and yet the crises they suffer or unleash can only be understood in systemic terms. Rather than view them under the aspect of the "failed state" paradigm and endogenetic bias of conventional social and historical science, they are products of a system that calls forth crises by subjecting them to the pressure of competition and imperative of withstanding core economic and political penetration to understand the processes of politicide, linguicide, democide, and ecocide that are critical to genocide studies.

Critical Genocide Studies

Genocide has been an enduring and profoundly disturbing feature of human history. Yet, scholars of organization and management have approached it in a rather limited and marginal way. Over the last two decades, the interdisciplinary field of genocide studies has dramatically expanded and matured. No longer in the shadow of Holocaust studies, it is now the primary subject of journals, textbooks, encyclopaedias, readers, handbooks, special journal issues, bibliographies, workshops, seminars, conference, Web sites, research centres, government agencies, non-governmental organizations, international organizations, and a unit at the United Nations. If not yet fully theorized, the discipline is characterized by a number of debates and approaches. As the outlines of the field emerge more clearly, the time is right to engage in critical reflections about the state of the field, or what might be called critical genocide studies. The goal is not to be critical in a negative sense but to consider, even as a canon becomes ensconced, what is said and unsaid, who has voice and who is silenced, and how such questions may be linked to issues of power and knowledge. It is, in other words, a call for critical thinking about the field of genocide studies itself, exploring our presuppositions, decentring our biases, and throwing light on blind spots in the hope of further enriching this dynamic field.

Critical genocide studies must also account for the radicalization of individual consciousness—that is, ideological radicalization—that attends genocide; we need to consider individual and social psychology, especially the role of paranoia and fantasy. Culture and psychology are not features of Wallerstein's work, but they also need to be considered in order to trace the manner in which the pressure of the international system is inscribed into individual subjectivity. Happily, Jacques Semelin's new book, Purify and Destroy: The Political Uses of Massacre and Genocide (2007) pays close attention to the social psychological aspect. The French political scientist, who has written extensively about massacres and genocide (2001, 2002a, b, 2003a, b, 2005), has been attempting to convince scholars, much like Martin Shaw in his What is Genocide? (2007), that moving away from the legal definition and invoking Weberian understandings of social action and interpretation will introduce precision and social scientific rigor into the discipline. We need to understand what the perpetrators thought they were doing, he suggests, an analytical imperative that necessarily leads to the dark world of delusion and paranoia, because they were convinced that external and internal enemies were conspiring to destroy their group. That is why they set out to massacre them. Semelin expands on Weber by invoking characteristically French intellectual tools to explore this world: René Girard's theory of sacrifice and the political *imaginaire* (or imaginary) as deployed by Georges Lefebvre in his analysis of the "Great Fear" in the summer of 1789. The impulse to purify the body politic of polluting elements is a function of nationalist elites that seek group regeneration, while the *imaginaire* of panic about putative threats is a necessary if not sufficient condition for genocidal action to take place (Semelin, 2007: 50, 92).

But why the fear in the first place? Here Semelin has recourse to the Italian psychologist Franco Fornani, who applies Kleinian psychoanalytical categories to warfare. The origin of paranoia lies in the universal experience of childhood, when the binary categories of good/bad and friend/enemy develop, and during which the infant worries, in certain circumstances, that it can only survive by destroying the threatening other. This is the famous "paranoid-schizoid position" of Melanie Klein, a theory put to good use by many scholars interested in political paranoia, whether of the political leader (Sagan, 1991) or the terrorist (Robins, 1986; Robins and Post, 1997; Bohleber, 2003, Young, 2003). A society regresses to this position in times of war when its leaders convince the population that national survival depends on the destruction of the (often fantasized) enemy. And such anxieties are fuelled by these leaders—"identity entrepreneurs," if you like—who believe that they are "victims of History," humiliated by rival powers, resentful at their subordinate status, and determined to defeat their enemies, including one's "own" people who are "traitors" and "betrayers" (Semelin: 2007, 24-32, 54). Semelin thus links psychology to politics: such leaders are given opportunities to purvey their delusional fantasies during moments of genuine social and political crisis when they have a ready audience (cf. Ferguson, 2006).

This short discussion cannot do justice to the richness of his important book, which, although social science, avoids the methodological shortcomings outlined above by taking three case studies—the Holocaust, Rwanda, and Yugoslavia—and relating them to many themes, rather than proceeding episodically according to an arbitrary definition. The appearance of this work, along with those of Levene, Kiernan and Shaw show that the limitations of the self-proclaimed "pioneers of genocide studies" (Totten and Jacobs, 2002) are being surmounted by scholars who have made themselves experts in a particular field before embarking on comparative research. The "historiography of genocide" (Stone, 2008) is in good shape because it has also become more critical and self-reflexive.

Bibliography

Bauman, Z., (1989), Modernity and the Holocaust, Ithaca, Cornell University Press.

Bohleber, Werner, 2003, "Collective Phantasms, Destructiveness, and Terrorism," in Sverre Varvin and Vamik D. Vokan, eds., *Violence or Dialogue? Psychoanalytic Insights on Terror and Terrorism.* London: International Psychoanalytic Association, 111-31.

Chalk, Frank, 1994, "Redefining Genocide," in George J. Andreopolous, ed., *Genocide: Conceptual and Historical Dimensions.* Philadelphia: University of Pennsylvania Press, 47-63.

Chalk, Frank, and Jonassohn, Kurt, eds., 1990, *The History and Sociology of Genocide: Analyses and Case Studies.* New Haven: Yale University Press.

Elder, T., (2005), 'What you see before your eyes: Documenting Raphael Lemkin's life by exploring his archival Papers, 1900 – 1959', Journal of Genocide Research, 7:4, 469 – 499.

Fein, H., (1979) 'Is Sociology Aware of Genocide? Recognition of Genocide in Introductory Sociology Texts in the US, 1947 – 1977," Humanity and Society, 3 (3), pp 177 193.

Fein, H., (1993), Genocide: A Sociological Perspective, London, Sage Publications.

Fein, H., (2002), Genocide: A Sociological Perspective in Hinton, A.L., (ed), (2002), Genocide: An Anthropological Reader, Oxford, Blackwell Publishers.

Fein, Helen, 1993, "Revolutionary and Antirevolutionary Genocides: A Comparison of State Murders in Democratic Kampuchea, 1975 to 1979, and in Indonesia, 1965 to 1966." *Comparative Studies in Society and History*, 35/4, 796-823.

Ferguson, R. Brian, 2006, "'Ethnic", and Global Wars," in Mari Fitzduff and Chris E. Stout, eds., *The Psychology of Resolving Global Conflicts: From War to Peace*, vol. 1, *Nature v. Nurture*, Westport, Conn., and London: Praeger Security International, 41-69.

Gellately, Robert, and Kiernan, Ben, eds., 2003, *The Specter of Genocide: Mass Murder in Historical Perspective*. New York: Cambridge University Press.

Harff, Barbara, 1986, "Genocide as State Terrorism," in *Government Violence and Repression*, ed. M. Stohl and G. A. Lopez, eds. New York: Greenwood Press.

Harff, Barbara, 2003, "No Lessons Learned from the Holocaust? Assessing Risks of Genocide and Political Mass Murder since 1955." *American Political Science Review*, 97, 57-73.

Harff, Barbara, and Gurr, Ted R., 1988, "Toward Empirical Theory of Genocides and Politicides." *International Studies Quarterly*, 32, 359-71.

Hirsch, H., (1995), Genocide and the Politics of Memory: Studying Death to Preserve Life, Chapel Hill, NC, University of North Carolina Press

Horowitz, I.L., (1982), Taking Lives: Genocide and State Power, New Brunswick, Transaction

Kuper, L., (1981), Genocide: Its Political Use in the Twentieth Century, New Haven, CT, Yale University Press

Kuper, Leo (1985). *The Prevention of Genocide*. New Haven, Conn.: Yale University Press

Lemkin, R., (1944), Genocide in Hinton, A.L., (ed), (2002), *Genocide: An Anthropological Reader*, Oxford, Blackwell Publishers.

Horkheimer, Max, 1992 [1937], "Traditional and Critical Theory," in Horkheimer, *Critical Theory: Selected Essays*. New York: Continuum.

Katz, Steven T., 1994, *The Holocaust in Historical Context*, vol. 1, New York: Oxford University Press.

Kiernan, Ben, 2007, *Blood and Soil: A World History of Genocide and Extermination from Sparta to Darfur*, Yale University Press.

Levene, Mark, 1999, "A Moving Target, the Usual Suspects and (Maybe) a Smoking Gun: The Problem of Pinning Blame in Modern Genocide," *Patterns of Prejudice*, 33/4.

Levene, Mark, 2004, "A Dissenting Voice: Part 1." *Journal of Genocide Research*, 6/2,153-66,

Levene, Mark, 2004, "A Dissenting Voice, Part 2." *Journal of Genocide Research*, 6/3, 431-45.

Levene, Mark, 2005, *Genocide in the Age of the Nation-State*. 2 vols. London: I.B. Tauris.

Mann, Michael, 2005, *The Dark Side of Democracy: Explaining Ethnic Cleansing*. Cambridge: Cambridge University Press.

McDonnell, Michael, and Moses, A. Dirk, 2005, "Raphael Lemkin as Historian of Genocide in the Americas." *Journal of Genocide Research*, 7/4, 501-29.

Moses, A. Dirk, 2002, "Conceptual Blockages and Definitional Dilemmas in the Racial Century: Genocide of Indigenous Peoples and the Holocaust," *Patterns of Prejudice*, 36, 7-36.

Moses, A. Dirk, 2006, "Why the Discipline of 'Genocide Studies' Has Trouble Explaining How Genocides End?" 22 December 2006, Social Sciences Research Council: [http://howgenocidesend.ssrc.org/Moses/- >http://howgenocidesend.ssrc.org/Moses/].

Moses, A. Dirk, 2008a, "Genocide and Modernity," in Dan Stone, ed., *The Historiography of Genocide*. Houndmills: Palgrave, MacMillan, 156-93.

Moses, A. Dirk, 2008b, "Empire, Colony, Genocide: Keywords and Intellectual History," in A. Dirk Moses, ed., *Empire Colony,*

Genocide: Conquest, Occupation, and Subaltern Resistance in World History. New York: Berghahn Books.

Mosse, George L., 1964, *The Crisis of German Ideology: Intellectual Origins of the Third Reich*, New York: H. Fertig, 1981.

Naimark, Norman, 2001, *Fires of Hatred: Ethnic Cleansing in Twentieth-Century Europe*. Cambridge, MA: Harvard University Press.

Power, Samantha, 2002, *"A Problem from Hell": America and the Age of Genocide*. New York: Basic Books.

Robins, Robert S., 1986, "Paranoid Ideation and Charismatic Leadership," *Psychohistory Review*, 5, 15-55.

Robins, Robert S., and Post, Jerrold M., 1997, *Political Paranoia: the Psychopolitics of Hatred*. New Haven: Yale University Press.

Sagan, Eli, 1991, *The Honey and the Hemlock: Democracy and Paranoia in Ancient Athens and Modern America*. Princeton: Princeton University Press.

Semelin, Jacques, 2001, "In Consideration of Massacres." *Journal of Genocide Research*, 3/3, 377-389.

Semelin, Jacques, 2002a, "Extreme Violence: Can We Understand It?" *International Social Science Journal*, 54/174, 429–431.

Semelin, Jacques, 2002b, "From Massacre to the Genocidal Process." *International Social Science Journal*, 54/174, 433-442.

Semelin, Jacques, 2003a, "Analysis of a Mass-Crime: Ethnic cleansing in the former Yugoslavia (1991-1999)," in Ben Kiernan and Robert Gellately, eds., *The Spectre of Genocide: Mass Murder in a Historical Perspective*, New York and Cambridge, Cambridge University Press, 353-370.

Semelin, Jacques, 2003b, "Toward a Vocabulary of Massacre and Genocide." *Journal of Genocide Research*, 5/2, 193-210.

Semelin, Jacques, 2005, "What is Genocide?" *European Review of History*, 12/1, 81-89.

Semelin, Jacques, 2007, *Purify and Destroy: The Political Uses of Massacre and Genocide*. New York: Columbia University Press.

Shaw, Martin, 2007, *What Is Genocide?* London. Polity.

Stern, Fritz, 1961, *The Politics of Cultural Despair: A study in the Rise of the Germanic Ideology*. Berkeley: University of California Press, 1961.

Stone, Dan, ed., 2007, *The Historiography of Genocide*. Houndmills. Palgrave MacMillan.

Totten, Samuel, Parsons, William S., and Charny, Israel W., eds., 2004, *A Century of Genocide: Critical Essays and Eyewitness Accounts*, 2nd ed. New York: Routledge.

Weitz, Eric D., 2003, *A Century of Genocide: Utopias of Race and Nation*. *Princeton*, NJ: Princeton University Press.

Volkan, Vamik, 1988, *The Need to Have Enemies: From Clinical Practice to International Relationships* (Northvale, N.J. and London: Jason Aaronson, 1988).

Volkan, Vamik, 1997, *Bloodlines: From Ethnic Pride to Ethnic Terrorism* Boulder, Colo.: Westview Press.

Volkan, Vamik, 2004, *Blind Trust: Large Groups and Their Leaders in Times of Crisis and Terror*, Charlottesville: Pitchstone Publishing.

Wallerstein, Immanuel, 1974, *The Modern World System: Capitalist Agriculture and the Origins of the European World Economy in the Sixteenth Century*. New York: Academic Press.

Wallerstein, Immanuel, 2004, *World Systems Analysis: An Introduction*. Durham: Duke University Press.

Young, Robert M., 2003, "Psychoanalysis, Terrorism, and Fundamentalism." *Psychodynamic Practice*, 9/3, 307-24.

Chapter Two

Conceptualizing Capitalism as Structural Genocide

Enslavement, massacres and mass killings of Africans in wars of religion, colonial conquest, genocide and the structural violence have marked the history of the continent. However, it is with the dawn of the capitalist system that we see the rise of nation states as we understand them today, sharing common languages and "culture." The very forging of such nation states involved the suppression of minorities, their cultures, religions, languages and dialects, often violently.

Karl Marx described the emergence of capitalism "dripping from head to toe, from every pore, with blood and dirt". The slave trade, that consumed the lives of an estimated 12 million black Africans, fuelled the industrial revolution. Settler-colonialism opened up the vast resources of the Americas and the Antipodes on the back of genocide of their indigenous peoples.

As the capitalist system developed, competition between capitals and states gave rise to what Marxists call "imperialism". This is not simply a matter of major powers exerting military might and domination over others but a system of economic and military competition that encompasses all states. It is from such an understanding of the world system that we need to examine how forms of violence such as ethnic cleansing and genocide emerge in Africa.

Capitalism's central motor force is the drive to accumulate capital and, thus, in the process, all other social and natural relationships are subordinated to this primary goal. As Paul Sweezey argued, it is 'both the subjective goal and the motor force of the entire economic system' (1989: 1–10). Once generalized commodity production is established, capital accumulation becomes, through the force of competition, a ceaseless and remorseless process, a kind of 'treadmill of accumulation' that respects no other cycles other than the business cycle (Foster, 2005). Consequently, the insatiable drive to accumulate capital and thus reap profits tramples all over natural cycles and processes and is no respecter of the natural rhythms of regeneration and recycling, as this imperative to accumulate on an ever expanding scale requires more and more of what ecologists term 'throughput of materials and energy' (Burkett, 1999:112).

The iron law of exponential growth under capitalism exacerbates the social metabolism of the capitalist system and places an ever greater strain on nature, eventually leading to metabolic rift. One feature of a system of universal commodity production for the market is that exchange values regulate the production of social wealth and validate particular labours as what Marx described as 'socially necessary labour time'. In other words, the intrinsic 'value' of a commodity, at least according to capitalism, is the amount of socially average labour that must go into its production. Critically, a market economy based on the organizing principle of exchange value presupposes that all producers cannot reproduce themselves independently of the market nexus and thus it assumes the social separation from the natural conditions of production (Burkett, Ibid.: 58). The social separation of the producers from the natural conditions of production makes possible a compulsion to perform surplus labour beyond immediate needs and ignore natural limits. It also rather palpably demonstrates one of the many ways that capitalism affects our alienation from nature and violates the nature-imposed conditions of social metabolism.

According to an essay excerpted from István Mészáros' book, *The Challenge and Burden of Historical Time: Socialism in the Twenty-First Century* (2009), the capitalist mode of production represents a great advance over all of the preceding ones, however problematical and indeed destructive this historical advance in the end turns out—and had to turn out—to be. By breaking the long prevailing but constraining direct link between human use and production, and replacing it with the commodity relation, capital opened up the dynamically unfolding possibilities of apparently irresistible *expansion* to which—from the standpoint of the capital system and of its willing personifications—there could be no conceivable limits. For the paradoxical and ultimately quite untenable inner determination of capital's productive system is that its commodified products "*are non-use-values for their owners and use-values for their non-owners. Consequently they must all change hands. . . .* Hence commodities must be realized as values *before they can be realised as use-values"* (Marx, 1992:85).

This self-contradictory inner determination of the capitalist system, which imposes the ruthless submission of human need to the alienating necessity of capital expansion, is what removes the possibility of overall rational control from this dynamic productive order. It brings with itself perilous and potentially catastrophic consequences in the longer run, transforming in due course a great *positive power* of earlier quite unimaginable economic development into a *devastating negativity*, in the total absence of the necessary reproductive restraint.

What is systematically ignored—and must be ignored, due to the unalterable fetishistic imperatives and vested interests of the capital system itself—is the fact that, inescapably, we live in a *finite world*, with its literally vital *objective limits*. For a long time in human history, including several centuries of capitalistic developments, those limits could be—as indeed they were—ignored with relative safety. Once, however, they assert themselves, as they emphatically must do in our irreversible historical epoch, no irrational and wasteful productive system, no matter how dynamic (in fact the more dynamic the worse) can escape the consequences. It can only disregard them for a while through reorienting itself toward the callous justification of the more or less openly destructive imperative of the system's self-preservation at all cost: by preaching the wisdom of "there is no alternative," and in that spirit brushing aside and, whenever need be, brutally suppressing even the most obvious warning signs that foreshadow the unsustainable future.

False theorization is the necessary consequence of this lopsided objective structural determination and domination of use value by exchange value not only under the most absurdly and blindly apologetic conditions of contemporary capitalism but also in the classical period of bourgeois political economy, at the time of the capital system's historical ascendancy. This is because under the rule of capital a *fictitiously limitless* production must be pursued at all cost, as well as theoretically justified as the only commendable one. Such pursuit is imperative even if there can be no guarantee whatsoever that: (1) the required and sustainable "changing of hands" of the supplied commodities will actually take place on the idealized market (thanks to the mysterious benevolence of Adam Smith's even more mysterious "invisible hand"); and (2) that the objective material conditions for producing the projected unlimited—and humanly unlimitable, since in its primary determination divorced from need and use—supply of commodities can be *forever secured*, irrespective of the destructive impact of capital's mode of social metabolic reproduction on nature.

The ideal suitability of the market for rectifying the unalterable structural defect indicated in point (1) above is a *gratuitous afterthought*, bringing with it many arbitrary assumptions and unfulfillable regulative projections in the same vein. The sobering reality underlying the market as a remedial afterthought is a set of insuperably adversarial power relations, tending to monopolistic domination and to the intensification of the system's antagonisms. Likewise, the grave structural defect of pursuing unlimited capital expansion—idealizing all-important "growth" as an end in itself—as put into relief in point (2) above, is complemented by an equally *fictitious afterthought* when it has to be admitted that some remedy might be in order. And the remedy thus projected—as an alternative to the system's collapse into the unredeemable negativity of the fateful *"stationary state"* theorized by bourgeois political economy in the nineteenth century—is simply the wishful advocacy of making *distribution* "more equitable" (and thereby less conflict-torn) while leaving the production system as it stands. This postulate, even if it could be implemented, which of course it cannot be, due to the fundamental hierarchical structural determinations of capital's social order itself, would not be able to solve any of the grave problems of *production* on which *also* the insurmountable contradictions of the capital system's incurable distribution are erected.

One of the principal representatives of liberal thought, John Stuart Mill, is as genuine in his concern about the "stationary state" of the future as he is hopelessly unreal in his proposed remedy to it. For he can only offer vacuous hope in his discussion of this problem which happens to be absolutely intractable from the standpoint of capital. He writes that "I sincerely hope, for the sake of posterity, that they will be *content to be stationary*, long before necessity compels them to it" (Mill,2004:751). In this way Mill's discourse amounts to no more than paternalistic preaching, because he can only acknowledge, in tune with his acceptance of the Malthusian diagnosis, the difficulties arising from population growth, but none of the contradictions of capital's reproductive order. His bourgeois self-complacency is clearly visible, depriving his analysis and paternalistic reforming intent of all substance. Mill peremptorily asserts that "It is only in the *backward countries of the world* that increased production is still an important object: in those most advanced, what is economically needed is a *better distribution*, of which one indispensable means is a *stricter restraint on population*" ill, Ibid.:749). Even his idea of "better distribution" is hopelessly unreal. For what Mill cannot possibly recognize (or acknowledge) is that the overwhelmingly important aspect of distribution is the untouchable exclusive distribution of the means of production to the capitalist class. Understandably, therefore, on such a self-serving operational premise of the social order a paternalist sense of superiority remains always prevalent in this that no solution can be expected "until *the better minds* succeeded in educating the others," (Mill,passim.749) so that they accept population restraint and a "better distribution" supposedly arising from such restraint. Thus people should forget all about changing the destructive structural determinations of the established social metabolic order which inexorably drive society toward a stagnating stationary state. In Mill's discourse the utopia of the capitalist millennium, with its *tenable stationary state*, will be brought into existence thanks to the good services of the enlightened liberal "better minds." And then, as far as the structural determinations of the established social reproductive order are concerned, everything can go on forever as before.

All this made some sense from capital's standpoint, however problematical and ultimately untenable that sense in the end had to turn out to be, due to the dramatic onset and relentless deepening of the system's structural crisis. But even that partial sense of the same wishful propositions could not be ascribed to the reformist political movement which claimed to represent the strategic interests of labour. Yet, social-democratic reformism at its inception took its inspiration from such naive, even if at first genuinely held, afterthoughts of liberal political economy. Thus, due to the internal logic of the adopted social premises, emanating from capital's standpoint and vested interests as the unchallengeable controller of the reproductive metabolism, it could not be surprising in the least that social-democratic reformism ended its course of development the way in which it actually did: by transforming itself into "New Labour" (in Britain; and its equivalents in other countries) and by abandoning completely any concern with even the most limited reform of the established social order. At the same time, in place of genuine liberalism the most savage and inhuman varieties of *neoliberalism* appeared on the historical stage, wiping out the memory of the once advocated social remedies—including even the wishful paternalistic solutions—from the progressive past of the liberal creed. And as a bitter irony of contemporary historical development, the "New Labour"–type former social-democratic reformist movements installed in government—not only in Britain but also everywhere else in the "advanced" and not so advanced capitalist world—did not hesitate to unreservedly identify themselves with the aggressive neoliberal phase of capital-apologetics. This capitulatory transformation clearly marked the end of the reformist road which was a blind alley from the outset.

In order to create an economically viable, and also on a long-term basis historically sustainable, social reproductive order it is necessary to radically alter the self-contradictory inner determinations of the established one, which impose the ruthless submission of human need and use to the alienating necessity of capital expansion. This means that the absurd precondition of the ruling productive system—whereby use values, by preordained and totally iniquitous ownership determinations, must be divorced from, and opposed to, those who create them, so as to bring about and circularly/arbitrarily legitimate capital's enlarged self-realization—has to be permanently relegated to the past. Otherwise the only viable meaning of *economy* as rational *economizing* with the available, necessarily finite, resources cannot be instituted and respected as a vital orienting principle. Instead, irresponsible *wastefulness* dominates in capital's socioeconomic—and corresponding political—order which invariably reasserts itself as *institutionalized irresponsibility*, notwithstanding its self-mythology of absolutely insuperable "efficiency." (To be sure, the kind of "efficiency" glorified in this way is in fact capital's ultimately self-undermining efficiency for blindly driving forward the adversarial/conflictual parts at the incorrigible

38

expense of the *whole*.) Understandably, therefore, the governmentally well-promoted fantasies of "market socialism" had to fizzle out in the form of a humiliating collapse, due to the acceptance of such presuppositions and capitalistically insuperable structural determinations.

The now dominant conception of the "economy," which happens to be quite incapable of setting limits even to the most grievous waste, in our time truly on a *planetary scale*, can only operate with self-serving *tautologies* and arbitrarily prefabricated, as well as simultaneously dismissed, *false oppositions and pseudo-alternatives*, devised for the same purpose of unjustifiable self-justification. As a blatant— and dangerously all-infecting—tautology, we are offered the arbitrary definition of *productivity as growth, and growth as productivity*, although both terms would require a historically qualified and objectively sustainable evaluation of their own.

Naturally, the reason why the obvious tautological fallacy is much preferable to the required proper theoretical and practical assessment is that by arbitrarily decreeing the *identity* of these two key terms of reference of the capital system the *self-evident validity and timeless superiority* of an extremely problematical—and ultimately even self-destructive—social reproductive order should look not only plausible but absolutely unquestionable. At the same time, the arbitrarily decreed *tautological identity* of growth and productivity is shored up by the equally arbitrary and self-serving false alternative between *"growth or no-growth."* Moreover, the latter is automatically prejudged in favour of capitalistically postulated and defined *"growth."* It is projected and defined with fetishistic quantification, as befits its way of *presupposing forever*, as self-commendingly *synonymous to growth itself*, nothing more specific and humanly meaningful than the abstract genericity of enlarged *capital-expansion* as the elementary *precondition* for satisfying human need and use.

That is where the incorrigible divorce of capitalistic growth from human need and use—indeed its potentially most devastating and destructive *counter-position* to human need—betrays itself. Once the fetishisitic mystifications and arbitrary postulates at the root of the categorically decreed false identity of *growth and productivity* are peeled away, it becomes abundantly clear that the kind of growth postulated and at the same time automatically exempted from all critical scrutiny is in no way inherently connected with sustainable objectives corresponding to human need. The only connection that must be asserted and defended at all cost in capital's social metabolic universe is the *false identity* of—aprioristically presupposed—*capital expansion* and circularly corresponding (but in truth likewise aprioristically presupposed) "growth," whatever might be the consequences imposed on nature and humankind by even the most destructive type of growth. For capital's real concern can only be its own *ever enlarged expansion*, even if that brings with it the destruction of humanity.

In this vision even the most lethal *cancerous growth* must preserve its conceptual primacy over (against) human need and use, if human need by any chance happens to be mentioned at all. And when the apologists of the capital system are willing to consider *The Limits to Growth* (Meadows, et al.,1972) as the "Club of Rome" did in its vastly propagandized capital-apologetic venture in the early 1970s, the aim inevitably remains the *eternalization of the existing grave* inequalities (Forrester, 1972) by fictitiously (and quixotically) freezing global capitalist production at a totally untenable level, blaming primarily "population growth" (as customary in bourgeois political economy ever since Malthus) for the existing problems. Compared to such callous hypocritical "remedial intent," rhetorically pretending to be concerned with nothing less than "the Predicament of Mankind," Mill's earlier quoted paternalistic preaching, with its genuine advocacy of somewhat more equitable distribution than what he was familiar with, was the paradigm of radical enlightenment.

The characteristically self-serving false alternative of "growth or no growth" is evident even if we only consider what would be the unavoidable impact of the postulated "no growth" on the grave conditions of inequality and suffering in capital's social order. It would mean the *permanent condemnation* of humanity's overwhelming majority to the inhuman conditions which they are now forced to endure. For they are now in a literal sense forced to endure them, by their thousands of millions, when there could be *created* a real alternative to it. Under conditions, that is, when it would be quite feasible to rectify at least the worst effects of global deprivation: by putting to humanly commendable and rewarding use the attained *potential* of productivity, in a world of now criminally wasted material and human resources.

To be sure, we can only speak of the positive *potential of productivity*, and not of its existing reality, as often predicated, with green-coloured good intentions but boundless illusions, by old fashioned single-issue reformers, wishfully asserting that we could do it "right now," with the productive powers at our disposal today, if we really decided to do so. Unfortunately, however, such a conception completely ignores the way in which our productive system is presently articulated, requiring in the future a radical rearticulation. For productivity wedded to *capitalist* growth, in the form of the now dominant reality of *destructive production*, is a most forbidding adversary. In order to turn the positive potentiality of productive development into a much needed reality, so as to be able to rectify many of the crying inequalities and injustices of our existing society, it would be necessary to adopt the *regulative principles* of a *qualitatively different* social order. In other words, humanity's now destructively negated *potential of productivity* would have to be liberated from its capitalist integument in order to become socially viable *productive power.*

The quixotic advocacy of freezing production at the level attained in the early 1970s was trying to camouflage, with vacuous pseudo-scientific model-mongering pioneered at the Massachusetts Institute of Technology, the ruthlessly enforced actual power relations of U.S. dominated postwar imperialism. That variety of imperialism was, of course, very different from its earlier form known to Lenin. For in Lenin's lifetime at least half a dozen significant imperialist powers were competing for the rewards of their real and/or hoped for conquests. And even in the 1930s Hitler was still willing to share the fruits of violently redefined imperialism with Japan and Mussolini's Italy. In our time, by contrast, we have to face up to the reality—and the lethal dangers—arising from *global hegemonic imperialism*, with the United States as its overwhelmingly dominant power (István Mészáros.2001). In contrast to even Hitler, the United States as the *single hegemon* is quite unwilling to share global domination with any rival. And that is not simply on account of political/military contingencies. The problems are much deeper. They assert themselves through the ever-aggravating contradictions of the capital system's deepening *structural crisis*. U.S. dominated global hegemonic imperialism is an—ultimately futile—attempt to devise a solution to

41

that crisis through the most brutal and violent rule over the rest of the world, enforced with or without the help of slavishly "willing allies," now through a succession of genocidal wars. Ever since the 1970s the United States has been sinking ever deeper into *catastrophic indebtedness*. The fantasy solution publicly proclaimed by several U.S. presidents was *"to grow out of it."* And the result: the diametrical opposite, in the form of astronomical and still growing indebtedness. Accordingly, the United States must grab to itself, by any means at its disposal, including the most violent military aggression, whenever required for this purpose, everything it can, through the transfer of the fruits of capitalist growth—thanks to the global socioeconomic and political/military domination of the United States—from everywhere in the world. Could then any sane person imagine, no matter how well armoured by his or her callous contempt for "the shibboleth of equality," that U.S. dominated global hegemonic imperialism would take seriously even for a moment the panacea of "no growth"? Only the worst kind of bad faith could suggest such ideas, no matter how pretentiously packaged in the hypocritical concern over "the Predicament of Mankind."

For a variety of reasons there can be no question about the importance of growth both in the present and in the future. But to say so must go with a proper examination of the concept of growth not only as we know it up to the present, but also as we can envisage its sustainability in the future. Our siding with the need for growth cannot be in favour of *unqualified growth*. The tendentiously avoided real question is: *what kind of growth* is both feasible today, in contrast to dangerously wasteful and even crippling capitalist growth visible all around us? For growth must be also *positively sustainable* in the future on a *long-term* basis.

As mentioned already, capitalist growth is fatefully dominated by the inescapable confines of *fetishistic quantification*. Ever-aggravating *wastefulness* is a necessary corollary of such fetishism, since there can be no criteria—and no viable *measure*—through the observance of which wastefulness could be corrected. More or less arbitrary *quantification* sets the context, creating at the same time also the illusion that once the required quantities are secured for the more powerful, there can be no further significant problems. Yet the truth of the matter is that self-oriented *quantification* in reality cannot be sustained at all as a form of productively viable strategy even in the short run. For it is partial and myopic (if not altogether blind), concerned only with quantities corresponding to the *immediate obstacles* hindering the accomplishment of a given productive task, but not with the necessarily associated *structural limits* of the socioeconomic enterprise itself which—whether you know it or not—ultimately decide everything. The capitalistically necessary confusion of *structural limits* with *obstacles* (which can be quantitatively overcome), in order to ignore the limits (since they correspond to the insurmountable determinations of capital's social metabolic order), vitiates the growth orientation of the entire productive system. To make growth viable would require applying to it profoundly *qualitative* considerations. But that is absolutely prevented by the unquestioning and unquestionable *self-expansionary drive* of capital at all cost, which is incompatible with the *constraining* consideration of *quality* and *limits*.

The great innovation of the capital system is that it can operate—*undialectically*—through the overwhelming domination of quantity: by subsuming *everything*, including living human labour (inseparable from the qualities of human need and use) under *abstract quantitative determinations*, in the form of value and exchange value. Thus everything becomes profitably commensurable and manageable for a determinate period of time. This is the secret of capital's—for a long time irresistible—socio-historical triumph. But it is also the harbinger of its ultimate unsustainability and necessary implosion, once the *absolute limits* of the system are fully activated, as they increasingly happen to be in our own historical epoch. Ours is the time when the undialectical domination of quality by quantity becomes dangerous and untenable.

For it is inconceivable to ignore in our time the fundamental, but under capitalism necessarily sidelined inherent connection of *economy as economizing* (which equals *responsible husbandry*). We have now arrived at a critical point in history when the ruling productive system's willing personifications do everything in their power to wipe out all awareness of that vital objective connection—opting for undeniable destructiveness, not only in the cult of extremely wasteful productive practices, but even glorifying their lethally destructive engagement in unlimited "preventive and preemptive wars."

43

Quality, by its very nature, is inseparable from *specificities*. Accordingly, a social metabolic system respectful of quality—above all of the needs of living human beings as its producing subjects— cannot be hierarchically regimented. A radically different kind of socioeconomic and cultural management is required for a society operated on the basis of such a qualitatively different reproductive metabolism, briefly summed up as *self-management*. Regimentation was both feasible and necessary for capital's social metabolic order. In fact the command structure of capital could not function in any other way. Structurally secured hierarchy and authoritarian regimentation are the defining characteristics of capital's command structure. The alternative order is incompatible with regimentation and with the kind of accountancy—including the strictly quantitative operation of *necessary labour time*—which must prevail in the capital system. Thus, the *kind of growth* necessary and feasible in the alternative social metabolic order can only be based on *quality* directly corresponding to *human needs*: the actual and historically developing needs of both society as a whole and of its particular individuals.

At the same time, the alternative to the restrictive and fetishistic time-accountancy of *necessary labour time* can only be the liberating and emancipating *disposable time* consciously offered and managed by the social individuals themselves. That kind of social metabolic control of the available human and material resources would—and actually could—respect both the overall limits arising from the orienting principle of economy as economizing; and at the same time it would also consciously expand such qualitative limits and needs as the historically developing conditions safely permitted. After all, we should not forget that "the first historical act was the creation of a new need" (Marx). Only capital's reckless way of treating the economy—not as rational economizing but as the most irresponsible legitimation of boundless waste—is what *totally perverts* this historical process: by substituting for the rich diversity of human needs capital's alienating one-and-only real need for enlarged self-reproduction at all cost, thereby threatening to bring to an end human history itself.

There can be not even *partial correctives* introduced into capital's operational framework if they are genuinely quality-oriented. For the only qualities relevant in this respect are not some abstract physical characteristics but the *humanly meaningful qualities inseparable from need*.

It is true, of course, as stressed before, that such qualities are always specific, corresponding to clearly identifiable particular human needs both of the individuals themselves and of their historically given and changing social relations. Accordingly, in their many sided specificity they constitute a *coherent and well defined set* of inviolable systemic determinations, with their own *systemic limits*. It is precisely the existence of such—very far from abstract—systemic limits which makes it impossible to transfer any meaningful operating determinations and orienting principles from the envisaged alternative social metabolic order into the capital system. The two systems are radically exclusive of each other. For the specific qualities corresponding to human need, in the alternative order, carry the indelible marks of their overall systemic determinations, as integral parts of a humanly valid social reproductive system of control. In the capital system, on the contrary, the overall determinations must be unalterably *abstract*, because capital's *value relation* must reduce all qualities (corresponding to need and use) to measurable generic quantities, in order to assert its alienating historical dominance over everything, in the interest of capital expansion, irrespective of the consequences.

The incompatibilities of the two systems become amply clear when we consider their relationship to the question of *limit itself*. The only sustainable *growth* positively promoted under the alternative social metabolic control is based on the *conscious acceptance of the limits* whose violation would imperil the realization of the chosen—and humanly valid—reproductive objectives. Hence *wastefulness* and *destructiveness* (as clearly identified limiting concepts) are *absolutely excluded* by the consciously accepted systemic determinations themselves, adopted by the social individuals as their vital orienting principles. By contrast, the capital system is characterized, and fatefully driven, by the—conscious or unconscious—*rejection of all limits, including its own systemic limits*. Even the latter are arbitrarily and dangerously treated as if they were nothing more than always superable *contingent obstacles*. Hence anything goes in this social reproductive system, including the possibility—and by the time we have reached our own historical epoch also the overwhelming grave probability—of *total destruction*.

Naturally, this mutually exclusive relationship to the question of limits prevails also the other way round. Thus, there can be no "partial correctives" borrowed from the capital system when creating and strengthening the alternative social metabolic order. The partial—not to mention general—incompatibilities of the two systems arise from the *radical incompatibility of their value dimension*. As mentioned above, this is why the particular value determinations and relations of the alternative order could not be transferred into capital's social metabolic framework for the purpose of improving it, as postulated by some utterly unreal reformist design, wedded to the vacuous methodology of "little by little." For even the smallest partial relations of the alternative system are *deeply embedded in the general value determinations* of an overall framework of human needs whose inviolable elementary axiom is the radical exclusion of *waste and destruction*, in accord with its *innermost nature*.

At the same time, on the other side, no partial "correctives" can be transferred from the operational framework of capital into a genuinely socialist order, as the disastrous failure of Gorbachev's "market socialist" venture painfully and conclusively demonstrated. For also in that respect we would always be confronted by the radical incompatibility of value determinations, even if in that case the value involved is destructive *counter value*, corresponding to the ultimate— necessarily ignored—limits of the capital system itself. The systemic limits of capital are thoroughly compatible with waste and destruction. For such normative considerations can only be *secondary* to capital. More fundamental determinations must take the precedence over such concerns. This is why capital's original *indifference to waste and destruction* (never a more positive posture than indifference) is turned into their most active promotion when conditions require that shift. In fact waste and destruction must be relentlessly pursued in this system in direct subordination to the *imperative of capital expansion*, the overwhelming systemic determinant. The more so the further we leave behind the historically ascending phase of the capital system's development. And no one should be fooled by the fact that frequently the preponderant assertion of *counter value* is misrepresented and rationalized as *"value neutrality"* by capital's celebrated ideologists.

It was therefore mind-boggling that at the time of Gorbachev's ill-fated "perestroika" his "ideology chief" (called officially by that name) could seriously assert that the capitalist market and its commodity relations were the instrumental embodiments of "universal human values" and a "major achievement of human civilization," adding to these grotesque capitulatory assertions that the capitalist market was even *"the guarantee of the renewal of socialism"* *(Vadim Medvedev. (1989):31-32)*. Such theorists kept talking about the adoption of the "market mechanism," when the capitalist market was *anything but* an adaptable neutral *"mechanism."* It was in fact *incurably value laden*, and must always remain so. In this kind of conception—curiously shared by Gorbachev's "socialist ideology chief" (and others) with the Friedrich von Hayeks of this world who violently denounced any idea of socialism as "The Road to Serfdom" — *exchange* in general was ahistorically and anti-historically equated with *capitalist exchange*, and the ever more destructive reality of the *capitalist market* with a fictionalized benevolent *"market"* in general. Whether they realized it or not, they capitulated thereby to idealizing the imperatives of a ruthless system of necessary *market domination* (ultimately inseparable from the ravages of imperialism) required by the inner determinations of capital's social metabolic order. The adoption of this capitulatory position was equally pronounced but even more damaging in Gorbachev's reform document. For he insisted that,

There are *no alternatives to the market*. Only the market can ensure the satisfaction of *people's needs*, the *fair distribution* of wealth, *social rights*, and the strengthening of *freedom and democracy*. The market would permit the Soviet economy to be *organically* linked with the world's, and give our citizens access to all the achievements of *world civilization (Gorbachev,1990)*.

Naturally, given the total unreality of Gorbachev's "no alternative" wishful thinking, expecting the generous supply "to the people" of all those wonderful would-be achievements and benefits, in all domains, from the global capitalist market, this venture could only end, most humiliatingly, in the disastrous implosion of the Soviet-type system.

It is not at all accidental or surprising that the proposition of *"there is no alternative"* occupies such a prominent place in the socioeconomic and political conceptions formulated from capital's standpoint. Not even the greatest thinkers of the bourgeoisie—like Adam Smith and Hegel—could be exceptions in this respect. For it is absolutely true that the bourgeois order either succeeds in asserting itself in the form of dynamic *capital expansion,* or it is condemned to ultimate failure. There can be really *no conceivable alternative* to endless capital expansion from capital's standpoint, determining thereby the vision of all those who adopt it. But the adoption of this standpoint also means that the question of *"what price must be paid"* for uncontrollable capital expansion beyond a certain point in time—once the ascendant phase of the system's development is left behind—cannot enter into consideration at all. The violation of *historical time* is therefore the necessary consequence of adopting capital's standpoint by internalizing the system's expansionary imperative as its most fundamental and absolutely unalterable determinant. Even in the conceptions of the greatest bourgeois thinkers this position must prevail. There can be no alternative future social order whose defining characteristics would be significantly different from the already established one. This is why even Hegel, who formulated by far the most profound historical conception up to his own time, must also arbitrarily bring history to an end in capital's unalterable present, idealizing the capitalist nation state as the insuperable climax of all conceivable historical development, despite his sharp perception of the destructive implications of the whole system of nation states. To quote one of Hegel's idealizing postulates: *"The nation state is mind in its substantive rationality and immediate actuality and is therefore the absolute power on earth"* (1991:212).

Thus, there can be no alternative to decreeing the pernicious dogma of *no alternative* in bourgeois thought. But it is totally absurd for socialists to adopt the position of endless (and by its nature uncontrollable) capital expansion. For the corollary idealization of—again characteristically unqualified—"consumption" ignores the elementary truth that from capital's uncritical self-expansionary vantage point there can be *no difference between destruction and consumption.* One is as good as the other for the required purpose. This is so because the commercial transaction in the capital relation—even of the most destructive kind, embodied in the ware of the military/industrial complex and the use to which it is put in its inhuman wars—successfully completes the cycle of capital's enlarged self-reproduction, so as to be able to open a new cycle. This is the only thing that really matters to capital, no matter how unsustainable might be the consequences. Consequently, when socialists internalize the imperative of capital expansion as the necessary ground of the advocated growth, they do not simply accept an isolated tenet but a whole "package deal." Knowingly or not, they accept at the same time all of the *false alternatives*—like "growth or no-growth"—that can be derived from the uncritical advocacy of necessary capital expansion.

The false alternative of *no growth* must be rejected by us not only because its adoption would perpetuate the most gruesome misery and inequality now dominating the world, with struggle and destructiveness inseparable from it. The radical negation of that approach can only be a necessary point of departure. The inherently *positive* dimension of our vision involves the fundamental redefinition of *wealth itself* as known to us. Under capital's social metabolic order we are confronted by *the alienating rule of wealth over society*, directly affecting every aspect of life, from the narrowly economic to the cultural and spiritual domains. Consequently, we cannot get out of capital's vicious circle, with all of its ultimately destructive determinations and false alternatives, without fully turning around that vital relationship. Namely, without *making society—the society of freely associated individuals—rule over wealth*, redefining at the same time also their relation to time and to the kind of *use* to which the products of human labour are put. As Marx (1993: 708) had written already in one of his early works:

> In a future society, in which class antagonism will have ceased, in which there will no longer be any classes, use will no longer be determined by the *minimum time of production*; but the time of production devoted to an article will be determined by the *degree of its social utility*.

This means an uncompromising departure from viewing wealth as a fetishistic material entity which must ignore the *real individuals* who are the creators of wealth. Naturally, capital—in its false claim to be identical to wealth, as the "creator and embodiment of wealth"—must ignore the individuals, in the self-legitimating service

49

of its own social metabolic control. In this way, by usurping the role of real wealth and subverting the potential use to which it could be put, capital is the *enemy of historical time*. This is what must be redressed for the sake of human survival itself. Thus all constituents of the unfolding relationships among the historically self-determining real individuals, together with the wealth they create and positively allocate through the conscious application of the only viable modality of time—*disposable time*—must be brought together in a qualitatively different social metabolic framework. To say it with Marx:

> *real wealth* is the developed productive power of all individuals. The measure of wealth is then not any longer, in any way, labour time, but rather *disposable time*. Labour time as the measure of value posits wealth itself as founded on poverty, and disposable time as existing in and because of the antithesis to surplus labour time; or, the positing of an individual's entire time as labour time, and his degradation therefore to mere worker, *subsumption under labour* (Marx, Ibid.).

Disposable time is the *individuals' actual historical time*. In contrast, necessary labour time required for the functioning of capital's mode of social metabolic control is *anti-historical*, denying the individuals the only way in which they can assert and fulfil themselves as *real historical subjects* in control of their own life-activity. In the form of capital's necessary labour time the individuals are subjected to time exercised as *tyrannical judge and degrading measure*, with no court of appeal, instead of being itself judged and measured in relation to qualitative human criteria "by the *needs* of the social individuals." Capital's perversely self-absolutizing anti-historical time thus superimposes itself over human life as fetishistic *determinant* which reduces living labour to *"time's carcase,"* as discussed elsewhere, in relation to "The Necessity of Planning."

The historical challenge is, then, to move in the alternative social metabolic order from the rule of capital's frozen time as alienating determinant to become freely determined by the social individuals themselves who consciously dedicate to the realization of their chosen objectives their incomparably richer resources of disposable time than what could be squeezed out of them through the tyranny of necessary labour time. This is an absolutely vital difference. For only social individuals can really determine their own disposable time, in sharp contrast to necessary labour time which dominates them. The adoption of disposable time is the only conceivable and rightful way in which time can be transformed from tyrannical determinant into autonomously and creatively determined constituent of the reproduction process.

This challenge necessarily involves the supersession of the structurally enforced hierarchical social division of labour. For so long as time dominates society in the form of the imperative to extract the surplus labour time of its overwhelming majority, the personnel in charge of this process must lead a substantially different form of existence, in conformity to its function as the willing enforcer of the alienating time imperative. At the same time the overwhelming majority of the individuals are "degraded to mere worker, subsumed under labour." Under such conditions, the social reproduction process must sink ever deeper into its structural crisis, with the perilous ultimate implications of no possible way of return.

The nightmare of the "stationary state" remains a nightmare even if one tries to alleviate it, as John Stuart Mill proposed, through the illusory remedy of "better distribution" taken in isolation. There can be no such thing as "better distribution" without a radical restructuring of the production process itself. The socialist hegemonic alternative to the rule of capital requires fundamentally overcoming the truncated dialectic in the vital interrelationship of production, distribution, and consumption. For without that, the socialist aim of turning work into "life's prime want" is inconceivable. To quote Marx:

> In a higher phase of communist society, after the enslaving subordination of the individual to the division of labour, and therewith also the antithesis between mental and physical labour, has vanished; after labour has become not only a means of life but life's prime want; after the productive forces have also increased with the all-round development of the individual, and all the springs of co-operative wealth flow more abundantly—only then can the narrow horizon of bourgeois right be crossed in its entirety and society inscribe on its banners: From each according to his ability, to each according to his needs! (1938:23).

These are the overall targets of socialist transformation, providing the compass of the journey and simultaneously also the measure of the achievements accomplished (or failed to be accomplished) on the way. Within such a vision of the hegemonic alternative to capital's social reproductive order there can be no room at all for anything like "the stationary state," nor for any of the false alternatives associated with or derived from it." The all-round development of the individuals," consciously exercising the full resources of their disposable time, within the framework of the new social metabolic control oriented toward the production of "co-operative wealth," is meant to provide the basis of a qualitatively different accountancy: the necessary socialist accountancy, defined by human need and diametrically opposed to fetishistic quantification and to the concomitant unavoidable waste.

This is why the vital importance of growth of a sustainable kind can be recognized and successfully managed in the alternative social metabolic framework. Such an alternative order of social metabolic control would be one where the antithesis between mental and physical labour—always vital for maintaining the absolute domination over labour by capital as the usurper of the role of the controlling historical subject—must vanish for good. Consequently, consciously pursued productivity itself can be elevated to a qualitatively higher level, without any danger of uncontrollable waste, bringing forth genuine—and not narrowly profit-oriented material— wealth of which the "rich social individuals" (Marx), as autonomous historical subjects (and rich precisely in that sense) are fully in control.

In the "stationary state," by contrast, the individuals could not be genuine historical subjects. For they could not be in control of a life of their own, in view of being at the mercy of the worst kind of material determinations directly under the rule of incurable scarcity.

Ever growing—and by its ultimate implications catastrophic— waste in the capital system is inseparable from the most irresponsible way in which the produced goods and services are utilized, in the service of profitable capital-expansion. Perversely, the lower their rate of utilization the higher the scope for profitable replacement— an absurdity emanating from capital's alienated vantage point whereby there can be no meaningful distinction drawn between

52

consumption and destruction. For totally wasteful destruction just as adequately fulfils the demand required by self-expansionary capital for a new profitable cycle of production as genuine consumption corresponding to use would be able to do. However, the moment of truth arrives when a heavy price must be paid for capital's criminally irresponsible husbandry, in the course of historical development. That is the point where the imperative to adopt an increasingly better and incomparably more responsible rate of utilization of the produced goods and services—and indeed consciously produced with that aim in mind, in relation to qualitative human need and use—becomes absolutely vital. For the only viable economy—one that economizes in a meaningful way and is thereby sustainable in the near and more distant future—can only be the kind of rationally managed economy, oriented toward the optimal utilization of the produced goods and services. There can be no growth of a sustainable kind outside these parameters of rational husbandry oriented by genuine human need.

To take a crucially important example of what is incurably wrong in this respect under the rule of capital, we should think of the way in which the ever growing numbers of motor cars are utilized in our societies. The resources squandered on the production and fuelling of motor cars are immense under "advanced capitalism," representing the second highest expenditure—after the mortgage commitments—in the particular households. Absurdly, however, the rate of utilization of motor cars is less than 1 percent, spuriously justified by the exclusive possession rights conferred upon their purchasers. At the same time the thoroughly practicable real alternative is not simply neglected but actively sabotaged by the massive vested interests of quasi-monopolistic corporations. For the simple truth is that what the individuals need (and do not obtain, despite the heavy financial burden imposed upon them) are adequate transport services, and not the economically wasteful and environmentally most damaging privately owned commodity which also makes them lose countless hours of their lives in unhealthy traffic jams.

Evidently, the real alternative would be to develop public transport to the qualitatively highest level, satisfying the necessary economic, environmental, and personal health criteria well within the scope of such a rationally pursued project, confining at the same time the use of—collectively owned and appropriately allocated, but not exclusively/wastefully possessed—motor cars to specific functions. Thus the individuals' need itself—in this case their genuine need for proper transport services—would determine the targets of the vehicles and communication facilities (like roads, railway networks, and navigation systems) to be produced and maintained, in accord with the principle of optimal utilization, instead of the individuals being completely dominated by the established system's fetishistic need for profitable but ultimately destructive capital expansion.

The unavoidable, but up to the present time tendentiously avoided, question of the real economy, corresponding to the considerations presented in this article, must be faced in the very near future. For in the so-called third world countries it is inconceivable to follow the wasteful "development" pattern of the past, which in fact condemned them to their precarious condition of today, under the rule of capital's mode of social metabolic reproduction. The clamorous failure of the much promoted "modernization theories" and their corresponding institutional embodiments clearly demonstrated the hopelessness of that approach.

7. In one respect, at least, we have seen alarm raised in this regard—characteristically pressing at the same time for the assertion and absolute preservation of the privileges of the dominant capitalist countries—in the recent past. It concerned the internationally growing need for energy resources and the competitive intervention of some potentially immense economic powers, above all China, in the unfolding process. Today that concern is primarily about China, but in due course also India must be added, of course, to the list of major countries unavoidably pressing for vital energy resources. And when we add to China the population of the Indian subcontinent, we are talking about more than two and a half billion people. Naturally, if they really followed the once grotesquely propagandized prescription of The Stages of Economic Growth (Rostow, 1960), with its simple-minded advocacy of "capitalist take-off and drive to maturity," that would have devastating consequences for all of us. For the fully automobilised society of two and a half billion people on the U.S. model of "advanced capitalist development," with more than 700 motor cars to every 1,000 people, would mean that

we would be all dead before long through the global "modernizing" benefits of poisonous pollution, not to mention the total depletion of the planet's oil reserves in no time at all. But by the same token, in an opposite sense, no one can seriously envisage that the countries in question could be left indefinitely where they stand today. To imagine that the two and a half billion people of China and the Indian subcontinent could be permanently condemned to their existing predicament, still in heavy dependency to the capitalistically advanced parts of the world in one way or another, defies all credulity. The only question is: whether humanity can find a rationally viable and truly equitable solution to the legitimate demand for social and economic development of the peoples involved. Otherwise, antagonistic competition and destructive struggle over resources are the way of the future, as befits the orienting framework and operating principles of capital's mode of social reproductive control.

Another respect in which the absolute imperative to adopt a qualitatively different way of organizing economic and social life appeared on the horizon in our time concerns the ecology. But again, the only viable way of addressing the increasingly grave problems of our global ecology—if we want to face up in a responsible way to the aggravating problems and contradictions of the planetary household, from their direct impact on such vital questions as global warming to the elementary demand for clean water resources and safely respirable air—is to switch from the existing order's wasteful husbandry of fetishistic quantification to a genuinely quality oriented one. Ecology, in this respect, is an important but subordinate aspect of the necessary qualitative redefinition of utilizing the produced goods and services without which the advocacy of humanity's permanently sustainable ecology—again: an absolute must—can be nothing more than pious hope.

The final point to stress in this context is that the urgency to face up to these problems cannot be underrated, let alone minimized, given capital's vested interests, sustained by its dominant imperialist state formations in their insuperable rivalry among themselves. Ironically, although there is so much propagandistic talk about "globalization," the objective requirements of making a rationally sustainable and globally coordinated reproductive order of social interchanges work are constantly violated. Yet, given the present stage of historical development, the irrepressible truth remains that with regard to all of the major issues discussed in this article we are really concerned with ever aggravating global challenges, requiring global solutions. However, our gravest concern is that capital's mode of social metabolic reproduction—in view of its inherently antagonistic structural determinations and their destructive manifestations—is not amenable at all to viable global solutions. Capital, given its unalterable nature, is nothing unless it can prevail in the form of structural domination. But the inseparable other dimension of structural domination is structural subordination. This is the way in which capital's mode of social metabolic reproduction always functioned and always must try to function, bringing with it even the most devastating wars of which we have much more than just a foretaste in our time. The violent assertion of the destructive imperatives of global hegemonic imperialism, through the formerly unimaginable destructive might of the United States as the global hegemon, cannot bring global solutions to our aggravating problems but only global disaster. Thus, the unavoidable necessity to address these global problems in a historically sustainable way puts the challenge of socialism in the twenty-first century—the only viable hegemonic alternative to capital's mode of social metabolic control—on the order of the day.

Conceptual Problems

Our thinking is unavoidably constrained by our conceptual structures. To the extent that we reflect on and reconstruct our concepts, however, we can sharpen our thinking. The theoretical and comparative focus of the field of genocide, however, led to a number of problems. For one, the literature became bogged down in rather tedious and ultimately irresolvable definitional debates, which were eventually only settled by disciplinary fiat. Clearly, these debates were unavoidable for one cannot compare cases without a common measure. But for reasons I will suggest shortly, leading genocide scholars took the Holocaust as the paradigm of genocide despite their ostensible rejection of Holocaust uniqueness. Ignoring or rejecting Raphael Lemkin's own capacious definition, which included non-murderous techniques of genocide, they redefined it as an

56

ideologically-motivated and state-executed program of mass killing. For instance, in their widely used book *The History and Sociology of Genocide* (1990), Chalk and Jonassohn criticized the UN Convention as inadequate because it omits political and social groups but includes non-lethal forms of group destruction. They wanted to confine genocide to mass killing: it is "a form of one-sided mass killing in which a state or other authority intends to destroy a group, as that group and membership in it are defined by the perpetrator" (1990: 23).

The prolific genocide scholar Barbara Harff echoed this line of thinking when she defined genocide "as a particular form of state terror ... mass murder, pre-meditated by some power-wielding group linked with state power." The background assumption was made explicit in her aside that "The Jewish Holocaust... is employed as the yardstick, the *ultimate criterion* for assessing the scope, methods, targets, and victims of [other] genocides" (1986: 165-66. Emphasis added). In an influential article, Harff and Ted Gurr followed the trend of excluding the non-lethal techniques of genocide in the UN Convention "because," as they wrote, "this extends the definition to innumerable instances of groups which have lost their cohesion and identity, but not necessarily their lives" (1988: 360).

The line we should follow was made clear by Chalk when he argued that "we must never forget that the great genocides of the past have been committed by [state] perpetrators who acted in the name of absolutist or utopian ideologies aimed at cleansing and purifying their worlds." (1994: 58). In its initial incarnation, then, genocide studies was really a version of totalitarianism theory because by definition a genocide—at least a true one—can only be committed by a totalitarian or at least authoritarian state.

Largely forgotten here were the colonial genocides about which Lemkin had written so much in his unpublished writing (McDonnell and Moses, 2005). It is to the lasting credit of Chalk and Jonassohn that they included colonial cases in their well-known anthology, but apart from outsiders like David Stannard in the USA and Tony Barta in Australia, colonial cases were not regarded as particularly interesting or important. There is a blindness at work here that led a prominent historian to concede that although "it was the hand-in-glove pressure of American settlers and the military might deployed by the government of the United States that destroyed large numbers of the American Indians," this fact revealed nothing about "the nature of American society" (Chalk, 1994: 56-57). If we are searching for what I have elsewhere called "conceptual blockages" in the discipline, here they are (Moses, 2002).

The restriction of the meaning of genocide in this way is not surprising. The Cambodian auto-genocide had occurred at the moment of the foundation of Genocide Studies, and the colonial period had long passed in the Anglophone settler colonies. There was also a Cold War imperative. Most North American genocide scholars are liberals for whom the answer to totalitarianism and genocide is the United States and its willing coalition partners. If the rest of the world were like the US, so the thinking goes, genocide would no longer occur. If the US is guilty of anything it is of sins of omission, as Samantha Power argued in her book, "*A Problem from Hell*" (2002).

This approach dovetails neatly with the implicit modernization theory in comparative Genocide Studies: genocides occur in societies—"failed states," we often hear today (Harff, 2003)—that have experienced perverted modernizations. Had they followed the western, preferably the North American, road to modernity, it is implied, they would not have become totalitarian states and perpetrated genocide on their own or neighbouring populations. Leaving aside the fact that this rosy view ignores the fate of the Native Americans, it can be identified as an American version of what we historians of Germany recognize immediately as the now highly suspect *Sonderweg* approach to comparative historical sociology.

Either way the US and, more generally, the West, is regarded as the redeeming power in world affairs, whether as the agent of liberalization or as the cavalry that rescues victims from genocidal elites and their militias in the "Third World." When Mark Levene suggested otherwise at the fourth biennial "International Association of Genocide Scholars" conference at the University of Minnesota on June 10, 2001, he was rebuked by leaders in the field with the epithets that he was anti-American, "ideological," and such heresies. Yet how ideological is a position that wants to ignore the genocidal foundation of settler colonies like the US and Australia, and question the theodicy that the westernization of the globe will lead to a world in which genocide has been banished?

Similar problems affect the comparative historical approach so common in the field. It proceeds *episodically* rather than studying broader and deeper processes. Consider two anthologies that cover the twentieth century: *The Specter of Genocide* (2003), edited by Robert Gellately and Ben Kiernan, and *A Century of Genocide* (2003) edited by Samuel Totten, Williams S. Parsons, and Israel Charny. Their chapters present global instances of genocide—the Kiernan/Gellately volume in particular includes cases that customarily receive less attention—but they do not give much of a sense of how they are related to one another except as instances of a definition. An integrated organization on ethnic cleansing is offered by the sociologist Michael Mann in his big work *The Dark Side of Democracy*. A neo-Weberian, Mann is reluctant to offer a single theory, and instead employs an ensemble of concepts of how nation states negotiate the tension between *ethnos* and *demos*, and the problem of national minorities – ranging from assimilation to extermination – to understand how and why states radicalize in the direction of ethnic cleansing and genocide. Like another Weberian, Reinhard Bendix, who wrote on nation and state formation in equally sweeping terms, Mann presents no overarching theory of what drives change and escalation on a global scale. In the end each chapter is a case study in the conventional mode of comparative sociology, in this case utilizing ideal types to categorize the material. Of the Holocaust, he admits that "it had too many peculiarities to fit easily into any general model" (503).

Progress has been made with two books by the American historians Norman Naimark and Eric Weitz. Because of their disciplinary background, perhaps, they are inclined to honour the specificity of individual cases and reluctant to subsume them mechanically under an overarching category. Naimark avers that "comparative reflection on the problems of ethnic cleansing also leads to the conclusion that each case must be understood in its full complexity, in its own immediate context, rather than merely as part of a long term historical conflict between nations" (2001: 16), while Weitz says he is averse to large scale generalization and lawmaking to which many social scientists are prone (2003: 11).

Both writers also attempt to situate ethnic cleansing and genocide in broader processes. Naimark thinks "its traces can be seen in every society, and its potentiality is part of us all," and he claims that the broader context is what he calls the "high modernism" of the nation state at its highest state of development (2001: 186). Similarly, Weitz maintains that genocides are "embedded in complex historical processes, notably, the emergence in the modern world of race and nation as the primary categories of political and social organization" (2003: 2) His aim is to write "a comparative study that tries to be faithful to the historian's propensity for detail, nuance, and contingency, but that also goes beyond an individual case to examine how, in the modern world, political models (not only capital and commodities) move in global space." And he goes so far to say that genocides lie at the centre of our "contemporary cultural crisis" (2003: 8-11).

As historians, both authors are also alive to the historically specific conjunctures that issue forth in genocide: they do not happen randomly at any time. Consequently, they embed the unfolding twentieth-century catastrophes—principally in Europe—in the First World War and its aftermath. To their credit, Naimark and Weitz – both experts on the history of European communism – raise the profile of ethnic cleansing and genocide in the Soviet Union—the fate of the North Caucasian Muslims, for instance—and the expulsion of ethnic Germans from central Europe after the Second World War. And yet, the break with the intellectual traditions of comparative genocide studies is incomplete. The continuing links manifest themselves in a number of ways:

➤ The nation-state remains the object of analysis rather than the process or crisis that they incarnate or to which they are responding. The broader context is background rather than foreground.

➤ The preoccupation with modern state, revolutionary politics, and utopian ideologies continues (Weitz, 2003: 6-7). Both books focus largely on totalitarian cases. Weitz, for instance, recognizes that pre-twentieth-century genocides include, as he puts it, "European settlers acting under the aegis of liberal states [who] annihilated indigenous populations in Australia and North America," as well as

60

German Southwest Africa and the Soviet deportations of the 1930s, noting that in "none of these states did genocide come to constitute the nearly exclusive, central motor of the systems" (2003: 10). So while not denying that they are genocides, he has deemed them less worthy of our intellectual attention.

➤ They are also preoccupied with illiberal elites in the manner of Helen Fein in her much-cited definition quoted above. Genocides "were ignited by the warped ambitions of modern politicians," writes Naimark (2001: 16). Utopianism is also a culprit for Weitz: "they shared a common orientation in their determination to remake fundamentally the societies and states they had either conquered or inherited" (2003: 237). No mention is made of the extensive literature on modernity and biopolitics that ascribes genocidal outcomes less to extreme ideologies than to logics inherent in the modern state itself (cf. Moses, 2008a).

➤ The whiff of an implicit rational choice theory, an idiosyncrasy of North American social science, is discernible in some passages in which war is depicted as an opportunity for the implementation of such ideologies. We are back to Fein's general theory of genocide with its various elements: ideologies of race and nation; revolutionary regimes with utopian aspirations of social or ethnic purity, moments of crisis generated by war and upheaval.

These two books, therefore, still exemplify the methodological assumptions of comparative sociology by proposing a general concept and offering case studies to bear it out. The danger of tautology is evident here when Weitz says that his "four case studies … display some notably common features, especially in relation to the historical origin and practice of genocide," a conclusion to which one can come depending on the selection of cases. The circularity is admitted in the statement that "The commonalities I have found among them may not apply to every single case of genocide; other historical factors may come into play in other situations" (2003: 251).

Here we see that the restriction of genocide to revolutionary utopian social projects can only be sustained by wilfully excluding cases that are not revolutionary utopian social projects. A final similarity is the insistence on contingency: genocide is not inevitable, nor does it follow any specific logics. Other regimes had multiracial ideologies, for instance. The nation-building process itself does not issue in genocide necessarily. "There is then," Weitz argues, a very substantial element of contingency to the emergence of genocides related to very specific conjunctures" (2003: 251). But if genocide is contingent upon a crisis of some kind, and we are in the middle of some kind of deeper "cultural crisis," as he puts it, should they and it not be the study of sustained reflection?

Conceptual Clarifications

In the normal course of perceiving and interpreting events, our concepts are, for the most part, invisible to us. Rather than reflecting on them, we see the world through them. In fact, it is only through concepts that we are able to identify and make sense of the various aspects of the world. What appear to us as objective representations imposed on our minds by reality itself are always in large part a function of the network of conceptions to which we have assimilated that reality. Thus, the nature of our concepts to a large degree determines not only our subjective interpretations but even our most elementary, and seemingly objective, observations and categorizations.

The unavoidable subjectivity of conceptual thought, however, does not entail a radical relativism that dismisses objectivity and truth as illusions. Despite their intrinsic subjectivity, our observations and interpretations are also a function of realities outside our minds. Although we cannot directly represent simple and absolute truths about the world, neither are we limited to illusions generated by arbitrary concepts. Perception is a joint function of the realities around us and the conceptions to which we assimilate those realities. Objectivity is not an achievable end but it remains an important epistemic ideal that can be approached by coordinating, reflecting on, and reconstructing our conceptual structures.

Antoine Laurent Lavoisier in 1789 instructed us that it is impossible to dissociate language from science or science from language. The reason is that every natural or social science always involves three things: the sequence of phenomena on which the science is based; the abstract concepts which call these phenomena to mind; and the words in which the concepts are expressed.

Genocide, however, is a confused and confusing concept. It may or may not include government murder, refer to wholly or partially eliminating some group, or involve psychological damage. If it includes government murder, it may mean all such murder or just some. Boiling all this down, genocide can have three different meanings. One meaning is that defined by international treaty, the Convention on the Prevention and Punishment of the Crime of Genocide. This makes genocide a punishable crime under international law, and defines it as: any of the following acts committed with intent to destroy, in whole or in part, a national, ethnical, racial or religious group, as such:

(a) Killing members of the group;
(b) Causing serious bodily or mental harm to members of the group;
(c) Deliberately inflicting on the group conditions of life calculated to bring about its physical destruction in whole or in part;
(d) Imposing measures intended to prevent births within the group;
(e) Forcibly transferring children of the group to another group.

Note that only the first clause includes outright killing, while the other clauses cover non-killing ways of eliminating a group. I will call this definition of genocide the *legal meaning*, since it is now part of international law. Regardless of this definition and doubtlessly influenced by the Holocaust, ordinary usage and that by students of genocide have tended to wholly equate it with the *murder and only the murder* by government of people due to their national, ethnical, racial or religious (or, what is called *indelible*) group membership. This way of viewing genocide has become so ingrained that it seems utterly false to say, for example, that the United States committed genocide against ethnic Hawaiians by forcing their children to study English and behave according to American norms and values. Yet, in the legal view of genocide, this is arguably true. The equating of genocide with the killing people because of their indelible group membership I will label the *common meaning* of genocide.

In some usage and especially among some students of genocide, the concept has been redefined to fill a void. What about government murdering people for other reasons than their indelible group membership? What about government organized death squads eliminating communist sympathizers, assassinating political opponents, or cleansing the population of anti-revolutionaries? What about simply fulfilling a government death quota (as in the Soviet Union under Stalin). None of such murders are genocide according the legal and common meanings. Therefore, some students of genocide have stretched its meaning to include all government murder, whether or not because of group membership. This may be aptly named the *generalized* meaning of genocide.

As obvious, the problem with the generalized meaning of genocide is that to fill one void it creates another. For if genocide refers to all government murder, what are we to call the murder of people because of their group membership? It is precisely because of this conceptual problem that Rummel (1994) created the concept of democide.

FIGURE 1A. The Relationship Between
Democide and the Legal Meaning of Genocide

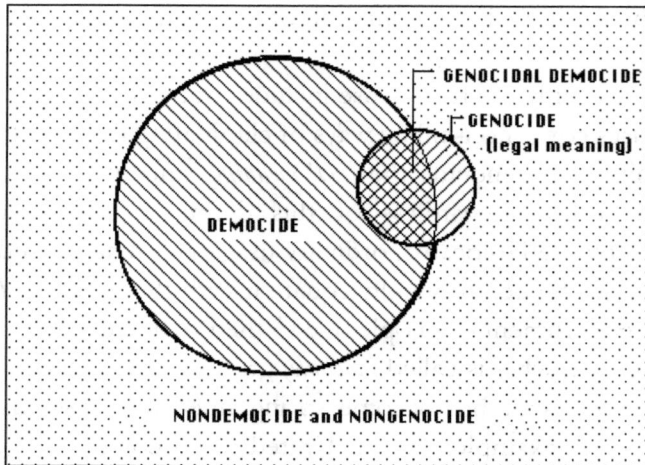

We now have three meanings of genocide: legal, common, and generalized. How do these related to democide? Let me try to make this clear through Venn Diagrams. Figure 1A shows two circles, one containing all cases of democide, the other all cases of genocide. Outside of the two circles are all other forms of behaviour that is

64

neither democide or genocide. Now, for the legal meaning of genocide, only part of the circle of genocide will overlap that of democide, as shown in the figure. This is because the legal meaning includes nonkilling, while democide includes only killing. The overlap portion of the circles comprise those cases of democide that are the genocidal murder of people in order to eradicate their group in whole or part. That part of the democide circle outside of the overlap contains those murdered for other reasons.

FIGURE 1B. The Relationship Between Democide and the Common Meaning of Genocide

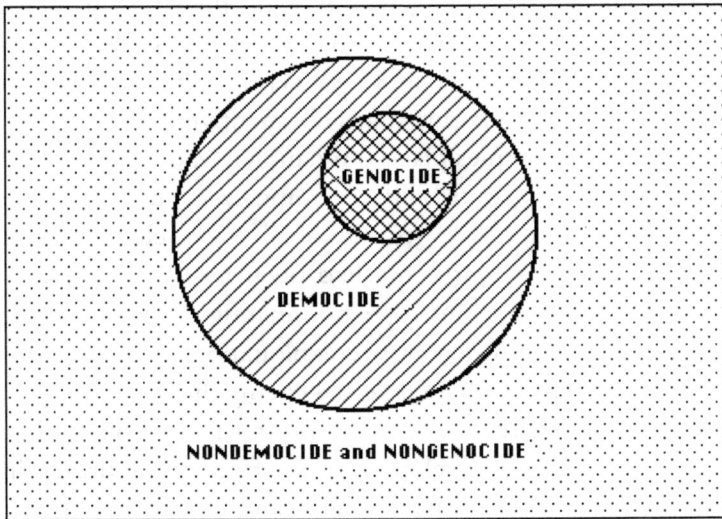

The progress of our knowledge of government murder depends fundamentally on the clarity and significance of our concepts. Especially, these concepts should refer to real world behaviour and events that can be clearly and similarly discriminated regardless of the observers and their prejudices. For if any area of social study is laden with predispositions and biases, it surely has to do with the who, why, when, and how of government murder (the meaning of "government" and "murder" are themselves concepts that require clarification. For these reasons I believe that both genocide in its common meaning and democide as I have defined it have an important role in understanding government murder. The legal view of genocide, however, is too complex and subsumes behaviour too different in kind, such as government murder, government induced psychological damage, government attempting to eliminate a group in whole or in part (what empirical meaning can we give to "in part "?), or government removing children from a group (removing what percentage constitutes genocide?), and so on. In the case of democide, the vast majority of government killing is manifestly murder--the intent to commit murder is inherent in the act itself. For example, soldiers lining up civilians against a wall and shooting them to death without a fair trial is manifestly government murder. And in its common meaning, most cases of genocide can be equally discriminated, as in the Holocaust or of the Armenian genocide in Turkey during 1915-1916. Indeed, genocide, then, is explained not by recourse to cultural or political contingencies endogenous to specific nation states, although the cultural perception of their elites remains important, but by the pressure that a competitive, indeed Darwinistic, system of state economies places on national leaderships to establish and maintain sovereign viability. In some cases, usually among the second tier late-comer states (postcolonial) to the club established by Westerners, desperate shortcuts had been taken to accelerate and institutional modernization: by exterminating a native people who live in an area desired for economic exploitation, or by exterminating a minority associated with an external enemy that is held responsible for endangering the nation in a security crisis, or holding back the country's independent development by effectively representing the interests of a competitor. Thus, under stable conditions, the empires of Eurasian tectonic plate could accommodate considerable national/ethnic diversity, but not when placed under geopolitical pressure by the West. Nor when it favoured minorities like the Armenians, who then, in Turkish eyes, became disloyal, indeed, dangerous subjects.

Democide is meant to define the killing by states as the concept of murder does individual killing in domestic society. Here intentionality (premeditation) is critical. This also includes practical intentionality. If a government causes deaths through a reckless and depraved indifference to human life, the deaths were as though intended. If through neglect a mother lets her baby die of malnutrition, this is murder. If we imprison a girl in our home, force her to do exhausting work fourteen hours a day, not even minimally feed and clothe her, and watch her gradually die a little each day without helping her, then her inevitable death is not only our fault, but our practical intention. It is murder. Similarly, for example, the Soviet system for forcibly transporting prisoners to labour camps was lethal. In transit hundreds of thousands of political prisoners died at the hands of criminals or guards, or from heat, cold, or inadequate food or water. Although not intended (indeed, this deprived the regime of their labour), the deaths were still murder. They were democide.

In sum, people are not united just by ethnicity, race and religion; rather, people can be united in political causes with greater passion than any other identifiable group. Therefore, it stands to reason that the definition of genocide should be expanded to include "any of the following acts committed with intent to destroy, in whole or in part, a national, ethnical, racial, political or religious group, as such: (a) killing members of the group; (b) causing serious bodily or mental harm to members of the group…" This new definition would serve the purpose of including horrific events, such as those in Darfur, with the definition of genocide. Then, once these events are identified as genocide, hopefully it will cause the rest of the world to honour their agreement and interfere.

Bibliography

Chalk, Frank, 1994, "Redefining Genocide," in George J. Andreopolous, ed., *Genocide: Conceptual and Historical Dimensions*. Philadelphia: University of Pennsylvania Press, 47-63.

Chalk, Frank, and Jonassohn, Kurt, eds., 1990, *The History and Sociology of Genocide: Analyses and Case Studies*. New Haven: Yale University Press.

Donella H. Meadows, et al. (1972). *The Limits to Growth: A Report for the Club of Rome Project on the Predicament of Mankind. London: Earth Island Limited. Professor Jay Forrester, of the Massachusetts Institute of Technology, contemptuously dismissed all concern with equality as a mere "shibboleth of equality." See his interview in* Le Monde, *August 1, 1972.*

Fein, Helen, 1990, *Genocide: A Sociological Perspective*. London: Sage Publications.

Fein, Helen, 1993, "Revolutionary and Antirevolutionary Genocides: A Comparison of State Murders in Democratic Kampuchea, 1975 to 1979, and in Indonesia, 1965 to 1966." *Comparative Studies in Society and History*, 35/4, 796-823.

István Mészáros. (2001). *Socialism or Barbarism: From the "American Century" to the Crossroads. Monthly Review Press.*

Vadim Medvedev. (1989). "The Ideology of Perestroika," in Perestroika Annual 2, Abel Aganbegyan, (ed.) London: Futura/Macdonald.

Gorbachev quoted in John Rettie, "Only Market Can Save Soviet Economy," The Guardian, October 17, 1990.

Gellately, Robert, and Kiernan, Ben, eds., 2003, *The Specter of Genocide: Mass Murder in Historical Perspective*. New York: Cambridge University Press.

Harff, Barbara, 1986, "Genocide as State Terrorism," in *Government Violence and Repression*, ed. M. Stohl and G. A. Lopez, eds. New York: Greenwood Press.

Harff, Barbara, 2003, "No Lessons Learned from the Holocaust? Assessing Risks of Genocide and Political Mass Murder since 1955." *American Political Science Review*, 97, 57-73.

Harff, Barbara, and Gurr, Ted R., 1988, "Toward Empirical Theory of Genocides and Politicides." *International Studies Quarterly*, 32, 359-71.

Hegel. G. W. F. (1991). The Philosophy of Right. Cambridge: Cambridge University Press.

John Bellamy Foster, 'The Treadmill of Accumulation', *Organization & Environment* 18, no. 1 (2005).

Katz, Steven T., 1994, *The Holocaust in Historical Context*, vol. 1, New York: Oxford University Press.

Kiernan, Ben, 2007, *Blood and Soil: A World History of Genocide and Extermination from Sparta to Darfur*, Yale University Press.

Marx. Karl. (1992). Capital, vol. 1. Penguin Classics. John Stuart Mill, Principles of Political Economy (Prometheus Books, 2004), 751.

Marx K. (1991). The Poverty of Philosophy, in Marx-Engels Collected Works, vol. 6, 134. Quoted in István Mészáros, "The Communitarian System and the Law of Value in Marx and Lukács" (chapter 19 of Beyond Capital), Critique, no. 23, 1991, 36. See also chapter 15 ("The Decreasing Rate of Utilization under Capitalism") and chapter 16 ("The Decreasing Rate of

Utilization and the Capitalist State") of *Beyond Capital*, which deal with some important related issues.

Marx, Karl. (1938*). Critique of the Gotha Programme, in Marx and Engels, Selected Works, vol. 2, 23.*

Paul Burkett, *Marx and Nature* (New York: St. Martin's Press, 1999), 112.

Paul Sweezy, 'Capitalism and the Environment', *Monthly Review* 41, no. 2 (1989): 1–10.

Levene, Mark, 1999, "A Moving Target, the Usual Suspects and (Maybe) a Smoking Gun: The Problem of Pinning Blame in Modern Genocide," *Patterns of Prejudice*, 33/4.

Levene, Mark, 2004, "A Dissenting Voice: Part 1." *Journal of Genocide Research*, 6/2,153-66,

Levene, Mark, 2004, "A Dissenting Voice, Part 2." *Journal of Genocide Research*, 6/3, 431-45.

Levene, Mark, 2005, *Genocide in the Age of the Nation-State*. 2 vols. London: I.B. Tauris.

Mann, Michael, 2005, *The Dark Side of Democracy: Explaining Ethnic Cleansing*. Cambridge: Cambridge University Press.

McDonnell, Michael, and Moses, A. Dirk, 2005, "Raphael Lemkin as Historian of Genocide in the Americas." *Journal of Genocide Research*, 7/4, 501-29.

Moses, A. Dirk, 2002, "Conceptual Blockages and Definitional Dilemmas in the Racial Century: Genocide of Indigenous Peoples and the Holocaust," *Patterns of Prejudice*, 36, 7-36.

Moses, A. Dirk, 2008a, "Genocide and Modernity," in Dan Stone, ed., *The Historiography of Genocide*. Houndmills: Palgrave, MacMillan, 156-93.

Moses, A. Dirk, 2008b, "Empire, Colony, Genocide: Keywords and Intellectual History," in A. Dirk Moses, ed., *Empire Colony, Genocide: Conquest, Occupation, and Subaltern Resistance in World History*. New York: Berghahn Books.

Mosse, George L., 1964, *The Crisis of German Ideology: Intellectual Origins of the Third Reich*, New York: H. Fertig, 1981.

Naimark, Norman, 2001, *Fires of Hatred: Ethnic Cleansing in Twentieth-Century Europe*. Cambridge, MA: Harvard University Press.

Power, Samantha, 2002, *"A Problem from Hell": America and the Age of Genocide*. New York: Basic Books.

Rummel, R.J. "Democide in Totalitarian States: Mortacracies and Megamurderers." In Israel Charny (Ed.), *The Widening Circle of Genocide: Genocide: A critical Bibliographic Review* Vol. 3, New Brunswick, New Jersey: Transaction Publishers, 1994.

Shaw, Martin, 2007, *What Is Genocide?* London. Polity.

Stern, Fritz, 1961, *The Politics of Cultural Despair: A study in the Rise of the Germanic Ideology.* Berkeley: University of California Press, 1961.

Stone, Dan, ed., 2007, *The Historiography of Genocide.* Houndmills. Palgrave MacMillan.

Totten, Samuel, Parsons, William S., and Charny, Israel W., eds., 2004, *A Century of Genocide: Critical Essays and Eyewitness Accounts,* 2nd ed. New York: Routledge.

Walt Rostow. (1960). *The Stages of Economic Growth: A Non-Communist Manifesto. Cambridge: Cambridge University Press.*

Weitz, Eric D., 2003, *A Century of Genocide: Utopias of Race and Nation. Princeton,* NJ: Princeton University Press.

Chapter Three

Genocide:
Slave Raids, Arabic and Trans-Atlantic Slave Trade, and Slavery

Overview

Over the course of more than three and a half centuries, the forcible transportation in bondage of at least twelve million men, women, and children from their African homelands to the Americas changed forever the face and character of the modern world. The slave trade was brutal and horrific, and the enslavement of Africans was cruel, exploitative, and dehumanizing. Together, they represent one of the longest and most sustained assaults on the very life, integrity, and dignity of human beings in history.

In the Americas, besides the considerable riches their free labour created for others, the importation and subsequent enslavement of the Africans would be the major factor in the resettlement of the continents following the disastrous decline in their indigenous population. Between 1492 and 1776, an estimated 6.5 million people migrated to and settled in the Western Hemisphere. More than five out of six were Africans. Although victimized and exploited, they created a new, largely African, Creole society and their forced migration resulted in the emergence of the so-called Black Atlantic.

The transatlantic slave trade laid the foundation for modern capitalism, generating immense wealth for business enterprises in America and Europe. The trade contributed to the industrialization of northwestern Europe and created a single Atlantic world that included Western Europe, western Africa, the Caribbean islands, and the main lands of North and South America. On the other hand, the overwhelming impact on Africa of its involvement in the creation of this modern world was negative. The continent experienced the loss of a significant part of its able-bodied population, which played a part in the social and political weakening of its societies that left them open, in the nineteenth century, to colonial domination and exploitation.

Introduction: The Birth of Slavery

It is virtually impossible to understand the new racial caste system in America—mass incarceration, without comprehending the history and legacy of racism in America. The story told in schools during Black History Month is usually triumphant, but the reality is more disturbing and pressing. The concept of race is relatively new—its origins are largely attributable to European imperialism over the last few centuries. In America, the modern conception of race developed as justification for exterminating American Indians, as well as to reconcile chattel slavery against the ideals of freedom whites preached in the new colonies.

Indentured servitude was originally the dominant means of securing cheap labour in the New World. According to historian Lerone Bennet Jr., whites and blacks together struggled to survive against "the big planter apparatus and a social system that legalized terror against black and white bondsmen." Black people brought to America were not initially all enslaved. Many lived as indentured servants, but as plantation farming grew, so too did demand for labour and land. Colonists met the increased demand for land by invading and stealing indigenous territory. Throughout this period, portrayals of American Indians in books, newspapers and magazines grew increasingly hostile. The depiction of indigenous people as "savages" became commonplace, providing the justification colonists needed for their extermination.

Slavery answered the call for increased labour demands. Indigenous people were not considered suitable slaves, because they presented too much of a risk. They could organize and fight back, which frightened plantation owners. European immigrants were not viable alternatives—not because of race, but because there were so few of them, and there were concerns that enslaving them would impede voluntary immigration to the new colonies. Africans met the selection criteria and became the ideal slaves. Systematic enslavement of Africans happened quickly and was intensified after events like Bacon's Rebellion. Nathaniel Bacon was a white property owner in

Jamestown, Virginia, who managed to unite slaves, indentured servants and poor white people in a revolt against the planter elite in 1675. Most free whites in the colonies at the time lived in abject poverty, and indentured servitude, while slightly higher on the rungs of social hierarchy, was still brutal and provided little room for mobility.

When planter elite refused to provide militia support for Bacon's scheme to seize Native American lands (for himself and others), he retaliated by attacking them, their homes and their property. He strategically condemned them for their oppression of the poor and forged an alliance of white and black bond labourers and slaves, who demanded an end to their servitude. The elite responded with force and false promises of amnesty, although many participants in the revolt were ultimately hanged. Although the threat of Bacon's Rebellion was quelled, the planter elite were left fearful of the multiracial alliance of bond workers and slaves. Word spread about the success of the revolt, and more uprisings of a similar nature occurred across the colonies.

The planter elite was shaken after Bacon's Rebellion. Scrambling to maintain dominance after the uprising, they shifted their focus onto black slaves instead of indentured servants. They recognized that non-English-speaking Africans would be easier to control (since they would be less familiar with European culture and language) and therefore less likely to form alliances with poor whites. But they feared this still wouldn't be enough, so they took it a step further.

A "racial bribe" was catalysed by the planter elite, wherein they extended exclusive privileges to poor whites, giving them a clear advantage over black slaves. Some of these privileges included granting whites greater access to Native American lands, allowing them to police slaves through patrols and militias, and generating boundaries to minimize competition between free labour and slave labour. The result of this shift was that poor whites now had personal stake in a race-based system of slavery; they were beneficiaries of a newfound kind of power, even though their conditions hadn't actually improved very much.

The strategy was a wild success. By the mid-1770s, a wedge was sufficiently driven between poor whites and black slaves, and a full racial caste system predicated on slavery had emerged. White colonists perpetuated and justified the degraded status of Africans on the same line of reasoning they invoked against American Indians—that they were an uncivilized lesser race—even as whites marched forward in creating a new nation based on "equality, liberty and justice for all." Chattel slavery in America was in full-effect before democracy was even born.

Race had an acute impact in defining the foundation of American society. The Constitution in many ways reflected an effort to preserve slavery and protect whites—particularly white property owners. A precondition for the Southern slaveholding colonies being willing to form a union was that the federal government wouldn't be able to interfere with their right to own slaves. Northern elites were sympathetic to this cause, in the sense that they also wanted their property interests protected. As one of the nation's Founding Fathers, James Madison, remarked, the nation should be constituted "to protect the minority of the opulent against the majority." The result was a Constitution designed for a weaker federal government, to protect states' rights and private property. The language was colourblind (a concept we'll return to later in detail—in this case referring to the absence of words such as "Negro" or "slave"), but the Constitution solidified the prevailing racial caste system. Even the Electoral College was created with slaveholder interests in mind; slaves under our nation's founding document were defined as three-fifths of a man. This is the structure upon which American democracy has unfolded.

Middle East Slavery

As old and as violent as the conflict is between Sunni and Shiite Muslims, slavery is even older. It predates the written historical record, Davis writes, and at critical turns was supported legally by the major religions of Judaism and Christianity. Islam followed. And as the teachings of the Koran spread from Mecca to the conquered lands of Africa and beyond, beginning in the seventh century, the lucrative slave trade expanded from Africa *back* to the Middle East. (For those who don't know, there are only 20 miles from the Horn of Africa to the Arabian Peninsula at its closest point, across the Babel-Mandeb Strait, linking the Indian Ocean and the Mediterranean by way of the Red Sea.)

Don't get me wrong: Africans were not just slaves in Mesopotamia. Some played key roles in the formation of Islam, as Leyla Keogh notes in her entry on the Middle East in *Africana: The Encyclopaedia of the African and African American Experience, Second Edition*. But, over time, the enslavement of African men and women went hand in hand with the maturation of Islam, and the caliphate's reliance on foreign, non-Arabic-speaking slaves, black and white, intensified as the empire grew.

Davis writes:

> The spectacular Arab conquests, like those of the earlier Romans, revolutionized geographic boundaries and produced an immense flow of slaves for employment as servants, soldiers, members of harems, eunuch chaperons, and bureaucrats. Thanks to such earlier innovations as the North Arabian saddle and camel caravans, Arabs, Berbers, and their converts made deep inroads into sub-Saharan Africa, thus tapping, through purchase or capture, an unprecedented pool of slave labour. According to some scholarship, this importation of black slaves into Islamic lands from Spain to India constituted a continuous, large-scale migration—by caravan and sea over a period of more than twelve centuries, beginning in the 600s— that may have equalled in total numbers all the African slaves transported to the Western Hemisphere. One French scholar, Raymond Mauny, estimates that as many as fourteen million African slaves were exported to Muslim regions.

But who exactly were the Zanj? Some identify them specifically as black slaves from east Africa—think *Zanzibar*—but it was a much looser term than that ("Zanj," an Arabic word, is often translated as "black"). The best book on the subject is *The Revolt of African Slaves in Iraq in the 3rd/9th Century* by Alexandre Popovic. (I had the pleasure of writing the introduction to the French-to-English translation in 1999.) As Popovic explains, Zanj was a label used for black slaves, specifically those tasked with the hardest, plantation-style work.

Key information on the Zanj work sites within Mesopotamia comes to us through Popovic by way of ninth-century Arab historian al-Tabari, who remembered the Zanj as black slaves who were forced to undertake the massive field project to drain the salt marshes of Lower Mesopotamia. It was backbreaking work, and the men were underfed and stuffed into labour camps of 500 to 5,000. While most slaves in Islamic countries were domestic workers, the Zanj toiled at the bottom of society at the bottom of the Arabian Peninsula.

Over time, their presence reinforced Arabs' negative stereotypes of blacks in general. Davis explains:

> [R]egardless of their continuing enslavement and purchase of white Christian infidels, medieval Arabs came to associate the most degrading forms of labour with black slaves—with the Zanj whom the medieval Arab writer Maqdisi described as 'people of black colour, flat noses, kinky hair, and little understanding or intelligence.' In fact, the Arabic word for slave, abd, came in time to mean only a black slave and, in some regions, referred to any black person whether slave or free. Many Arab writers echoed the racial contempt typified by the famous fourteenth-century Tunisian historian Ibn Khaldun when he wrote that black people 'are, as a whole submissive to slavery, because Negroes have little that is essentially human and have attributes that are quite similar to those of dumb animals.'

Throughout history, the hardest work has had a way of landing on the lowliest workers, who, in turn, are bestialized by the master class in order to justify the very conditions they imposed. It is important to remember that this process, historically throughout the world, has not always been based on differences of colour or "race," though it became color-coded early on in the history of the British colonies, just as it had in the Middle East. And many white immigrant groups—such as the earliest Irish immigrants—were demeaned and stereotyped in very similar ways to the treatment of black people. The quickest way to justify exploiting an entire race, nationality or religious group is to represent them as subhuman. As Georgia congressman John Lewis recently tweeted about the United States, "In many ways this country was built by slaves and immigrants, something we should not forget in our 'debate' about immigration." Except that we always do.

The Caliphate

What the caliphate of the ninth century failed to remember, to its detriment, was that however long and cruelly a master might use his slaves as "tool[s] or instrument[s]," he can never erase their will to survive—and be free. As Davis writes, "The slave is of course an independent centre of consciousness, a unique human mind often aware of an owner's weaknesses and capable of defiance, retaliation, or subtle triumphs that uncloak a master's pretensions to godhood."

In other words, the Zanj camps were a powder keg.

According to Popovic, two Zanj insurrections failed under the previous Umayyad Caliphate: One in 689-690 was small and local, and the prisoners were beheaded. Another, in 694, led by the "Lion of the Zanj," took two military offenses to defeat. It was followed by two centuries of silence.

When the Umayyad Caliphate was cast out by the rival Abbasid Caliphate in 750, slavery persisted. A confluence of factors made the year 869 ripe for another push for freedom. The central government was mired in divisions among Turkish military leaders, Arab lawmakers and Persian civil servants, Popovic explains. The empire also was increasingly spread thin defending its positions abroad, while, internally, independent governors were becoming ever more independent. "[A]ll that was lacking," Popovic writes, "was a leader capable of stirring up the Zanj and lighting the fire."

The Master of the Zanj

Enter Ali bin Muhammad, the matchstick of the Zanj revolt. Muhammad was not Zanj himself, but of Arab or Persian descent. Little is known about his early life except that he was a poet who claimed to have a direct line to the Almighty with instructions to lead a great crusade. He also was clever enough to assure his followers that his family tree included connections to the Prophet Muhammad. According to Popovic, Ali bin Muhammad moved restlessly around the empire searching for a people to lead. He found them in the lower canal region of Mesopotamia in September 869.

What began as a local revolt escalated when the fearful word spread from Basra to the central government. Heading to the fray was Ali bin Muhammad, who established himself as leader by promising the Zanj freer, better lives. Muhammad wrapped his message in a strain of Islam at once stark and egalitarian. According to *Britannica Online*, "Ali's offers became even more attractive with his subsequent adoption of a Khārijite religious stance: anyone, even a black slave, could be elected caliph, and all non-Khārijites were infidels threatened by a holy war."

Before long, Muhammad became known ironically as the Master of the Zanj. Popovic, via the historian al-Tabari, returns us to a fateful first encounter: "Ali b. Muhammad assembled his followers, whose numbers continued to grow, under the flag for prayer. In an address to them, he spoke of their miserable condition and assured them that God had chosen him to be the instrument of their deliverance. He also told them that he, 'Ali b. Muhammad, wanted to improve their lot so that one day they, too, might have beautiful homes and slaves. After the oath, and before leaving, he asked those who had understood to translate for anyone who did not speak Arabic.' "

Muhammad's flag became the flag of the Zanj, and unlike future slaves who failed to show up for John Brown at Harpers Ferry (Brown's 1859 rebellion was so close to the capital in Washington that it was easy to telegraph for help and send troops before the uprising had a chance to breathe out), the Zanj rallied, wave after wave, and they weren't interested in abolition, but in taking their masters' places. That included enslaving others in their wake.

Was Muhammad using them? On some level, yes. He was an ambitious leader, Popovic writes. But the Zanj's response and resiliency indicate something much larger at play. In fact, in one early episode, according to al-Tabari, a rumour spread that Muhammad had been approached by an Abbasid general who offered him clemency and five dinars for each slave returned to bondage.

Here's how Popovic describes Muhammad's response to quell his followers' anger:

> That very night he assembled his men and, through an interpreter, swore that none of them would ever be returned to their former masters. 'May some of you remain with me and kill me if you feel that I am betraying you.' Then he called together those who spoke Arabic

and solemnly promised to lead them in battle personally and risk his life with them. He assured them that it was not for the wealth and honour of this world that he had rebelled. The Zanj were calmed down by his words.

The Revolt of the Zanj

The Zanj formed a rag-tag, yet relentless, army. In the initial fighting, Popovic writes, "[a] troop of four-thousand men attacked the rebels. The Zanj 'army' was poorly equipped to fend them off with only three sabers in its arsenal. One rebel was seen dashing into battle carrying only his plate as a weapon.

"Nevertheless, the Zanj won another victory and put the enemy to fight. One member of the attacking force was killed; others died of thirst. On orders from Ali b. Muhammad, prisoners were beheaded. The Zanj carried away the severed heads on their own mules."

There were great victories and terrible defeats along the way, but as the Zanj revolt spread, the port city of al-Uballa fell into their hands in 870. Then, dramatically, in 871, Basra fell under their control, with the Zanj massacring most of the city's residents. By 873, the Master of the Zanj had consolidated the making of an independent state in Lower Mesopotamia. According to Kent Krause, author of the entry on the Zanj rebellion in *Africana*, Muhammad "controlled the canal region of southern Iraq. He built a capital in al-Mukhtara and set up an independent government that collected taxes and minted its own coins."

But, of course, as in *Star Wars*, the empire struck back. In 880, the Abbasid Caliphate's military brother, al-Muffawaq, assembled a second army to crush the rebellion. They set out from al-Firk and built a city of their own from which to lay siege to the Zanj stronghold, al-Mukhtara. For two years, al-Muffawaq's army, including his son Abu l-Abbas, tightened the grip.

The Zanj revolt ended for good in 883 for a variety of reasons: promises of amnesty, offers to the Zanj to join the other side and, most consequently, the death of Ali bin Muhammad (either by suicide, beheading or in battle). Three years later, other Zanj leaders were executed—their bodies crucified. All told, Krause estimates, "[b]etween 500,000 and 2.5 million people died during the fourteen-year war." No slave rebellion on American soil ever came close to matching the intensity or duration of the Zanj.

The big question remaining, though: Was this technically a slave revolt? David Brion Davis uses that term. Others point out that it wasn't a war fought for abolition: The Zanj enslaved others and were brutal in their attack. Instead, Popovic says he thinks the rebellion was closer to a "political (power struggle) and social (betterment of certain class living conditions) revolt." And it wasn't strictly racial or for racial ends. That last point was advanced in a landmark 1977 article in The International Journal of African Historical Studies, "The Zanj Rebellion Reconsidered," by Ghada Hashem Talhami, who argued:

> [T]he Zanj Rebellion was not restricted to slaves of East African origin; in fact, it was not even a slave rebellion in the strict sense of the word. Ali ibn [bin] Muhammad was definitely head of a religious uprising with social overtones in which slaves provided much of the manpower. In return, as individual converts and as soldiers of the religious cause of Kharijism, they were able to win their freedom. The protest made no concerted attack on the institution of slavery as such. Moreover, its participants included Bahranis, Bedouins, and lower-class artisans as well as black slaves, some Arabic-speaking and some still speaking their native tongues.

One would, however, agree with Davis's usage. Operationally, the revolt involved masses of slaves, even if part of a diverse lot; the rebellion was distinguished by the Zanj's willingness to fight; and they helped give the revolt's leaders the numbers they needed to fend off the military for 14 years. We also must bear in mind, as Popovic does, that "to be surprised that the Zanj revolt did not aim at abolishing slavery is perhaps asking too much. I do not see how it would have been possible, in the Muslim Middle Ages, to contemplate suppression of an institution that was tolerated by the Qur'an and accepted by custom." And, in the aftermath, did slavery persist? Of course it did, but there were important temporary consequences. As Krause explains:

Despite its ultimate fate of the rebellion, the Zanj uprising had a lasting significance. The work camps of southern Iraq were abandoned and the living conditions of slaves in the region improved. The large-scale Abbasid importation of slaves from East Africa was effectively halted. Moreover, those Africans who had defected to the caliph's army were not returned to slavery. A precursor to the slave rebellions in Latin America and the Caribbean centuries later, the Zanj rebellion demonstrated the powerful potential of a captive population that rises up in solidarity.

Other consequences were damaging and long lasting, I'm afraid, well after the Mongols sacked the caliphate in the 13th century. Davis puts it this way: "While much further research is needed, it seems probable that racial stereotypes were transmitted, along with black slavery itself, from Muslims to Christians and from the eastern Mediterranean to that melting pot of religions and cultures, the Iberian Peninsula." And as we learned in last week's column, the Portuguese and Spanish had no qualms about exporting race-based slavery to the New World.

In sum, why does this matter? After all, slavery, as an institution steeped in racial difference, only strengthened with time and space. And because the Zanj were based in and around the canals of Lower Mesopotamia, archaeology holds little hope of discovering their physical footprint 1,400 years later. Many mysteries remain.

Still, Davis writes that the Zanj revolt does matter, and that is more than good enough for me. Here's what he concludes: "Though the Zanj revolt must be understood within an Islamic social and political context, the Arabs and their Muslim allies were the first people to develop a specialized, long-distance slave trade from sub-Saharan Africa. This fact widens the geographic boundaries for a full understanding of racial slavery in the New World."

Causes and results of slavery

A main cause of the trade was the colonies that European countries were starting to develop. In America, for instance, which was a colony of England, there was a demand for many labourers for the sugar, tobacco and cotton plantations.

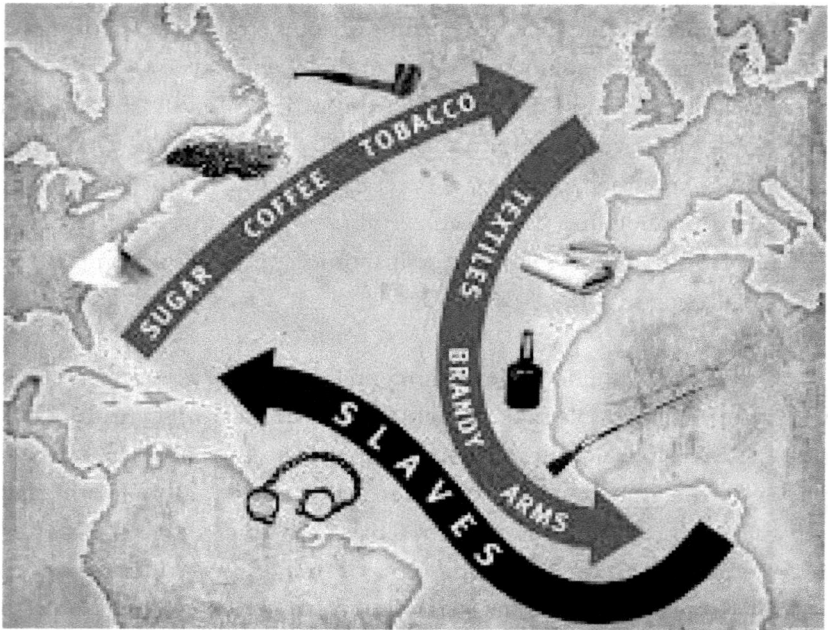

Paid labourers were too expensive, and the indigenous people had largely been wiped out by disease and conflict, so the colonizers turned to Africa to provide cheap labour in the form of slaves. The first shipment of slaves from West Africa to the Americas, across the Atlantic Ocean, was in the early 1500s. European, Arab and African merchants were now selling humans as well as gold, ivory and spices (**Anstey,** 1975).

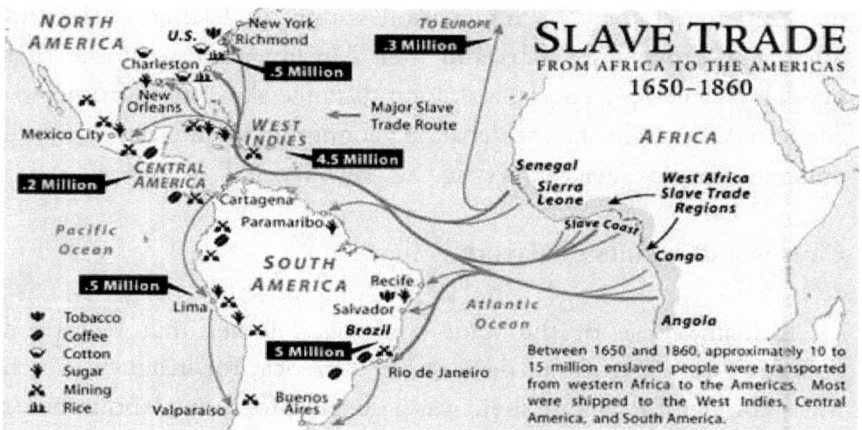

SLAVE TRADE FROM AFRICA TO THE AMERICAS 1650–1860

Between 1650 and 1860, approximately 10 to 15 million enslaved people were transported from western Africa to the Americas. Most were shipped to the West Indies, Central America, and South America.

But responsibility for the slave trade is not simple. On the one hand, it was indeed the Europeans who purchased large numbers of Africans, and sent them far away to work in their colonies. On the other hand, Africans bear some responsibility themselves: some African societies had long had their own slaves, and they cooperated with the Europeans to sell other Africans into slavery. The Europeans relied on African merchants, soldiers and rulers to get slaves for them, which they then bought, at convenient seaports.

Africans were not strangers to the slave trade, or to the keeping of slaves. There had been considerable trading of Africans as slaves by Islamic Arab merchants in North Africa since the year 900. When Leo Africanus travelled to West Africa in the 1500s, he recorded in his *The Description of Africa and of the Notable Things Therein Contained* that, "slaves are the next highest commodity in the marketplace. There is a place where they sell countless slaves on market days." Criminals and prisoners of war, as well as political prisoners were often sold in the marketplaces in Gao, Jenne and Timbuktu. Perhaps because slavery and slave trading had long existed in much of Africa (though perhaps in forms less brutal than the slavery practiced in the Americas), Africans were "untroubled" by selling slaves to Europeans (Curtin, 1967).

Case study: The kingdom of Kongo and the slave trade

At the same time as Great Zimbabwe was powerful, there was a large and powerful kingdom along the Congo River in Central Africa, known as the Kongo. Kongo was ruled by a *manikongo*, or king, and was divided into six provinces, each administered by a governor.

The kingdom had an organized system of labour, taxation and trade, especially in iron and salt. It also had a currency, in the form of *nzimbu* shells from a nearby island. The Kongo Kingdom had been in place for around 200 years when the first Portuguese arrived on the coast.

Artist's depiction of the Kingdom of Kongo. Picture source: The Abolition Project, abolition.e2bn.org

In 1482, Diego Cão, a Portuguese explorer, visited the kingdom. The reigning *manikongo*, Nzinga Nkuwu, was impressed by the Portuguese and sent a delegation to visit Portugal. As a result, Portuguese missionaries, soldiers and artisans were welcomed to Mbanza, the capital of the kingdom. The missionaries targeted the Kongo leaders, and managed to convert Nzinga Nkuwu to Christianity. This led to divisions between the new Christians and followers of the traditional religions. The next *manikongo*, Alfonso I, was raised as a Christian. He expanded trade links with the Portuguese, which included becoming involved in the slave trade. His people would raid neighbouring villages and states, selling the prisoners to the Europeans for a good price. This made the kingdom very wealthy for some years.

However, the slave trade eventually took its toll on the Kongo kingdom. Although the slave trade made some chiefs enormously wealthy, it ultimately undermined local economies and political stability as villages' vital labour forces were shipped overseas and slave raids and civil wars became commonplace. To meet the huge demand for slaves, the Kongolese began raiding further afield, and several groups fought back, including the Téké and the Kuba. This constant conflict distracted them from trade and weakened their defences. They soon became dependent on the Portuguese for assistance, especially in the Jaga Wars of 1568. The Kongo Kingdom never regained its former power. In the years that followed, the Kongo fought both for and against the Portuguese, eventually being colonized in 1885. A breakaway group, the Ndongo, moved southwards. They called their kings *angola*. They were also later colonized by the Portuguese.

The Development of Slave Trade

In the mid-fifteenth century, Portuguese ships sailed down the West African coast in a manoeuvre designed to bypass the Muslim North Africans, who had a virtual monopoly on the trade of sub-Saharan gold, spices, and other commodities that Europe wanted. These voyages resulted in maritime discoveries and advances in shipbuilding that later would make it easier for European vessels to navigate the Atlantic. Over time, the Portuguese vessels added another commodity to their cargo: African men, women, and children.

For the first one hundred years, captives in small numbers were transported to Europe. By the close of the fifteenth century, 10 percent of the population of Lisbon, Portugal, then one of the largest cities in Europe, was of African origin. Other captives were taken to islands off the African shore, including Madeira, Cape Verde, and especially São Tomé, where the Portuguese established sugar plantations using enslaved labour on a scale that foreshadowed the development of plantation slavery in the Americas. Enslaved

Africans could also be found in North Africa, the Middle East, Persia, India, the Indian Ocean islands, and in Europe as far as Russia.

English and Dutch ships soon joined Portugal's vessels trading along the African coast. They preyed on the Portuguese ships, while raiding and pillaging the African mainland as well. During this initial period, European interest was particularly concentrated on Senegambia. Culturally and linguistically unified through Islam and in some areas, Manding culture and language, the region and Mali to its east had a long and glorious history, centred on the ancient Kingdom of Ghana and the medieval empires of Mali and Songhay. Its interior regions of Bure and Bambuk were rich in gold. It reached the Mediterranean and hence Europe from Songhay. The slave trade was closely linked to the Europeans' insatiable hunger for gold, and the arrival of the Portuguese on the "Gold Coast" (Ghana) in the 1470s tapped these inland sources.

Later, they developed commercial and political relations with the kingdoms of Benin (in present-day Nigeria) and Kongo. The Kongo state became Christianized and, in the process, was undermined by the spread of the slave trade. Benin, however, restricted Portuguese influence and somewhat limited the trade in human beings.

Starting in 1492, Africans were part of every expedition into the regions that became the American Spanish colonies. By the beginning of the sixteenth century, they were brought as slaves to grow sugar and mine gold on Hispaniola, and were forced to drain the shallow lakes of the Mexican plateau, thereby finalizing the subjugation of the Aztec nation. In a bitter twist, the Africans were often forced to perform tasks that would help advance the genocide that would resolve the vexing "Indian question."

By the middle of the seventeenth century, the slave trade entered its second and most intense phase. The creation of ever-larger sugar plantations and the introduction of other crops such as indigo, rice, tobacco, coffee, cocoa, and cotton would lead to the displacement of an estimated seven million Africans between 1650 and 1807. The demand for labour resulted in numerous innovations, encouraged opportunists and entrepreneurs, and accrued deceptions and barbarities, upon which the slave trade rested. Some slave traders - often well-respected men in their communities - made fortunes for themselves and their descendants. The corresponding impact on

Africa was intensified as larger parts of west and central Africa came into the slavers' orbit.

The third and final period of the transatlantic slave trade began with the ban on the importation of captives imposed by Britain and the United States in 1807 and lasted until the 1860s. Brazil, Cuba, and Puerto Rico were the principal destinations for Africans, since they could no longer legally be brought into North America, the British or French colonies in the Caribbean, or the independent countries of Spanish America. Despite this restricted market, the numbers of deported Africans did not decline until the late 1840s. Many were smuggled into the United States. At the same time, tens of thousands of Africans rescued from the slave ships were forcibly settled in Sierra Leone, Liberia, and several islands of the Caribbean.

Capture and Enslavement

War, slave raiding, kidnapping, and politico-religious struggle accounted for the vast majority of Africans deported to the Americas. Several important wars resulted in massive enslavement, including the export of prisoners across the Atlantic, the ransoming of others, and the use of enslavement within Africa itself. The Akan wars of the late seventeenth century and the first half of the eighteenth century were a struggle for power among states in the Gold Coast hinterland. Akwamu, Akyem, Denkyira, Fante, and Asante groups battled for more than half a century for control of the region. By the mid-eighteenth century, Asante emerged as the dominant force.

By 1650, Oyo had become a consolidated imperial power in the interior of the Bight of Benin by defeating the Bariba and Nupe in the north and other Yoruba states to the south (Adediran, 1984). The wars between various Gbe groups resulted in the rise of Dahomey and its victory over Allada in 1724. The winners occupied the port of Whydah three years later but were then forced to pay tribute to the more powerful Oyo. These wars accounted for the deportation of over a million Africans along the Bight of Benin coast (Adamu, 1979). The sixty-year period of the Kongo civil wars, ending in 1740, was responsible for the capture and enslavement of many. Among them were the followers of the Catholic martyr Beatrice of Kongo, who tried to end the wars through pacifist protest.

The spread of militant Islam across West Africa began in Senegambia during the late seventeenth century. The jihad led to two major political transformations: the emergence in the late eighteenth century of the Muslim states of Futa Jallon in the Guinea highlands and Futa Toro on the Senegal River. The jihad movement continued into the nineteenth century, especially with the outbreak of war in 1804 in the Hausa states (northern Nigeria) under the leadership of Sheikh Usman dan Fodio. These wars in turn exacerbated political tensions in Oyo, which resulted in a Muslim uprising and the collapse of the Oyo state between 1817 and 1833. New strongholds were created at Ibadan, Abeokuta, and Ijebu, and the conflict intensified over attempts to replace or resurrect the Oyo state.

After 1700, the importation of firearms heightened the intensity of many of the wars and resulted in a great increase in the numbers of enslaved peoples. European forces intervened in some of the localized fighting and in warfare all along the Atlantic coast. They sought to obtain captives directly in battle or as political rewards for having backed the winning side. Working from their permanent colonies at Luanda, Benguela, and other coastal points, the Portuguese conducted joint military ventures into the hinterlands with their African allies.

Africans also became enslaved through non-military means. Judicial and religious sanctions and punishments removed alleged criminals, people accused of witchcraft, and social misfits through enslavement and banishment. Rebellious family members might be expelled from their homes through enslavement. Human pawns, especially children, held as collateral for debt were almost always protected from enslavement by relatives and customary practices. However, debts and the collateral for those debts were sometimes subjected to illegal demands, and pawned individuals, especially children, were sometimes "sold" or otherwise removed from the watchful eyes of the relatives and communities that had tried to safeguard their rights.

Africans were also kidnapped, though kidnapping was a crime in most communities, and sold into slavery. Captives were sometimes ransomed, but this practice often encouraged the taking of prisoners for monetary rewards. As the slave trade destroyed families and communities, people tried to protect their loved ones. Various governments and communal institutions developed means and policies that limited the trade's impact. Muslims were particularly concerned with protecting the freedom of their co-religionists. Qur'anic law stated that those of the Faith born free must remain free. But this precept was often violated.

Throughout Africa, people of all beliefs tried to safeguard their own. Some offered themselves in exchange for the release of their loved ones. Others tried to have their kin redeemed even after they had been shipped away. Resistance took the form of attacks on slave depots and ships, as well as revolts in the forts, in barracoons, and on slave ships. But at a higher level, the political fragmentation - many small centralized states and federations governed through secret societies - made it virtually impossible to develop methods of government that could effectively resist the impact of the slave trade. Even the largest states, such as Asante and Oyo, were small by modern standards. Personal gain and the interests of the small commercial elites who dominated trade routes, ports, and secret societies also worked against the freeing of captives, offenders, and displaced children, who could easily end up in the slave trade.

Dehumanization of Africans by Europeans during the Slave trade.

Dehumanization is the act of making someone less of a person. Europeans have attempted various ways to dehumanize Africans. First, Europeans ripped Africans off their identity. They have introduced European religious belief and ways of life and condemned the traditions of the African people. This has resulted in the loss of many original African traditions as they turn to follow European style of life. This has dehumanized the people of Africa because they were made to believe their culture was not good and their lifestyle was primitive so they ended up living other people's life, that of Europeans.

Europeans also dehumanized Africans by killing and enslaving them. On arrival at the coast of Africa, Europeans bought slaves from local African chiefs and kings to work for them on their sugar plantation islands of Cape Verde, Canary, Azores and later on the new found land of America. Europeans at times obtained slaves by kidnapping them from their villages as if they were animals or other living or non-living things considered lower than human beings. Europeans tempted local African chiefs with wares in other to coerce them to sell their fellow Africans to them. Even though internal slavery existed long ago before the first Europeans, Portuguese, reached the coast of Africa, slavery at that time was not that intensive and many slave owners obtained slaves after overcoming another tribe in a tribal war. Slaves obtained by Europeans became completely dehumanized, they had no right and were forced to work against their will till they wore out and died. They were beaten, maltreated, cheated on, and killed just like animals. The African slaves were properties of the European slave masters rather than equal living beings with a voice. This dehumanized Africans as they had been totally reduced to property rather than living as free persons that could make self-decisions of life and live as they wished.

To conclude, Africans responded to the dehumanization efforts by Europeans in many different ways. Some African slaves couldn't stand the abuse so they starved themselves to death. Other African slaves stayed stronger and united in slavery and waited for a day when the humiliation would be over. The enslaved Africans learned to fight against invasion by other groups on their settlements and avoided a second capture or enslavement different from their current situations. This type of humiliation and depletion of the population of Africa affected the continent beyond repairs and the main reason why the continent has very high poverty and lack of unity and trust among the people.

Dehumanization of the African was displayed during slavery. In order to transport slaves over the Atlantic to America, the white men needed a fast, practical means of transportation in order to move the slaves, their merchandise, from one continent to another. The best way to do this, they decided, was to use cargo ships. According to the power point presentation in class, the slaves were crammed into the bottom of these ships like sardines. A 'light-load' would be when the slaves are all lying on their backs with one stacked on top of the other. When the slave owners were in a rush and needed a lot of 'merchandise', the slaves would be packed on their sides. They were unable to move except for the hour that they were allowed outside on the deck. In many instances, one third of the slaves being transported would die on the way to America.

The lucky ones who survived the trip were forced to endure years of hatred and oppression. This is a prime example of dehumanization. Humans are forced to withstand a three-month trip in minimal conditions just so they can be bought and sold like animals for work. People are not meant to be treated like cattle. It is abusive, demoralizing and degrading to be treated like this. What's worse is that when the slaves arrived in America, they were thrown into prisons and auctioned off like objects. They would literally stand on a podium and have white men brush past them and feel them and check them out. The black people had to first endure a gruelling trip across the ocean, and then they had to be auctioned off like workhorses. It was very dehumanizing because the slaves were forced to work. They had no rights, therefore they were not free.

Dehumanization was shown during the civil war as well. As a country, we were reduced to nothing because we were fighting amongst ourselves over such a very immoral, dehumanizing topic of slavery. We nearly lost half of our land to people who believed in using black people as objects and making them work. Thanks to Abraham Lincoln and the Emancipation Proclamation, slavery was abolished, and the War Between the States was over. The damage had been done, however. Brothers were forced to fight against brothers, and friends against friends. So much blood was shed for such a despicable cause. It is a clear example of dehumanization when a country is on the verge of downfall and the citizens are at war over a topic such as slavery.

Theorizing Systematic Dehumanization

Around the globe, a network of killing centres is eliminating "unwanted" human beings at a staggering rate—relying on the same basic arguments that were once used to justify slavery and the Holocaust. One of history's most tragic lessons is that human beings have a remarkable capacity for abusing each other. When this abuse is severe enough, and moves beyond the mistreatment of a few individuals, we call it a crime against humanity. These are not crimes of passion; these are crimes of precision. They are not the result of accidental, momentary impulses; they are thought-out and rationalized. The scale of such crimes cannot be carried out by individuals. They require systematic cooperation and consent. Crimes against humanity are almost always built on the assertion that certain human beings do not deserve protection under the law. The most notorious example is the Jewish Holocaust, in which six million European Jews were executed for their alleged racial inferiority.

Raphael Lemkin, a Polish-Jewish lawyer, is the man responsible for making the annihilation of entire people groups an international crime. In 1933, influenced by his knowledge of the slaughter of Armenians by the Turks in WWI and the more recent slaughter of Christian Assyrians by Iraqis, he appeared before The Legal Counsel for the League of Nations in Madrid and proposed to make the extermination of human groups an international crime, calling such crimes "acts of barbarity" (1933). His proposal was not accepted. Ten years later, in 1943, he coined the term "genocide" in an effort to more specifically describe the Nazi attempt to annihilate entire ethnic groups. The term appeared in print for the first time in 1944, in Lempkin's *Axis Rule in Occupied Europe (1944:* 79-95).

The word "genocide" combines the Greek word for race (geno) with the Latin word for killing (cide). The Nuremberg trials (2010), which concluded in 1946, used Lemkin's term "genocide" in their indictment against top Nazi officials who were convicted for their collective "crimes against humanity." In 1948, the United Nations officially made genocide an international crime at the Convention on the Prevention and Punishment of the Crime of Genocide. The Convention defined genocide as any of a series of acts designed to "destroy, in whole or in part, a national, ethnical, racial or religious group" (UN, 1948). The acts listed include: causing serious bodily or mental harm to members of the group, imposing measures intended to prevent births within the group, or forcibly transferring children out of the group. Since then, the term "genocide" has been applied to other historic and contemporary crimes against humanity. In some instances, such as Pol Pot's Cambodian genocide, the victims have been targeted for non-racial reasons. This broadening definition of genocide is reflected in *Webster's New World Encyclopaedia*:

gen·o·cide - *n*.

The deliberate and systematic destruction of a national, racial, religious, political, cultural, ethnic, or other group defined by the exterminators as undesirable (Webster's New World Encyclopedia,1992). This definition of genocide is broad enough to include abortion, and some organizations have made a compelling case that abortion *is* genocide. Abortion is certainly deliberate and systematic. By the latest count, close to 20% of American unborn children are aborted (United States, 2013." Morbidity and Mortality Weekly Report, 2016). In New York City, there is one abortion for every 1.7 births Ibid.). Each day, roughly 2,500 abortions are performed in the United States Ibid.,2015), and close to 60 million American unborn children have lost their lives to abortion since the Supreme Court struck down all state prohibitions in 1973 (http://www.nrlc.org/uploads/factsheets/FS01AbortionintheUS.pdf).

Approximately 93% of abortions occur in free-standing abortion clinics (Meckstroth, 2009: 135). The largest network of abortion clinics belongs to Planned Parenthood, which accounts for a third of all U.S. abortions (Planned Parenthood. Annual Report, 2014). The specific group of human beings that abortion targets is unwanted, unborn children—a victim class defined by the pro-abortion mantra,

"Every Child a Wanted Child." Planned Parenthood's *Final Solution* for unwanted, unborn children is extermination.

Though the appropriateness of calling abortion "genocide" depends on how broadly you define the term, there is no getting around the fact that abortion has systematically destroyed millions of innocent and helpless human beings. Gregory H. Stanton is a research professor in Genocide Studies and the president of Genocide Watch. He describes genocide as something that develops in eight stages, the third of which is dehumanization. What does this look like in practice? According to Dr. Stanton, "One group denies the humanity of the other group" by equating it with "animals, vermin, insects or diseases." This allows those in the first group to overcome "the normal human revulsion against murder" (Stanton, 1998).

If you've ever listened to someone try to explain why it is morally acceptable to kill a living human being before it is born, you've probably already heard unborn children described in the terms above. If not, public examples are not hard to come by. Warren Hern is one of the most prominent abortionists in the world. He wrote the textbook, *Abortion Practice*. His central premise is this: *unborn children should be viewed not as people, but as a disease.* He writes that "the relationship between the [mother] and the [baby] can be understood best as one of host and parasite" (Stanton,, 1990:14). Famed astrophysicist Carl Sagan joined this chorus by comparing unborn children to segmented worms, fish, tadpoles, reptiles, and pigs" (Sagan and Druyan, 1990:5). That is the language of dehumanization. Even the word "foetus" has become a term of derision used by those who want to deemphasize the humanity of unborn children.

The reason so many people take offense at comparing abortion to historic atrocities is the same reason so many white Americans were scandalized when Martin Luther King Jr. compared the abuse of black Americans to the Holocaust (1963). It is easy to condemn injustice that is far away—by distance or time; it is much harder to condemn injustice that sits in your own backyard, especially when it provides a material benefit. Abortion supporters are infuriated at the notion that abortion is comparable to the Holocaust because they incessantly argue that human embryos and foetuses are not actually people. This is the argument that is *always* made to justify crimes against humanity. It is the same rationale that drove Hitler's mistreatment of the Jews and America's scandalous three-fifths compromise, which reckoned enslaved African-Americans as 3/5 of a person (1787). David Livingstone Smith, the author of *Less Than Human*, notes that society is all too willing to "gerrymander the category of humans in ways that suit us" (2011).

Though there are differences between abortion and historic forms of genocide, there are also huge similarities. If we can't compare atrocities past to atrocities present, then the term "never again" loses all meaning—and we will continue our sad legacy of dehumanizing and abusing those who get in our way or have something we want.

Slave Traders and Slave Trade

Western European countries established distinct national trades. The European port cities most involved in this growth industry were Bristol, Liverpool, and London in England; Amsterdam in Holland; Lisbon, the Portuguese capital; and Nantes, located on the western French coast (Drescher, 1977). On the African side most captives were traded from only a few ports: Luanda (Angola), Whydah (Bight of Benin), Bonny (Bight of Biafra); and the adjacent "castles" at Koromantin and Winneba on the Gold Coast accounted for at least a third of the Africans transported to the Americas. Other major ports included Old Calabar (Bight of Biafra), Benguela (Southern Angola), Cabinda (north of the Congo River), and Lagos in the Bight of Benin. These nine ports accounted for at least half of all the Africans deported to the Americas.

The European countries attempted, though not successfully, to regulate the trade by chartering various national companies established under royal decree or parliamentary order. But these efforts to create monopolies, such as England's Royal African Company (RAC), were soon undermined by private merchant companies and pirates who opened up new markets in the Bight of Biafra and the northern Angola coast, and challenged the RAC on the Gold Coast and in the Gambia.

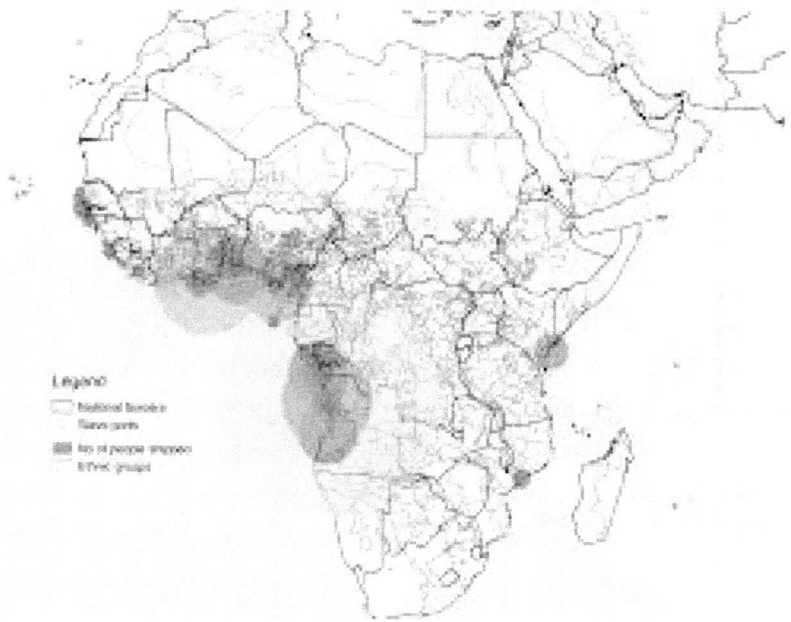

Legend
National borders
Slave ports
No. of people enslaved
Ethnic groups

Each of the nations and their slave ports experimented with innovative marketing and trading techniques. Sometimes this competition required the maintenance of trading depots and forts - the slave "castles" or factories - as was the case in the Gold Coast and the Bight of Benin, as well as in lesser ports along the Upper Guinea Coast, Senegambia, and Angola.

The trade was propelled by credit flowing outward from Europe and used by merchants to purchase men, women, and children in West Africa. They advanced goods on credit in lieu of payment in captives. The wares sent to Africa in exchange for captives included those that could be used as money: cowry shells, strips of cloth (often imported from India), iron bars, copper bracelets (manillas), silver coins, and gold. These goods also had value as commodities: cloth could be turned into clothing, iron into hoes and other tools. Consumer goods included textiles, alcohol, and jewellery. Their importation supplemented but did not replace the local production of these items. Alcohol was regarded as a luxury, except in Muslim communities, where it was prohibited.

Military goods, principally firearms, were also exchanged for captives. They were instrumental in the eighteenth-century Gold Coast wars that enslaved multitudes and led to the Asante people's political ascendancy in the region. With the exception of the Gold Coast wars, guns played little role at first in local conflicts, due in part to the difficulty of keeping powder dry in tropical regions. For example, the rise of Oyo, which became the dominant slaving power in the interior of the Bight of Benin, was mostly effected by the use of cavalry.

Merchants experimented with various trading methods. In some places, such as Old Calabar and the minor ports of the Upper Guinea Coast, individuals who were often the relatives of local merchants and officials were accepted by ship captains as collateral for credit. These individuals were human pawns who could be enslaved if debts were not paid.

In Angola and Senegambia, European merchants married or otherwise cohabited with local women, and these women sometimes amassed considerable fortunes as agents and merchants in their own right. Their mixed offspring became an intermediate class of merchants along the coast, but especially concentrated along the Upper Guinea Coast as far as Senegambia, and in Luanda, Benguela, and their commercial outposts in the interior of Angola.

The trade was a high-risk enterprise. The commodity was people; they could escape, be murdered, commit suicide, or fall victim to epidemics or natural disasters. Local traders could disappear with their payment and never produce the captives stipulated in the contract. Since the slave trade went across political and cultural frontiers, there was little recourse to courts and governments in the event of commercial dishonesty. No international court or judicial system existed to handle the extraordinary violations of human rights that defined every aspect of the slave trade.

The slave trade was driven by both demand and greed. The customers in the Americas who could afford it desperately needed labour and did not care how it was obtained. Traders could benefit immensely from theft, plunder, kidnapping, ransoming, and the sale of human beings as commodities. These slavers took advantage of African political troubles, religious differences, legal technicalities, economic crises, and outright callousness to exploit helpless individuals.

The Middle Passage

On the first leg of their three-part journey, often called the Triangular Trade, European ships brought manufactured goods to Africa; on the second, they transported African men, women, and children to the Americas; and on the third leg, they exported to Europe the sugar, rum, cotton, and tobacco produced by the enslaved labour force. There was also a direct trade between Brazil and Angola that did not include the European leg. Traders referred to the Africa-Americas part of the voyage as the "Middle Passage" and the term has survived to denote the Africans' ordeal.

Well over 30,000 voyages from Africa to the Americas have been documented. But numbers and statistics alone cannot convey the horror of the experience. However, the records provide detailed information on some aspects of this tragedy.

The dreadful Middle Passage could last from one to three months and epitomized the role of violence in the trade. Based on regulations, ships could transport only about 350 people, but some carried more than 800 men, women, and children. Branded, stripped naked for the duration of the voyage, lying down amidst filth, enduring almost unbearable heat, compelled by the lash to dance on deck to straighten their limbs, all captives went through a frightening, incredibly brutal and dehumanizing experience. Men were shackled under deck, and all Africans were subjected to abuse and punishment.

Some people tried to starve themselves to death, but the crew forced them to take food by whipping them, torturing them with hot coal, or forcing their mouths open by using special instruments or by breaking their teeth.

The personal identity of the captives was denied. Women and boys were often used for the pleasure of the crew. Ottobah Cugoano, who endured the Middle Passage in the eighteenth century, recalled: "it was common for the dirty filthy sailors to take the African women and lie upon their bodies." Mortality brought about by malnutrition, dysentery, smallpox, and other diseases was very high. Depending on the times, upwards of 20 percent died from various epidemics or committed suicide. Venture Smith, describing his ordeal, wrote: "After an ordinary passage, except great mortality by the small pox, which broke out on board, we arrived at the island of Barbadoes: but when we reached it, there were found out of the two hundred and sixty that sailed from Africa, not more than two hundred alive." It was not unusual for captains and crew to toss the sick overboard; and some even disposed of an entire cargo for insurance purposes.

On board slave ships, in the midst of their oppression, the Africans, who were often as much strangers to each other as to their European captors, forged the first links with their new American identities. Relationships established during the Middle Passage frequently resulted in revolts and other forms of resistance that bound them in new social and political alliances. Ottobah Cugoano described the attempted revolt organized on the ship that took him from the Gold Coast to Grenada: "when we found ourselves at last taken away, death was more preferable than life; and a plan was concerted amongst us, that we might burn and blow up the ship, and to perish all together in the flames . . . . It was the women and boys which were to burn the ship, with the approbation and groans of the rest; though that was prevented, the discovery was likewise a cruel bloody scene."

The special relations created on the ship lasted a lifetime and were regarded by the deported Africans, torn from their loved ones, as strongly as kinship. They had special names for those who had shared their ordeal. They were called *bâtiments* in Creole (from the French for ship), *sippi* in Surinam (from ship), and shipmate in Jamaica. Far from wiping out all traces of their cultural, social, and personal past, the Middle Passage experience provided Africans with opportunities to draw on their collective heritage to make themselves a new people.

Africans in America

Of the estimated ten million men, women, and children who survived the Middle Passage, approximately 450,000 Africans disembarked on North America's shores. They thus represented only a fraction - 5 percent-- of those transported during the 350-year history of the international slave trade. Brazil and the Caribbean each received about nine times as many Africans. The labour of enslaved Africans proved crucial in the development of South Carolina, Georgia, Virginia, and Maryland and contributed indirectly through commerce to the fortunes of New York, Massachusetts, and

Pennsylvania. Though the enforced destination of Africans was primarily to plantations and farms for work in cash crop agriculture, they were also used in mining and servicing the commercial economy. They were placed in towns and port cities as domestic servants; and many urban residents performed essential commercial duties working as porters, teamsters, and craftsmen.

In eighteenth-century America, Africans were concentrated in the agricultural lowlands of South Carolina and Georgia, especially in the Sea Islands, where they grew rice, cotton, indigo, and other crops. In Louisiana, they laboured on sugarcane plantations. They were employed on tobacco farms in the tidewater region of Virginia and Maryland. The tidewater, together with the Georgia and South Carolina lowlands, accounted for at least two-thirds of the Africans brought into North America prior to the end of legal importation in 1807.

Ethnicities in the United States

The largest number of Africans in the lowlands (34 percent) came from Bantu-speaking regions of west-central Africa. Twenty percent were transported from Senegambia, while the Gold Coast and Sierra Leone each accounted for about 15 percent of the total number. Others came from the Bight of Biafra and the Windward Coast.

The enslaved population of Virginia/Maryland was composed mostly of Africans from the Bight of Biafra, some 39 percent. Senegambia accounted for 21 percent of the Africans in this region. Another 17 percent were of Bantu origin, and 10 percent were originally from the Gold Coast.

Therefore, nearly 90 percent of the Africans in these two major regions came from only four zones in Africa. Most came from the west-central area of Angola and Congo where languages - Kikongo, Kimbundu and culture (often referred to as Bantu) were closely related. Many more ended up in the tidewater than in the lowlands, but they comprised nearly a third of all migrants in both sectors.

The Senegambians were much more prominent in North America than in South America and the Caribbean. Senegambia was strongly influenced by Islam, to a greater degree than any other coastal region where enslaved Africans originated. More Muslims were enslaved in North America - except for Brazil - than anywhere else in the New World. Their presence was especially pronounced in Louisiana, to which many Manding people - almost all males - had been transported. This state also had a large presence of non-Muslim Bambara from Mali.

The Upper South had a considerable population of people from the Bight of Biafra, as did lowland South Carolina and Georgia. In all probability, a large number of the many Africans whose origins are not known actually came from this area. These Igbo and Ibibio people would develop a distinct subculture. Women made up a relatively high number among those groups. They gave birth to a new generation, ensuring some transmission of their cultural values and beliefs.

Men and women from Sierra Leone and the adjacent Windward Coast were heavily concentrated in the low country, and most were involved in cultivating rice. Noticeably absent from North America's African population were substantial numbers of people from the Slave Coast (Togo, Benin, and western Nigeria). Contrary to Brazil and Cuba, the United States received very few Yoruba.

What Slavery Cost Slaves

Slavery cost slaves income and wealth. They made no wages, although some masters paid bonuses as incentives for good work. Lacking wages, slaves could not save. Slaves had no legal right to hold property, and without wages, they were seldom able to accumulate property. As in the case of wages, some masters offered favoured slaves the use of property. Sojourner Truth's parents, for instance, lived in a cottage they considered their own and kept a garden they considered theirs. But possession remained strictly contingent upon the owner's pleasure. Slaves had no rights in such property and could not pass on cottage or garden to their children. Without wages, savings, or property, Africans and their descendants could not send money back to their African villages of origin, as did millions of immigrants from Asia and Europe (**Annexture II**).

Educating slaves in or out of school was illegal in the nineteenth-century South, but not in the North and West. Nonetheless formal education remained outside the reach of most African Americans for several reasons beyond their enslavement. Few black people, slave or free, were allowed in schools; rural areas offered schooling to almost no one, for poor children of all races and ethnicities were destined for the workforce, not the schoolroom. A small minority of the enslaved did learn to read, write, and figure. Often their owners, particularly their mistresses (as in the cases of Frederick Douglass and Harriet Jacobs) helped bright slave children learn their letters. Owners also valued the assistance of slaves who could read or keep accounts. Upgrading one's skill, however, rewarded the owner far more than the slave.

Because slaves could not change employers of their own volition, they could not use the skills they acquired to better their situation by finding improved working conditions or jobs that paid more. They could not work their way up or purchase a share in their business. Closely supervised, they seldom exercised control over their working conditions. Although slaves lacked unions and therefore lacked grievance procedures, they sometimes successfully appealed overseers' orders to their owners. Appeals could go no higher than the master, for masters exercised powers directly on their farms, plantations, and households and indirectly through slave patrols on the roads and other public places. In the South, local governments nearly always deferred to owners, who exercised police power over the land and people they owned.

The combination of physical violence and the requirement to remain cheerful before one's owners bred habits of deceit and anger that turned against oneself and one's own family. Child and spouse abuse were constant dangers in Southern families. One of the most famous works of the late nineteenth-century black poet Paul Laurence Dunbar (1872–1906) commemorates the need to conceal emotions: "We Wear the Mask."

We wear the mask that grins and lies,
It hides our cheeks and shades our eyes,—
This debt we pay to human guile;
With torn and bleeding hearts we smile,
And mouth with myriad subtleties. . . .
(Claude Clark, 1946; Joyce Scott, 1991).

Physical Trauma

By the end of the eighteenth century, branding, amputation, and other extremely brutal forms of punishment became rare as means of controlling slaves. But beating continued, causing slaves' most catastrophic physical and psychological trauma. Every ex-slave narrative includes scenes of physical torture inflicted by owners (female as well as male), overseers, and fellow slaves forced to administer their masters' punishments. The narratives also comment on the emotional pain of parents, children, and spouses, forced to watch their kin being beaten. Artists have depicted the physical torture of slavery in countless images, such as "Slave Lynching" by Claude Clark (1915–2001). The enslaved woman's nakedness before a crowd of onlookers adds further humiliation to the physical pain of the beating.

In addition to physical injury caused by beating, slaves suffered from the chronic conditions caused by overwork, scanty rations, and insufficient clothing. Frederick Douglass recalled going barefoot and ill clothed all winter and suffering from frostbite as a child. Stealing food to stanch constant hunger earned many a slave a whipping. Years of hard work, often in swampy conditions, left their signs within slaves' bodies. The skeletons of enslaved children and adults working in eighteenth-century New York City bore the traces of lesions denoting excessive, repetitive stress. The remains found in the African burial ground in lower Manhattan indicate that about 50 percent of New York's colonial Africans died before the age of twelve, and 30 to 40 percent of those children died in infancy. Many of the 40 percent of the skeletons in the burial ground belonged to preadolescent children and show the thickening of the skull associated with anaemia and osteomalacia (weakening of the bones due to poor diet and nutrition). The skeletons' enlarged muscle attachments are attributable to the heavy loads children were forced to carry. The skeletons also show signs of arthritis in the neck bones and lesions on the thighbones from muscle and ligament tears, caused by carrying heavy loads.

Psychological Trauma

Slaves and, to a certain extent, their owners paid the psychological costs of a society based on violence, obedience, and submission. As the slave Isabella in the Hudson River Valley, Sojourner Truth neglected her own children to work for her owners, including their children. "No Mommy Me (1)" by Joyce Scott (b. 1948) captures the tragedy of the neglected black child. While the mother plays with the white child in her charge, her own child, disregarded, clings to her skirt. Slave owners placed great value on slaves' demeanour, which was to remain cheerful and submissive at all times. Above all, slaves were not to appear to be thinking for themselves or to display the anger inevitably flowing from physical violence, whether being beaten oneself or witnessing someone else's torture. The signs of this repressive regime appeared in advertisements for runaway slaves. Slaves were described as stutterers, as people who always looked down, who seemed depressed, who drank liquor excessively, who alternated between periods of withdrawal and outbursts of fierce, uncontrollable rage.

Some slaves suffered from what is now termed post-traumatic stress syndrome, and some inflicted their pain on their kin. But every slave was vulnerable psychologically, and every slave was at risk of falling victim to psychological trauma. The enslaved bore the brunt of emotional pain, but their owners did not escape unscathed.

Whites as well as blacks noticed slavery's detrimental effects on white people. Thomas Jefferson could only speak vaguely of "odious peculiarities." Mistresses and slaves spelled out the evils, physical and emotional: Absolute power over other people bred sadism; absolute power over other people also bred sexual abuse. The rape of slave women translated into the pain of adultery for mistresses. Harriet Jacobs, herself the sexual prey of her middle-aged master when she was less than fourteen, summed up slavery's costs to white families: "I was twenty-one years in that cage of obscene birds. I can testify, from my own experience and observation, that slavery is a curse to the whites as well as to the blacks. It makes the white fathers cruel and sensual; the sons violent and licentious; it contaminates the daughters, and makes the wives wretched. And as for the coloured race, it needs an abler pen than mine to describe the extremity of their sufferings, the depth of their degradation."

Impact of the Slave Trade on Africa

The negative impact of the international slave trade on Africa was immense. It can be seen on the personal, family, communal, and continental levels. In addition to the millions of able-bodied individuals captured and transported, the death toll and the economic and environmental destruction resulting from wars and slave raids were startlingly high. In the famines that followed military actions, the old and very young were often killed or left to starve.

Forced marches of the captives over long distances claimed many lives. A large number of the enslaved were destined to remain in Africa - many were transported across the Sahara to the north - which heightened the impact of the slave trade on the continent. It is estimated that the population of Africa remained stagnant until the end of the nineteenth century.

Besides its demographic toll, the slave trade, and the Africans' resistance to it, led to profound social and political changes. Social relations were restructured and traditional values were subverted. The slave trade resulted in the development of predatory regimes, as well as stagnation or regression. Many communities relocated as far from the slavers' route as possible. In the process, their technological and economic development was hindered as they devoted their energy to hiding and defending themselves.

The disruption was immense: the relationships between kingdoms, ethnic groups, religious communities, castes, rulers and subjects, peasants and soldiers, the enslaved and the free, were transformed. In some decentralized societies, people evolved new styles of leadership that led to more rigid, hierarchical structures, thought to better ensure protection. In addition, European powers intervened in the political process to prevent the rise of the African centralized states that would have hampered their operations. In the end, the slave trade left the continent underdeveloped, disorganized, and vulnerable to the next phase of European hegemony: colonialism.

Legacies in America

The slave trade and slavery left a legacy of violence. Brutality, often of near-bestial proportions, was the principal condition shaping the character of the enforced migration, whether along a trade route, on board ship, or labouring on an American plantation. The degree of power concentrated in the hands of North American slave owners, interested only in maximizing their profits, allowed excessive levels of physical punishment and the perpetuation of sexual abuse and exploitation that have marked in many ways the development of the African-American community.

There was a marked sexual component to the assaults: rape was common. Kinship was disregarded, particularly the paternity of children. Their status reflected the enslaved status of their mothers, no matter who their father might have been. Slave owners treated their unpaid, overworked labour forces as mere chattel.

Avoiding and resisting violence were determining characteristics of the responses of the Africans to their forced migration experience. Individuals attempted to evade physical abuse through strategies of accommodation, escape, and on several occasions, violent rebellion. The preservation and adaptation of African cultural forms to respond to the new needs of the enslaved population was also an act of resistance to the imposition of European norms.

Unlike earlier slave systems, in the Americas racial distinctions were used to keep the enslaved population in bondage. Contrary to what happened in Latin America, where racial stratification was more complex, in North America, any person of identifiable African descent, no matter the degree of "white" ancestry, was classified as coloured, Negro, or black. A racial caste system was established, and as a result racialized attitudes and racism became an inherent and lasting part of North American culture.

Though enslaved individuals came from widely different backgrounds and the number of ethnic groups and markers of identity were extensive, certain ethnicities, cultural forms, and languages - usually in pidgin and creolized forms - as well as religions proved sustainable and were maintained, sometimes exaggerated and manipulated during the process of adjusting to enslavement in the Americas.

The overarching result of African migration during the slavery era was an "American" culture, neither "European" nor "African," created in a political and economic context of inequality and oppression. The African contribution to this new culture was a towering legacy, hugely impacting on language, religion, music, dance, art, and cuisine. Most importantly, an enduring sense of African-American community developed in the face of white racism.

Slavery broke the world in half, it broke it in every way. It broke Europe. It made them into something else, it made them slave masters, it made them crazy. You can't do that for hundreds of years and it not take a toll. They had to dehumanize, not just the slaves but themselves" (Gilroy, 1933: 221).

In order to comprehend acts of oppression such as the slave trade, not to mention the atrocities which accompanied it, an investigation into the psychological reasoning of the oppressors must be considered. People are not inherently evil; however, all human beings have the capacity to commit evil acts (Waller, 2002:133). Dehumanization is commonplace in instances of persecution. John Wade describes dehumanization as a "psychological state and linguistic transition which occurs during conflict which both justifies past behaviour; and encourages future aggressive conflict" (Wade, 2000). In another definition; to dehumanize is to deprive a person or group of human qualities, stripping them of their personal identity and individuality (Wade, 2010). In instances of persecution, dehumanization serves as a justification and rationalization of past and future behaviour. With these definitions in mind, slavery is the epitome of dehumanization. Many take for granted the dehumanization of slaves. However, the power of this psychological spur must be considered in depth, chiefly because dehumanization is still taking place and leading to disastrous consequences such as genocide and mass murder in the twenty-first century.

Dehumanization cannot be hailed as the sole psychological motivation of oppression. A plethora of internal (dispositional) and external (situational) factors also go hand in hand with dehumanization in times of oppression or persecution (Waller, 2002:133). The question of how ordinary people can commit extraordinary acts presents the historian with a complex problem. And as James Waller points out, for each complex question, there is a simple, neat and often incorrect answer (Waller, 2007:137). Dehumanization of victims should be considered a small, yet compelling part of the slave trade. The role which was filled by dehumanization allowed and condoned the continuation of the trade for over two hundred years. Oppression and brutality were made viable by a common consensus which promoted the inferiority of Africans, a consensus which portrayed them as less than human, and often as animals.

The dehumanization of victims is a theme which persistently rears its ugly head in many instances of persecution; including oppression, genocide and mass murder. It is in fact extremely difficult, if not impossible, to recall an example where dehumanization has not preceded a genocidal policy or been used to justify inhumane acts in history. As a justification of persecution, dehumanization is a profoundly effective tool. Successfully serving as an ideology which allows the perpetrator, and indeed society, to avoid guilt, condone actions and override their conscience. If the victim is not human, then the actions cannot be inhumane.

The dehumanization of victims of persecution has proved so powerful and disastrous an instrument that the shockwaves can still now be felt in modern day society. The repercussions of past ideologies; in particular, the belief that Black people were inferior, incredibly still exists to some degree in the twenty-first century dehumanization of minority groups in the past, gives way to racism in the future (Wilson, 1996: 46). Assumptions pertaining to certain minority groups have stuck like glue. Modern day racism can be traced back to the first instances of the dehumanization of Black people. Many like to believe our society has grown past these racial prejudices and ideologies. But really, just how true is this statement? The power of ideology is profound. Perceptions, assumptions and beliefs can prove as unshakable as the strongest foundations, as persistent as the strongest will. No one individual or collective people can be blamed for the origin, constancy or evolution of dehumanization. Its mere existence reflects the very essence of human nature itself and actually champions the presence of morality in the psychological make-up of human beings.

It is not the historians place to judge perpetrators or bystanders of persecution. What needs to be achieved is an understanding of why and how events which we deem immoral today were able to occur then. People are influenced by their culture, upbringing, society and religion. Societies are formed and ideals are shaped through popular culture and ideologies. Assumptions and stereotypes filter down through generations and deep-set beliefs form over many years. As sure as the sky was blue, so too Black people were inferior. The slave owners were not evil, society was not corrupt. Fundamentally, people are a reflection of their culture and environment.

> If only there were evil people somewhere insidiously committing evil deeds, if only it were necessary to separate them from the rest of us, but the line dividing good and evil cuts through the heart of every human being. It is, after all, only because of the way things worked out that they were the executioners and we weren't. (Solzhenitsyn, 1974: 168).

Dehumanization successfully acts as a bulwark in times of oppression or persecution, safeguarding the perpetrator from their conscience. In the case of the Atlantic Slave Trade, the merchants and public alike were protected by a sound belief that Black people were not suitable for anything other than slavery. In fact, it was widely accepted that Black Africans were better off under the control of Europeans-dehumanization of Black Africans during the slave trade occurred as a result of a psychological need to justify and rationalize the treatment and enslavement of millions of people. The alluring economic incentive meant that Africans were far too valuable a commodity to be slaughtered *en masse*, a climax which often occurs as a consequence of dehumanization (**Annexture III**).

Bibliography

Adamu, Mahdi, "The Delivery of Slaves from the Bight of Benin in the eighteenth and nineteenth centuries," in H.A. Gemery and J.S. Hogendorn (eds.), *The Uncommon Market: Essays in the Economic History of the Atlantic Slave Trade* (New York; Academic Press, 1979), 163-80. "Abortion Surveillance — United States, 2013." Morbidity and

Mortality Weekly Report (Centres for Disease Control and Prevention, November 25, 2016): Table 2
https://www.cdc.gov/mmwr/volumes/65/ss/ss6512a1.htm

Adediran, Biodun, "Yoruba Ethnic Groups or a Yoruba Ethnic Group? A Review of the Problem of Ethnic Identification," *Africa: Revista do Centro de Estudos Africanos da USP*, 7 (1984), 57-70

Anstey, Roger, *The Atlantic Slave Trade and British Abolition, 1760-1810* (London, 1975)

Bühnen, Stephan, "Ethnic Origins of Peruvian Slaves (1548-1650): Figures for Upper Guinea," *Paiduema*, 39, (1993), 57-110.

Carl Sagan and Ann Druyan, "Is It Possible To Be Pro-Life and Pro-Choice?" Parade Magazine. April 22, 1990.

Claude Clark, Image credits: "Slave Lynching," 1946. Permission to reproduce Slave Lynching by Claude Clark is granted by the Claude Clarke Estate (2) Joyce Scott, "No Mommy Me (1)," 1991. Collection Susan & Michael Hort / @Scott

Nell Irvin Painter is the Edward Professor of American History at Princeton. A former Director of Princeton's Program in African-American Studies, she is the author of Creating Black Americans: African-American History and Its Meanings, 1619 to the Present; Sojourner Truth: A Life, A Symbol; Standing at Armageddon: The United States 1877-1919. Read Nell Irvin Painter's essay on the difficulty of tracking down the artwork in Creating Black Americans at Beatrice.com.

Curtin, Philip D., ed., *Africa Remembered: Narratives of West Africans from the Era of the Slave Trade* (Madison: University of Wisconsin Press, 1967).

Curtin, Philip D., *The Atlantic Slave Trade: A Census* (Madison: University of Wisconsin Press, 1969).

Curtin, Philip D., *Economic Change in Precolonial Africa: Senegambia in the Era of the Slave Trade* (Madison: University of Wisconsin Press, 1975), 2 vols.

Curtin, Philip D., *The Rise and Fall of the Plantation Complex. Essays in Atlantic History* (Cambridge: Cambridge University Press, 1990).

Curto, José C. and Lovejoy, Paul E., eds., *Enslaving Connections: Changing Cultures of Africa and Brazil during the Era of Slavery* (Amherst NY: Humanity Books, 2004).

Daaku, Kwame Yeboah, *Trade and Politics on the Gold Coast 1600- 1720: A study of the African Reaction to European Trade* (Oxford: Clarendon, 1970)

Dantzig, Albert van, "Effect of the Atlantic Slave Trade on some West African Societies," *Revue francaise d'histoire d'outre-mer*, 62:1-2 (1975), 252-69.

David Livingstone Smith. Interview with Neal Conan. *Talk of the Nation*. NPR, March 29, 2011: http://www.npr.org/2011/03/29/134956180/criminals-see-their-victims-as-less-than-human.

Davidson, Basil, *The African Slave Trade* (Boston, 1961).

Diouf, Sylviane. *Servants of Allah: African Muslims Enslaved in the Americas* (New York: New York University Press, 1998).

——————. (ed.), *Fighting the Slave Trade: West African Strategies* (Athens: Ohio University Press, 2003).

Donnan, E. (ed.), *Documents Illustrative of the Slave Trade to America* (Washington, D.C., 1930-35), 4 vols.

Drescher, Seymour. 1977. *Econocide: The British Slavery in the Era of Abolition*. Pittsburgh.

Eltis, David, "The Volume and Structure of the Transatlantic Slave Trade: A Reassessment," *William and Mary Quarterly*, 58, 1 (2001), 17-46.

Eltis, David, *Economic Growth and the Ending of the Transatlantic Slave Trade* (New York and Oxford, 1987).

Eltis, David and Engerman, Stanley L., "Was the slave trade dominated by men?" *Journal of Interdisciplinary History*, 23 (1992), 237-57.

Eltis, David and Engerman, Stanley, L., "Fluctuations in sex and age ratios in the transatlantic slave trade, 1663-1864," *Economic History Review*, 46 (1993), 308-23.

Eltis, David, and Richard, David, Behrendt, Stephen, and Klein, Herbert S., *The Atlantic Slave Trade. A database on CD-ROM* (Cambridge: Cambridge University Press, 1999).

Eltis, David and Walvin, James (eds.), *The Abolition of the Atlantic Slave Trade*. (Madison: University of Wisconsin Press, 1981).

Engerman, S. L. and Genovese, E. D. (eds.), *Race and Slavery in the Western Hemisphere: Quantitative Studies*. (Princeton: Princeton University Press, 1975).

Equiano, Olaudah, *Olaudah Equiano: The Interesting Narrative and Other Writings* (Vincent Carretta, ed.) (New York: Penguin Books, 1995).

Fage, J.D., "Slaves and society in Western Africa. c.1445-c.1700," *Journal of African History* 21, 3 (1980), 289-310

Florentino, Manolo G. "About the Slaving Business in Rio de Janeiro, 1790-1830: A Contribution," in François Crouzet, Philippe Bonnichon, and Denis Rolland, eds., *Pour l'histoire du Brésil: hommage à Katia de Queirós Mattoso* (Paris: L'Harmattan, 2000), pp. 397-416.

Gemery, Henry and Hogendorn, J.S., eds., *The Uncommon Market: Essays in the Economic History of the Atlantic Slave Trade* (New York: Academic Press, 1979).

GILROY, P. (1933). The Black Atlantic: Modernity and Double Consciousness (London: Verso, 1993) p. 221.

Gomez, Michael. *Exchanging our Country Marks: The Transformation of African Identities in the Colonial and Antebellum South* (Chapel Hill: University of North Carolina Press, 1998)

Hair P. E. H. "Ethnolinguistic Continuity on the Guinea Coast". *Journal of African History,* 1967, VIII, 2 pp.247-268.

Hall, Gwendolyn, *African Ethnicities in the Americas: Restoring the Links* (Chapel Hill: University of North Carolina Press, 2004)

Handler, Jerome S., "Life Histories of Enslaved Africans in Barbados," *Slavery and Abolition*, 19:1 (1998), 129-141

Herskovits, Melville J., "The Significance of West Africa for Negro Research," *Journal of Negro History,* 21 (1936), 15-30.

Herskovits, Melville J., "On the Provenience of New World Negroes," *Social Forces,* 12 (1933), 247-62

Heywood, Linda, ed., *Central Africans and Cultural Transformations in the American Diaspora* (New York: Cambridge University Press, 2001)

Higman, B. W., "African and Creole Slave Family Patterns in Trinidad," Journal *of family History,* 3 (1978), 163-180

Higman, B. W. "Growth in Afro-Caribbean Slave Populations", American *Journal of Physical Anthropology,* 50 (1979), 373-385.

Hern, Warren M. (1990). Abortion Practice. Philadelphia: J.B. Lippincott Company.

Hogendorn, Jan and Johnson, Marion, *The Shell Money of the Slave Trade* (Cambridge: Cambridge University Press, 1986).

"Induced Abortion in the United States." Guttmacher Institute (May 2016): bullet point #2 https://www.guttmacher.org/fact-sheet/induced-abortion-united-states

Inikori, Joseph E., *Africans and the Industrial Revolution in England: A Study in International Trade and Economic Development* (Cambridge: Cambridge University Press, 2002)

Inikori, Joseph E. and Engerman, Stanley L. (eds.), *The Atlantic Slave Trade: Effects on Economies, Societies, and Peoples in Africa, the Americas, and Europe* (Durham: University of North Carolina Press, 1992)

Jones, Adam, "Recaptive Nations: Evidence Concerning the Demographic Impact of the Atlantic Slave Trade in the Early Nineteenth Century," *Slavery and Abolition*, 11:1 (1990), 43-57

Karasch, Mary C., "Central Africans in Central Brazil, 1780-1835," in Linda Heywood, ed., *Central Africans and Cultural Transformations in the American Diaspora* (New York: Cambridge University Press, 2001), 117-151.

Karen Meckstroth MD, MPH, and Maureen Paul MD, MPH, "First-Trimester Aspiration Abortion," Management of Unintended and Abnormal Pregnancy. Ed. Paul, Lichtenberg, Borgatta, Grimes, Stubblefield and Creinin. (Wiley-Blackwell, 2009)

Kea, Raymond, 1982. *Settlements, Trade, and Politics in the Seventeenth-Century Gold Coast*. Baltimore

Klein, Herbert S., *The Middle Passage: Comparative Studies in the Atlantic Slave Trade* (Princeton: Princeton University Press, 1978)

Klein, Martin A. "Slavery, the International Labour Market and the Emancipation of Slaves in the Nineteenth Century." *Slavery and Abolition*, 1994, Vol.15, No. 2, pp.197-220.

Klein, Martin. *Slavery and Colonial Rule in French West Africa* (Cambridge: Cambridge University Press, 1998)

Kulikoff, Allan. "The Origins of Afro-American Society in Tidewater Maryland and Virginia, 1700 to 1790." *The William and Mary Quarterly*, 1978, Vol. 35, pp. 226-59.

Law, Robin. "Ethnicity and the Slave Trade: "Lucumi" and "Nago" as Ethnonyms in West Africa". *History in Africa*, 1997, Vol. 24, pp.205-219.

Law, Robin. *The Slave Coast of West Africa 1550-1750.* (Oxford: Clarendon Press, 1991)

Law, Robin. "Slaves, Trade, and Taxes: The Material Basis of Political Power in Precolonial West Africa," *Research in Economic Anthropology* 1 (1978): 37-52

Law, Robin. *The Oyo Empire, c.1600-c.1836: A West African Imperialism in the Era of the Atlantic Slave Trade* (Oxford: Clarendon Press, 1977)

Law, Robin (ed.), *The Ports of the Slave Trade (Bights of Benin and Biafra).* Stirling

Law, Robin. "The Chronology of the Yoruba Wars of the Early Nineteenth Century: A Reconstruction," *Journal of the Historical Society of Nigeria* 5 (1970)

Law, Robin, *The Oyo Empire, c. 1600 - c. 1836: A West African Imperialism in the Era of the Atlantic Slave Trade* (Oxford: Clarendon, 1977)

Law, Robin, "Royal monopoly and private enterprise in the Atlantic trade: the case of Dahomey," *Journal of African History*, 18, 4 (1977), 555-77

Law, Robin, "Slaves, trade and taxes: the material basis of political power in pre-colonial West Africa," *Research in Economic Anthropology*, 1 (1978), 37-52

Law, Robin, *The Horse in West African History* (Oxford: Clarendon, 1980)

Law, Robin, *The Kingdom of Allada* (Leiden, 1997)

Law, Robin (ed.), *From Slave Trade to 'Legitimate' Commerce: The Commercial Transition in Nineteenth-Century West Africa* (Cambridge: Cambridge University Press, 1995)

Law, Robin and Lovejoy, Paul E., ed., *The Biography of Mahommah Gardo Baquaqua: His Passage from Slavery to Freedom in Africa and America* (Princeton: Markus Wiener Publisher, 2001)

Lovejoy, Paul E., ed. *Identity in the Shadow of Slavery* (London: Cassell Academic, 2000)

Lovejoy, Paul E. "The Clapperton-Bello Exchange: The Sokoto *Jihad* and the Trans-Atlantic Slave Trade, 1804-1837," in A.E. Willey and C. Wise, eds. *The Desert Shore: Literatures of the African Sahel* (Boulder: Lynne Rienner, 2000)

Lovejoy, Paul E. *Transformations in Slavery: A History of Slavery in Africa* (Cambridge: Cambridge University Press, 2nd ed., 2000)

Lovejoy, Paul E. "Cerner les identities au sein de la diaspora africaine, l'islam et l'esclavage aux Ameriques," *Cahiers des Anneaux de la Memoire* 1 (1999): 249-78.

Lovejoy, Paul E. "Biography as Source Material: Towards a Biographical Archive of Enslaved Africans," in R. Law, ed. *Source Material for Studying the Slave Trade and the African Diaspora.* (Stirling: Centre for Commonwealth Studies, 1997)

Lovejoy, Paul E. "Background to Rebellion: The Origins of Muslim Slaves in Bahia," *Slavery and Abolition* 15 (1994): 151-80

Lovejoy, Paul E. "The Impact of the Atlantic Slave Trade on Africa: A Review of the Literature," *Journal of African History,* 30 (1989): 365-94

Lovejoy, Paul E., ed. *Africans in Bondage* (Madison: African Studies Program, 1986)

Lovejoy, Paul E., ed. *The Ideology of Slavery in Africa* (Beverly Hills, Calif.: Sage Publications, 1981)

Lovejoy, Paul E., ed., *Slavery on the Frontiers of Islam* (Princeton: Markus Wiener Publisher, 2004)

Lovejoy, P.E. and Hogendorn, J.S. 1979, "Slave Marketing in West Africa," in H.A Gemery and J.S. Hogendorn (eds.), *The Uncommon Market: Essays in the Economic History of the Atlantic Slave Trade* (New York: Academic Press, 1979), 213-35

Lovejoy, Paul E. and Richardson, David. "The Initial 'Crisis of Adaptation': The Impact of British Abolition on the Atlantic Slave Trade in West Africa, 1808-1820," in R. Law, ed. *From Slave Trade to "Legitimate" Commerce: The Commercial Transition in Nineteenth-Century West Africa* (Cambridge: Cambridge University Press, 1995)

Lovejoy, Paul E. and Richardson, David. "Competing Markets for Male and Female Slaves: Slave Prices in the Interior of West Africa, 1780-1850," *International Journal of African Historical Studies* 28:2 (1995)

Lovejoy, P.E. and Trotman, David V., eds. *Trans-Atlantic Dimensions of Ethnicity in the African Diaspora* (London: Continuum, 2003)

Lovejoy, Paul E. and Trotman, David V. "Enslaved Africans and their Expectations of Slave Life in the Americas: Towards a

Reconsideration of Models of 'Creolisaton'," in Verene A. Shepherd and Glen L. Richards (eds.), *Questioning Creole: Creolisaton Discourses in Caribbean Culture* (Kingston: Ian Randal, Publishers, 2002), 67-91

Manning, Patrick, *Slavery and African Life. Occidental, Oriental and African Slave Trades* (Cambridge: Cambridge University Press, 1990).

Martin Luther King Jr. "Letter from Birmingham Jail." (April 16, 1963)

Miers, Suzanne, *Britain and the Ending of the Slave Trade* (New York, 1975)

Miers, S. and Kopytoff, I. (eds.), *Slavery in Africa: Historical and Anthropological Perspective* (Madison: University of Wisconsin Press, 1977)

Miers, Suzanne and Roberts, Richard (eds.). 1988. *The End of Slavery in Africa*. Madison

Miller, Joseph C. "Central Africa During the Era of the Slave Trade, c. 1490s-1850s," in Linda Heywood, ed., *Central Africans and Cultural Transformations in the American Diaspora* (New York: Cambridge University Press , 2001), 21-69.

Miller, Joseph C. "History and Africa/Africa and History," *American Historical Review* 104, 1 (1999): 1-32.

Miller, Joseph C., *Way of Death. Merchant Capitalism and the Angolan Slave Trade, 1730-1830* (Madison: University of Wisconsin Press, 1988)

Miller, Joseph C. 1999. *Slavery and Slaving in World History. A Bibliography, 1900-1996* (Armon, NY. 2nd edition., 1999), 2 vols.

Mintz, Sidney W. and Price, Richard. *An Anthropological Perspective to the Afro-American Past: A Caribbean Perspective* (Philadelphia: Institute for the Study of Human Issues, 1976)

Morgan, Philip. "The Cultural Implications of the Atlantic Slave Trade: African Regional Origins, American Destinations and New World Developments," *Slavery and Abolition*, 18:1 (1997)

Morgan, Philip, *Slave Counterpoint* - full details needed

Northrup, David, *Trade without Rulers: pre-Colonial Economic Development in South-Eastern Nigeria* (Oxford: Clarendon, 1978)

Palmer, Colin A. "From Africa to the Americas: Ethnicity in the Early Black Communities of the Americas" *Journal of World History*, 6:2 (1995), 223-237.

Pavy, David. "The Provenience of Columbian Negroes." *Journal of Negro History*, 52 (1967), 35-58.

Price, Richard. "Resistance to Slavery in the Americas: Maroons and Their Communities" *Indian Historical Review*, 15:1/2, (1988-89), 71-95.

Raphael Lemkin, Special Report presented to the 5th Conference for the Unification of Penal Law in Madrid (October 14 -20, 1933) http://www.preventgenocide.org/lemkin/madrid1933-english.htm

Raphael Lemkin, *Axis Rule in Occupied Europe* (Washington, D.C. Carnegie Endowment for International Peace, 1944), 79-95.

Rodney, Walter. "Upper Guinea and the Significance of the Origins of Africans Enslaved in the New World." *The Journal of Negro History*, 1969, Vol. 54, No. 4.

Rodney, Walter, "Slavery and other forms of social oppression on the Upper Guinea Coast in the context of the Atlantic slave trade," *Journal of African History*, 7, 4 (1966), 431-43.

SOLZHENITSYN, A. I., The Gulag Archipelago, 1918-1956: An Experiment in Literary Investigation (London: HarperCollins, 1974).

Stanton, Gregory H. (1998). "The 8 Stages of Genocide." Genocide Watch http://www.genocidewatch.org/aboutgenocide/8stagesofgenocide.html

Sweet, James H. *Recreating Africa: Culture, Kinship and Religion in the African-Portuguese World, 1441-1770*. Chapel Hill: University of North Carolina Press, 2003.

The Three-Fifths compromise of 1787 was reached after those in the North demanded that slaves not be counted for enumeration purposes while those in the South wanted slaves counted as full-persons. Since slaves were not allowed to vote, counting them as only 3/5 of a person gave Southern states less voting power than if slaves had been counted as full persons, but far more than if slaves hadn't been counted at all.

Thornton, John, *Africa and Africans in the Making of the Atlantic World, 1400-1800* (Cambridge: Cambridge University, 2nd ed., 1998).

This percentage was arrived at by dividing the total number of abortions performed at Planned Parenthood (323,999 according to their 2014 - 2015 Annual Report) by the total number of abortions performed in the United States (approximately 983,000 in 2014).

Thornton, John K. "African Dimensions of the Stono Rebellion" *American Historical Review,* 1991, 1101-1113.

Thornton, John K., "I Am the King of Congo': African Political Ideology and the Haitia Revolution," *Journal of World History,* 4:2 (1993), 181-214

Trouillot, Michel-Rolph. "Culture on the Edges: Creolization in the Plantation Context." *Plantation Society in the Americas,* 5:1 (1998), 8-28.

United Nations, General Assembly Resolution 1021, "Convention on the Prevention and Punishment of the Crime of Genocide" (AUSTRALIA, BULGARIA, CAMBODIA, CEYLON, CZECHOSLOVAKIA, etc.) 9 Dec 1948. https://treaties.un.org/doc/Publication/UNTS/Volume%2078/volume-78-I-1021-English.pdf

UNKOWN, 'The Free Dictionary by Farlex', thefreedictionary.com, Unknown date, 10 February 2010, http://www.thefreedictionary.com/dehumanization

WADE, J., 'Negotiation and Mediation Concepts and Terminology', Mediate.com, September 2000, Bond University, 10 February 2010, http://www.mediate.com/articles/bondV2sept99.cfm

WALLER, J., Becoming Evil (Oxford: Oxford University Press, 2002).

Warner-Lewis, Maureen, "Posited Kikoongo origins of some Portuguese and Spanish words from the slave era," *América Negra,* 7:13 (1997), 83-97

Warner-Lewis, Maureen, *The History of the Congo Peoples in the Caribbean* [correct title]

Webster's New World Encyclopaedia, Prentice Hall General Reference, 1992.

Wilks, Ivor. *Forests of Gold: Essays on the Akan and the Kingdom of Asante* (Athens: Ohio University Press, 1993).

WILSON, C. A., Racism: From Slavery to Advanced Capitalism (London: Sage Publications, 1996).

Chapter Four

The Dynamics of European Colonial Genocidal Terror in Africa

Overview

European colonial terrorism and genocide in Africa confound scholars, practitioners, and laypersons alike. Despite the carnage of the twentieth century, our understanding of genocidal terror remains partial. Popular, moralizing accounts have done their share to hinder understanding by attempting to advance simple truths in an area where there are none. This chapter focuses on certain elements of the European genocidal terror legacy in Africa that were crucial in framing the turn of the twenty-first century and marking the "western" picture of the world during that period. In addition, these elements were major factors in enabling the perpetration of atrocities on the African continent on a scale that invites comparison with the Holocaust – that is, the first and the last genocides of the twentieth century.

This chapter therefore discusses genocide and mass violence in Africa during the colonial period. While European colonial rule lasted only several decades, it had a profound impact on Africa. The history of European colonialism in Africa is of unprecedented socio-economic, political, and cultural change, genocidal mass violence, and exploitation. Until recently, the historiography of colonialism and genocide has portrayed the Africans as passive and apathetic victims of European power and violence. But Africa did not degenerate into a graveyard because of the Europeans' attempt to brutally transform the continent and its inhabitants according to their ideas. European colonialism did not succeed in completely destroying African cultures and identities. Africans always found ways to preserve their cultures and to reconstitute their social organizations, however totalitarian and coercive the colonizers' policies and fantasies about absolute power were confirmed.

Introduction

For centuries, beginning with the slave trade, Western Europe has ruthlessly exploited the African continent. As Karl Marx (1977, 915, http://www.marxists.org/archive/marx/wor...) described it, "the turning of Africa into a commercial warren for the hunting of black skins" was one of the chief sources of "primitive accumulation" that "signalled the rosy dawn of the era of capitalist production". But the abduction and enslavement of millions of Africans was only the start of genocidal exploitation and dehumanization of the African. In the late nineteenth century, in what became known as the "scramble for Africa," the continent was arbitrarily carved up into colonies by the leading European powers, which violently subjected its people and plundered the continent of its rich natural resources. In the post-independence eras, African states became weak pawns in the European imposed capitalist world economy, subject to Cold War rivalries, their path to development largely blocked by their debilitating colonial past. More recently, the West has choked Africa with an onerous debt regime, forcing many nations to pay more in interest on debts to the World Bank and International Monetary Fund (IMF) than on health care, education, infrastructure, and other vital services combined.

The legacy of Western domination has left Africa devastated with crippling rates of poverty, hunger, and disease. The continent today has a gross national per-capita yearly income of $829—below that of the 1950s and 1960s in most African countries—and an average life expectancy of only fifty years (Average world gross national income is $7,748. Source: World Bank Key Development Data and Statistics, http://web.worldbank.org/WBSITE/EXTERNAL...). Si xty-two percent of Africans have no access to standard sanitation facilities, and two-thirds of the total world population suffering from HIV/AIDS (25.8 million people) live in Africa (Global Aids Statistics, Global AIDS Alliance, http://www.globalaidsalliance.org/info/f...). It remains a continent abundant in human and natural resources, but these manage to enrich only a handful of African rulers and foreign capitalists.

This is the historical legacy, in the words of Patrick Bond, "of a continent *looted*":

[T]rade by force dating back centuries; slavery that uprooted and dispossessed around 12 million Africans; precious metals spirited away; the 19th century emergence of racist ideologies to justify colonialism; the…carve-up of Africa into dysfunctional territories in a Berlin negotiating room; the construction of settler-colonial and extractive-colonial systems—of which apartheid, the German occupation of Namibia, the Portuguese colonies and King Leopold's Belgian Congo were perhaps only the most blatant…; Cold War battlegrounds—proxies for U.S./U.S.S.R. conflicts—filled with millions of corpses; other wars catalysed by mineral searches and offshoot violence such as witnessed in blood diamonds and coltan; poacher-stripped swathes of East, Central and Southern Africa…; societies used as guinea pigs in the latest corporate pharmaceutical test; and the list could continue (Bond, 2006:2).

You might think a track record of this kind would lead to some self-reflection on the part of Western powers regarding their genocidal violent history in Africa. But you would be wrong. Robert Calderisi, a former World Bank Africa chief and author of *The Trouble With Africa: Why Foreign Aid Isn't Working* (2006) offers diagnoses and prescriptions for Africa that are no less paternalistic than those given by the colonialists of old:

[Some Africans] believe all of Africa's problems are basically rooted in Western nastiness: colonialism, slavery, debt, and the like. But my own sense is that opinion has shifted tremendously in Africa over the last ten years, that there's greater openness to accepting that African problems have roots in Africa…. [O]ne of the good legacies of colonialism [is that] there are Western nations that could have turned their backs on Africa a long time ago if they didn't have some historical, economic, and sentimental connection…. For me to suggest that we reduce rather than increase aid to Africa will sound to many people like spitting in the face of a dying man, but I see it as analogous to dragging a dope addict to his feet and bringing him to a rehabilitation clinic (Calderisi, 2006). Others, like former British Prime Minister Gordon Brown, are no less direct in their unapologetic defence of imperialism. "The days of Britain having to apologize for its colonial history are over," he said arrogantly during a tour of Africa, "We should celebrate much of our past rather than apologize for it (Pilger, 2007). The simple way to distinguish between

123

colonialism and imperialism is to think of colonialism as practice and imperialism as the idea driving the practice. Colonialism is the implanting of settlements on a distant territory.

Understanding Colonialism

A colony is a part of an empire and so colonialism is closely related to imperialism. Assumptions are that colonialism and imperialism are interchangeable, however Robert J. C. Young suggests that imperialism is the concept while colonialism is the practice. Colonialism is based on an imperial outlook, thereby creating a consequential relationship. Through an empire, colonialism is established and capitalism is expanded, on the other hand a capitalist economy naturally enforces an empire. In the next section Marxists make a case for this mutually reinforcing relationship.

Marxism views colonialism as a form of capitalism, enforcing exploitation and social change. Marx thought that working within the global capitalist system, colonialism is closely associated with uneven development. As defined in the *Dictionary of Human Geography*, "Colonialism" is an "instrument of wholesale destruction, dependency and systematic exploitation producing distorted economies, socio-psychological disorientation, massive poverty and neocolonial dependency." Colonies are constructed into modes of production. The search for raw materials and the current search for new investment opportunities is a result of inter-capitalist rivalry for capital accumulation. Lenin regarded colonialism as the root cause of imperialism, as imperialism was distinguished by monopoly capitalism via colonialism and as Lyal S. Sunga (1997: 90) explains: "Vladimir Lenin advocated forcefully the principle of self-determination of peoples in his "Theses on the Socialist Revolution and the Right of Nations to Self-Determination" as an integral plank in the program of socialist internationalism "and he quotes Lenin who contended that "The right of nations to self-determination implies exclusively the right to independence in the political sense, the right to free political separation from the oppressor nation. Specifically, this demand for political democracy implies complete freedom to agitate for secession and for a referendum on secession by the seceding nation." Non-Russian Marxists within the RSFSR and later the USSR, like Sultan Galiev and Vasyl Shakhrai, meanwhile, between 1918 and 1923 and then after 1929, considered the Soviet Regime a renewed version of the Russian imperialism and colonialism.

In his critique of colonialism in Africa, the Guyanese historian and political activist Walter Rodney (1973) states:

"The decisiveness of the short period of colonialism and its negative consequences for Africa spring mainly from the fact that Africa lost power. Power is the ultimate determinant in human society, being basic to the relations within any group and between groups. It implies the ability to defend one's interests and if necessary to impose one's will by any means available ... When one society finds itself forced to relinquish power entirely to another society that in itself is a form of underdevelopment ... During the centuries of pre-colonial trade, some control over social political and economic life was retained in Africa, in spite of the disadvantageous commerce with Europeans. That little control over internal matters disappeared under colonialism. Colonialism went much further than trade. It meant a tendency towards direct appropriation by Europeans of the social institutions within Africa. Africans ceased to set indigenous cultural goals and standards, and lost full command of training young members of the society. Those were undoubtedly major steps backwards ... Colonialism was not merely a system of exploitation, but one whose essential purpose was to repatriate the profits to the so-called 'mother country.' From an African view-point, that amounted to consistent expatriation of surplus produced by African labour out of African resources. It meant the development of Europe as part of the same dialectical process in which Africa was underdeveloped" (149, 224).

"Colonial Africa fell within that part of the international capitalist economy from which surplus was drawn to feed the metropolitan sector. As seen earlier, exploitation of land and labour is essential for human social advance, but only on the assumption that the product is made available within the area where the exploitation takes place" (Schwarz; Ray, *2004:271*).

According to Lenin, the new imperialism emphasized the transition of capitalism from free trade to a stage of monopoly capitalism to finance capital. He states it is, "connected with the intensification of the struggle for the partition of the world". As free trade thrives on exports of commodities, monopoly capitalism thrived on the export of capital amassed by profits from banks and industry. This, to Lenin, was the highest stage of capitalism. He goes on to state that this form of capitalism was doomed for war between the capitalists and the exploited nations with the former inevitably losing. War is stated to be the consequence of imperialism. As a continuation of this thought G.N. Uzoigwe states, "But it is now clear from more serious investigations of African history in this period that imperialism was essentially economic in its fundamental impulses" (Adu, 1985:11).

Colonialism is therefore the establishment, exploitation, maintenance, acquisition, and expansion of colony in one territory by a political power from another territory. It is a set of unequal relationships between the colonial power and the colony and often between the colonists and the indigenous population. The European colonial period was the era from the 16th century to the mid-20th century when several European powers established colonies in Asia, Africa, and the Americas. At first the countries followed mercantilist policies designed to strengthen the home economy at the expense of rivals, so the colonies were usually allowed to trade only with the mother country. By the mid-19th century, however, the powerful British Empire gave up mercantilism and trade restrictions and introduced the principle of free trade, with few restrictions or tariffs. Historians often distinguish between two overlapping forms of colonialism:

Settler colonialism involves large-scale immigration, often motivated by religious, political, or economic reasons. Exploitation colonialism involves fewer colonists and focuses on access to resources for export, typically to the metropole. This category includes trading posts as well as larger colonies where colonists would constitute much of the political and economic administration, but would rely on indigenous resources for labour and material. Prior to the end of the slave trade and widespread abolition, when indigenous labour was

126

unavailable, slaves were often imported to the Americas, first by the Portuguese Empire, and later by the Spanish, Dutch, French and British. Plantation colonies would be considered exploitation colonialism; but colonizing powers would utilize either type for different territories depending on various social and economic factors as well as climate and geographic conditions. Surrogate colonialism involves a settlement project supported by colonial power, in which most of the settlers do not come from the mainstream of the ruling power. Internal colonialism is a notion of uneven structural power between areas of a nation state. The source of colonial capitalist exploitation comes from within the state in any capitalist society.

General Theories of Capitalist Society

General theories of capitalist society are many but the main ones are the following: First there are the works of the classical economists of which *Wealth of Nations* (Smith 1977) is the most important and still highly relevant example. Second are the theories of capitalism which arise from the work of Karl Marx in Marx 1992. Marx develops his famous labour theory of value in which, in contrast to Smith, labour power rather than labour is the source of exchange value and its exploitation in the labour process is the source of surplus value. The third group of theories is those derived from marginal utility theory which, influenced by Bentham's utilitarianism, developed toward the latter part of the 19th century and which are best represented in the work of Alfred Marshall in Marshall 2009. This is the source of modern day micro-economics and neo-classical theory which looks at the economy principally from the point of view of maximizing the interests of the individual consumer or firm. Fourthly, there is Keynesianism in Keynes 2007. Influenced by Cambridge aestheticism, Keynes in effect transforms the individualist perspective of the marginalists into a social utility in which social consumption and aggregate demand play a pivotal role. The issue now is how to stabilize the capitalist system as a whole in such a manner that the cycles of boom and bust are evened out. The final group of works stress the cultural consequences of capitalism—of particular importance for anthropologists. The two preeminent books here are Durkheim 1997 (*Division of Labour in Society*) and Weber 1978 (*Protestant Ethic*). Durkheim, influenced by 19th century thinkers like Herbert Spencer as well as by Henry Maine, argues that capitalism produces a potential for a new form of social solidarity ("organic") which is based on the mutual interdependence of differentiated social institutions. Giddens 1971, drawing on the Durkheimian tradition, presents a synthetic summary of contemporary capitalism in which the potential for capitalism to be stabilized by normative reforms is emphasized. In contrast to this basically optimistic view of the political-cultural future of capitalism, Max Weber presents a pessimistic and ironic narrative of a system which, having been originally inspired by a deep-seated sense of individual ethical commitment, now finds itself descending into an iron cage of bureaucracy which threatens to stifle all liberal and human values. Here one can detect that tragic sense of resignation and alienation which some characterize as "modernist" and a hallmark of late capitalist culture—public, private, and aesthetic—in the 20th and 21st centuries.

Capitalism and the Expansion of Imperialism

Throughout the nineteenth and twentieth centuries, European and Western nations scrambled to the far corners of the globe seeking to establish vast imperial networks through both the conquest and exploitation of indigenous populations. By 1914, virtually no country, continent, nor locality found itself unscathed from the imperial ambitions of the West. What explains this dramatic expansion of imperialism and competition among the European powers? Did these ambitions result from a political and nationalist desire for glory and prestige? Or was the expansion of imperialism linked to more economic factors instead – in particular, a desire for wealth and greater trade? While answers to these questions may never be fully resolved by historians, this article seeks to address the potential economic elements that led to imperialism through a cross-comparison of figures such as Karl Marx, J.A. Hobson, and Vladimir Lenin. Why did these individuals blame the growth of capitalism for the expansion of imperialism? More specifically, why did they feel as though imperialism was inextricably linked to the growth of capitalism during the nineteenth-century? Finally, and perhaps most importantly, how have modern historians interpreted the connection between capitalism and imperialism during this period of world history?

According to Karl Marx, the expansion of imperialism was directly linked to a growth in capitalism due to one fundamental reason: the fact that capitalism was a worldwide system and unable to be constrained within the boundaries of a single country or nation-state (Chandra: 39). This viewpoint of Marx is reiterated by historian Bipan Chandra who states: "by its very nature capitalism could not exist in only one country...it expanded to encompass the entire world, including the backward, non-capitalist countries...it was a world system" (Chandra, 39). In accordance with this view, Marx argued that capitalism required an "international division of labour," in which the capitalists sought to convert "one part of the globe into a chiefly agricultural field of production, for supplying the other part which remains a chiefly industrial field" (Chandra: 43). Thus, according to Marx, imperialism served as a means to extract a large amount of "raw materials" and resources in a relatively cheap manner – all at the expense (and exploitation) of the indigenous peoples of the world that came into contact with the imperial powers. Ironically, Marx viewed the expansion of capitalist societies into the world as a necessary evil that would, ultimately, shift societies toward the path of communism. For Marx – who believed that society followed a series of progressing epochs – imperialism was simply the next (and unavoidable) step for capitalism's relentless expansion.

In 1902, J.A. Hobson – a social democrat – argued along similar lines of Marx by stating that the growth of imperialism was directly correlated with an expansion of capitalism as well. According to Hobson, imperialism resulted from a capitalist desire for additional (outside) markets. As production capabilities in capitalist countries increased over time (due to competition with the rapidly developing industries of Western nations), Hobson believed that overproduction eventually outgrew consumer needs on the home-front. Hobson argued that overproduction, in turn, leads to a system in which "more goods can be produced than can be sold at a profit" (Hobson: 81). As a result, Hobson believed that the financiers of industry – concerned only with expanding their margin of profit – began to seek out foreign regions to invest their large savings that had been acquired through years of "surplus capital" (Hobson: 82). As he states, "Imperialism is the endeavour of the great controllers of industry to broaden the channel for the flow of their surplus wealth by seeking foreign markets and foreign investments to take off the goods and capital they cannot sell or use at home" (Hobson: 85). According to Hobson, an expanded market would afford financiers an opportunity to further expand production, while also lowering their costs; thus, allowing for an upsurge in profits since consumption would be expanded from populations in these oversea ventures (Hobson: 29). Moreover, by expanding into foreign regions protected by their governments (through imperial colonization), industries would gain a competitive edge over rival European companies seeking to expand their own consumption rates (Hobson: 81).

Unlike Marx, however, Hobson viewed these imperial endeavours as both unnecessary and avoidable. Hobson viewed imperialism – particularly in Great Britain – as a detriment to society as he felt that it led to a system in which governments were largely controlled by financiers and industrial giants. In pulling the strings of the government in this manner, Hobson's theory alludes to an inherent risk involved with imperialism; the risk of driving European powers into potential conflict (and war) over territorial claims and rights in the future.

In a similar manner to Hobson, Vladimir Lenin also linked the desire for foreign markets and imperial expansion to a growth in capitalism as well. However, in contrast to Hobson, Lenin viewed the advent of imperialism as "a special stage of capitalism" – an unavoidable transition that inevitably set the stage for global revolution (www.marxists.org). As capitalist corporations continued to grow over time, Lenin believed that banks, companies, and industries were quickly developing into monopolies involving "cartels, syndicates and trusts" that would expand and "manipulate thousands of millions" across the globe (www.marxists.org). According to Lenin, the growth of monopolies was, in effect, destroying capitalist "free competition…creating large-scale industry and forcing out small industry" (www.marxists.org). Eager to exploit "limited and protected markets" for maximum profits, Lenin's theory argues that financiers under the monopoly-capitalist system had discovered that "it was more profitable to employ surplus capital abroad than in domestic industry," thus, setting the stage for intense "overseas investment" through imperialist measures of colonization (Fieldhouse: 192). According to historian, D.K. Fieldhouse, Lenin firmly believed that only through complete colonization "could really comprehensive economic and political controls be imposed which would give investments their highest return" (Fieldhouse: 192). As a result of these desires, Lenin believed that imperialism represented the final stage of capitalism and marked the beginning of a worldwide revolution toward socialism and communism.

While it is clear that Marx, Hobson, and Lenin all understood imperialism to be a by-product of capitalism, historians remain divided over the effects that this intertwining of capitalism and imperialism had upon the world at large. This issue is particularly evident with the discussion of British rule in India from the eighteenth to the twentieth-century, as scholars continue to debate whether British rule should be categorized as either a positive or negative period for Indian history.

For historians such as Morris D. Morris, British rule introduced both values and political order to India and can be viewed as a positive step for Indian society. As he states, the British ushered in an era of "stability, standardization, and efficiency...in administration" for the Indians (Morris: 611). Moreover, Morris believed that British rule "probably stimulated economic activity in a way which had never been possible before" (Morris: 611). While Morris states that "the policies of the state [British Raj] were not sufficient to permit the development during the century of all the fundamental underpinnings of an industrial revolution," he argues that imperial conquest of India created a basis "for a renewed upward surge after [Indian] Independence" (Morris: 616).

In comparison to this view, historian Bipan Chandra found great faults with Morris' line of reasoning. Through his analysis of Morris' interpretation on British rule in India, Chandra rejects nearly all the positive assertions made by Morris and argues instead that "British rule was imperialistic" and that "its basic character...was to subserve Indian interests to British interests" (Chandra, 69). Chandra argues that "rationalized taxation, the pattern of commerce, law and order, and judicial system" implemented by the British all "led to an

131

extremely regressive…agrarian structure" for India (Chandra, 47). Historian, Mike Davis' book, *Late Victorian Holocausts: El Nino Famines and the Making of the Third World* offers a similar interpretation of British imperialism through his discussion of famines that were amplified by improper British rule in India. Davis points out that not only did the British use famine and drought as a means of gaining a stronger hold over the Indians (both economically and politically), but their supposed use of free-market principles served only "as a mask for colonial genocide" in that millions of Indians perished from starvation and disease from mismanagement under imperial rule (Davis: 37). Such exploitation was not limited to only the British, however. Davis points out that other empires used drought and famine to expand their power and influence over indigenous peoples during this time as well. In a brief discussion of the Portuguese, Germans, and Americans, Davis argues that "global drought was the green light for an imperialist land rush" in which these empires would use drought and disease to suppress largely powerless people into submission (Davis: 12-13). Consequently, Davis views the millions of worldwide deaths inflicted by imperial policies as "the exact moral equivalent of bombs dropped from 18,000 feet" (Davis: 22).

In sum, the link between a growth in capitalism and the expansion of imperialism remains a highly relevant issue for historians today. While it is true that political factors may have also played a role in the decision to colonize foreign lands, one cannot ignore the potential economic elements of imperialism as well. In the end, historians will likely never agree on the consequences and impact of imperialism on the world at large – particularly in regions such as Africa and India. However, given the size and scope of imperialism across the nineteenth and twentieth centuries, it is difficult to view the policies of European expansion in a positive light when one considers the tremendous exploitation and death that followed in the wake of European conquest.

The Capitalism-Genocide Nexus

The study of capitalism and its genocidal effects covers a wide range of issues from the economic to the civilizational which can easily overwhelm scholars. Capitalism is a familiar word. I suspect, however, that even in Western democracies where capitalist economic arrangements are most familiar, advanced and dominant, most citizens would be hard-pressed to put together a coherent definition, description, explanation and justification of capitalism. Suffice here to say that it is an economic system in which the principal form of ownership dictates that the means of production and distribution of goods and services are held mostly in private hands—whether individual and corporate.

For the purposes of clarity capitalism is therefore best defined as an economic system based on private ownership of the means of production and in which goods and services are freely exchanged by means of the market mechanism. It can be contrasted to various models of "state socialism" in which the means of production are collectively owned either through the state or in a cooperative relationship at the plant level and in which economic production and exchange are centrally planned and controlled. It is also to be distinguished from "market socialism" which is a hybrid economic system in which critical areas of the economy, especially finance and core production functions, are collectively owned by the state but a large range of consumer enterprises are privatized allowing market exchange to play a major role in economic transactions albeit within a framework of selective central planning and administrative oversight and regulation. The outstanding case of a capitalist economy today is the United States; the classical case of "state socialism" was the Soviet Union; and the best current example of "market socialism" is the Chinese economy. Given the vital issues of human development, political freedom, and ideology which are involved, these distinctions are highly controversial and contested. For example, there is an ongoing debate as to whether China is to be understood as a market socialist economy or simply a capitalist economy with a veneer of socialist rhetoric and an authoritarian political structure. Notwithstanding these debates which cannot be avoided, the distinctions made above offer a useful point of departure to embark on the study of capitalism in an organized and logically coherent fashion

Genocide is also a familiar word. It is generally understood to be the intentional destruction, usually by violent means, of a group of people by some organized adversary, most often a government or at least well-organized paramilitary forces. Of course, there are variants including the previously mentioned phenomenon of "cultural genocide," which entail the extinguishment of a culture and its people, typically by means of forced assimilation. Still, the basic idea is clear enough: genocide is the attempt to significantly devastate or eradicate an entire people.

In the capitalist market, of course, it is the power of those who own and control capital that takes precedence over the consumer needs and desires, but even here there is wiggle room, for the needs and desires are said to be "demanded" by consumers who vote with their dollars and pay extortionist prices because it is *their* needs and desires that are being met. The market premise, therefore, both assures the continuation of the *fundamental* inequity of ownership and control and justifies it in terms of allegedly free choice. In the end, of course, it is easy to see how many so-called consumer needs and desires are manufactured through massive advertising campaigns for specific products and by the underlying propaganda for material consumption in general. Private purchases are celebrated, even though they eventually substitute for personality, character, social relations and a sense of meaning in a society in which people are alienated from nature, from their communities, their work, their intimate relations and finally from themselves. We are what we buy. (Fromm, 1955; Fromm, 1961: 1-85).

To many citizens in liberal democracies, the logical necessity of genocide as a corollary of economic market mechanisms may seem like an untenable stretch. Nonetheless, let us look at a number of persuasive case studies to prove his point. He reveals the North American Free Trade Agreement to be an instrument whereby American-based agribusiness has destroyed local Mexican agriculture and led to death and dispossession among thousands of the rural poor. He points to India where the government's own figures show that over 200,000 Indian farmers have been driven to suicide by the effects of policies imposed by the World Trade Organization, the World Bank and the International Monetary Fund. In Africa, too, investment from the "North" according to rules manufactured in the interest of advanced capitalist countries have deformed development, ruined indigenous farmers and prioritized edible crops for export while allowing citizens of those countries to fall below subsistence living and to starve.

Practices such as the annihilation of a whole or a part of a population either by direct armed attack or the deprivation of the necessities of life (food, medicine, etc.) are well established as crimes against humanity in international law. We have seen such crimes, mainly in the peripheral countries, too often in the past century; so, the fact of genocide is plainly one with which we are familiar in the contemporary world. What might remain questionable in the minds of sticklers for technicalities is the question of *mens rea.* Is imperial genocide the *intentional* act of capitalist nations? For Leech, no claim of innocence through ignorance will do. Even if not premeditated, as Jean-Paul Sartre (1971, p. 545) is recruited to protest: "genocidal intent is implicit in the facts." Over half a century of postcolonial carnage permits no government or citizenry—no matter how dim and discredited—to claim exemption.

There's more. Assuming a capitalist model in which demand is the engine of the economy, what is to be done about those people who lack the resources to make demands on the system? Almost twenty years ago, Arthur Kroker and Marilouise Kroker (1996: 36) put the matter poignantly. On the same weekend that the United Nations "safe haven" the former Yugoslavia was destroyed, Bill Gates made a very big splash in the pond of personal computing. They write (Kroker & Kroker, 1996: 36):

"Windows-95 opens up onto the dominant ideology and privileged life position of digital flesh. It installs the new codes of the master occupants of virtual worlds: frenzied devotion to cyber-business, life in a multi-media virtual context, digital tunnel vision, and, most of all, embedded deep in the cerebral cortex of the digital elite, an I-chip: I, that is, for complete indifference. Technological acceleration is accompanied by a big shutting-down of ethical perception."

The Bosnian Muslims were massacred because they didn't fit into the new digitized economy. They had nothing to add to the virtual market. They were "ethnically cleansed" because they had already been "technically cleansed … They were surplus to world domination in a cyber-box."

Whether by military or economic means, the extermination of peoples is at least foreseeable. We have, after all, a lengthy history of transforming whole societies into subhuman stereotypes, making their removal a matter of capitalist logic. If they cannot "demand" commodities and are not internally productive according to the monetary logic of capitalist development, they cease to exist as creatures of concern.

The consequences of capitalism from the end-of-the sixteenth-century to the mid-seventeenth century *Enclosures Acts* in England, to the *Highland Clearances* in Scotland and the "potato famine" in Ireland in the mid-nineteenth century are well known to anyone willing to be attentive and to understand such matters. Today's *maquiladoras* in Mexico, the unknown thousands of casualties of the insane "war on drugs" in Latin America, the roughly four million internally displaced persons who are victims of military and paramilitary operations in support of global megaprojects, and the millions who have perished from easily cured diseases resulting from contaminated water are ignored by the mainstream media in wealthy countries, but they are surely well-known by the victims and perpetrators of the crimes against them, all committed in the name of intellectually indolent citizens of the advanced (post)industrial world.

The Partition of Africa

The task of this conference was to ensure that each European country that claimed possession over a part of Africa must bring civilization, in the form of Christianity, and trade to each region that it would occupy. Also a country's claim of a territory was valid only if it informed the other European powers and established some occupying force on the ground. This occupying force was often a few military outposts on the coast and interior waterways with little to no actual settlement. Specific lands were obtained by having African indigenous rulers sign an "x" to a general agreement for protection by a European power. Often these rulers had no idea what they were signing since most could not read, write, or understand European languages.

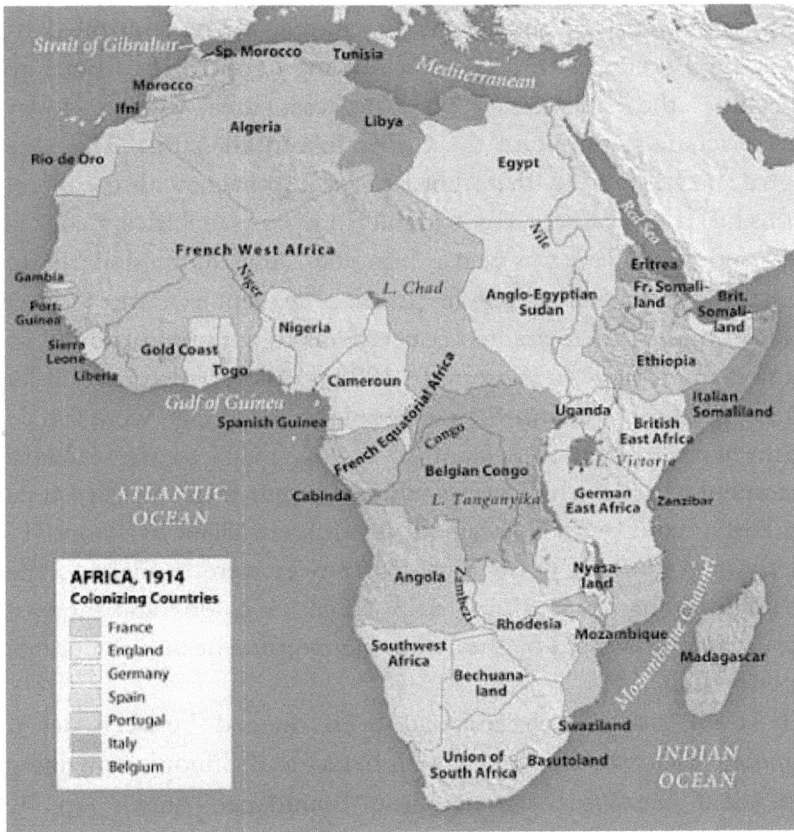

Strait of Gibraltar — Sp. Morocco · Tunisia · *Mediterranean*

Morocco
Ifni
Algeria · Libya
Rio de Oro
Egypt
Nile
French West Africa
Gambia
Port. Guinea
Niger
L. Chad
Anglo-Egyptian Sudan
Eritrea
Fr. Somaliland
Brit. Somaliland
Sierra Leone
Liberia
Gold Coast
Togo
Nigeria
Cameroun
Ethiopia
Gulf of Guinea
Spanish Guinea
French Equatorial Africa
Congo
Uganda
Italian Somaliland
British East Africa
L. Victoria
Belgian Congo
ATLANTIC OCEAN
Cabinda
L. Tanganyika
German East Africa
Zanzibar
Nyasaland
AFRICA, 1914
Colonizing Countries
France
England
Germany
Spain
Portugal
Italy
Belgium
Angola
Zambezi
Rhodesia
Mozambique
Mozambique Channel
Madagascar
Southwest Africa
Bechuanaland
Swaziland
Union of South Africa
Basutoland
INDIAN OCEAN

The conference only dealt with territories yet to be acquired in Africa. This meant that the interior of Africa, about which little was known, was the land area available. Most coastal land had already been claimed by various European countries, as had much of Southern Africa and Africa north of the Sahara. Few Europeans had set foot into the interior of sub-Saharan Africa prior to this conference. Following the Berlin Conference there was still little exploration into the interior of Africa beyond gaining initial treaties. Most Europeans continued to stay on the coastal regions while a few missionaries followed rivers inland to find Christian converts. By 1900, though, more Europeans moved into the African interior to extract raw materials such as rubber, palm oil, gold, copper, and diamonds. These natural resources made Africa a vital resource for the European economy.

Although most of these African colonies were controlled by nations, the Berlin Conference allowed King Leopold II of Belgium to become the sole owner of the vast area that is today the Democratic Republic of the Congo in central Africa. This area was given to Leopold by the other European powers with the intent that this be an area of Free Trade for all Europeans in Africa. Leopold agreed to this stipulation as well as bringing Christian missionaries to the interior of this area, but in practice he kept out most other European traders as he granted concessions to various corporations to exploit the region's resources. In 1908 it was revealed that under King Leopold's instructions native people of the Congo were forced to farm wild rubber as a form of tax payment to the colonial government. Those who were unable to reach their rubber quota often had a hand or foot chopped off, or were killed by Leopold's agents. Once news of these abuses of power were brought to the public light, King Leopold was stripped of his colony and the vast Congo region was ruled by the Belgium government until it became independent in 1960.

By 1914, 90% of Africa had been divided between seven European countries with only Liberia and Ethiopia remaining independent nations. Many of the boundaries drawn up by Europeans at the Berlin Conference still endure today with little regard to natural landmarks or historic ethnic or political boundaries established by the Africans themselves. The disregard of these boundaries, most of which were retained after independence, often continues to generate conflict in Africa today.

European Presence in Africa

Since as early as the fifteenth century and continuing to the present day, European colonies have always viewed Africa as an economic object with a wealth of resources waiting to be extracted and exploited through colonization or by whatever means necessary. The recent history (500 years) of the world justifies the conclusion that Europeans have always sought to assert superiority over people of darker pigmented complexions (all of who just happen to be non-Europeans) by the free and unrestrained assertion of their will and authority, unfettered by any moral constraints on human conduct. As

138

a substitute for any notion of a "humane" code of conduct, the European psychology operated a regime based upon the principles and practices used to control and domesticate lower forms of animal life. In the beginning, the slave trade was the main attraction of these European nations because they saw a law filled with cheap labour and always felt that Africa was uncivilized country begging for colonization. There was undeniable thirst for Africa, deeply rooted in racism. The European nations saw Africa as empty and undiscovered land simply because there were no Europeans present. Judging by the particularly heinous treatment of the Congolese people, it is far to posit that these Europeans believed there were no humans present, only varieties of wild animal life to be domesticated. The 1885 Berlin Conference is perhaps the most notorious example of this self-proclaimed superiority complex. It was at this conference that the European powers met to partition Africa and resolve any territorial conflicts. It was at this conference that the future of Africa was decided; yet no Africans were present to help decide it.

In *The Partition of Africa*, by Robert Collins, the author proposes a similar perspective to this European self-proclaimed superiority complex. Collins argues that the military and economic disparity that existed between the European and African nations precipitated the exploration of Africa and instilled a definite arrogance and confidence. The nineteen-century was marked by not just European territorial expansion, but European expansion with regards to technological innovation of the material world. Advancements were being made continuously in the technological and science fields that "upset the balance of power between Europe and Africa" (Collins: 2) Collins asserts that these advancements gave the European powers a false sense of superiority over Africans, and thus was one contributing factor in the colonization of Africa. "The expansion of knowledge, the triumphs of science and technology, and the improvement in the standard of living of the many produced a cultural self-confidence in Europe that found popular and political expression in nationalism."(Collins 2) Thus, Europeans felt that their financial and alleged "mental" superiority gave them an excuse for conquering a group of people. He then continues to show that the self-proclaimed superiority gave them a defining arrogance, which helped to propel them through their conquest of Africa and its people. It is of course fair to reverse the argument and claim that our ability to physically dominate and destroy and kill justifies the assertion that one is superior.

"Technological superiority was often confused with national superiority, and it certainly helped to create a rationale for conquering technologically primitive peoples and an Olympian confidence in the superiority of European rule over them. National self-confidence was characteristic of all the European powers..." (Collins: 2-3).

This "national self-confidence" laid the foundation for many of the colonial problems that would later be encountered within Africa. Thus this confidence was a racist arrogance disguised as nationalism, which empowered these European nations with a feeling of entitlement to the land in Africa. "During the nineteenth-century European drive for possessions in Africa... people justified colonialism in various ways, claiming that it Christianized the heathen or civilized the savage races or brought everyone the miraculous benefits of free trade."(Hochschild 38) This further reveals that the European imperialism in Africa was motivated the sense of superiority given that these European powers deemed its inhabitants to be inferior. Even some researchers have explored the idea that Europe's occupation of Africa was rationalized by an arrogant thinking that these nations had a duty and an obligation to explore and colonize this continent. "Africa was no longer viewed as a bottomless reservoir of slaves for the plantations of the New World. Africa was viewed as an untapped source of raw materials for European industries and the target of Europeans God-given mission to spread the gospel of civilization."(Gandola: 16)

In the grand scheme, the European presence in Africa did not help to improve the wellbeing of the people nor did it help to improve the societies already in place, but instead slowed both the political and economic growth of the countries. In fact, there was never any pretext at improving the lot of the African nations. As a result, many African countries, such as the Congo, are still experiencing problems today which stem from the European occupation. The African countries were merely exploited by these foreign nations in order for them to amass even greater wealth and fortune. "The partition of Africa did not create a set of uniform colonies each resembling the other in a constitutional stereotype. On the contrary, the establishment of colonial rule was varied and pragmatic."

European Colonization of Africa

European colonial period was the period 1500-1900 in most of the European powers to colonize Africa, America and Asia. Designed to boost the bottom of the first region of the national economy at the expense of rivals, the colonies are usually allowed to deal only with the mother nation. By mid-19th century, the great British Empire as trade restrictions mercantilism and established the principle of free trade, the conditions of the restrictions or charges.

Classical colonialism in Africa started in the nineteenth century. Like the colonization of the Americas and the Atlantic Slave Trade, it was *systemic violence*—organized, continuous, methodic, and wilful. It was not only integral to capitalism, but also coexistent with racism, cultural domination, and European self-aggrandizement. Continuing injustices and denial of rights of indigenous peoples are part of the long legacy of colonial domination. Parallel processes of exploitation and injustice can be identified in relation to non-human species and/or aspects of the natural environment. International law can address some extreme examples of the crimes and harms of colonialism through the idea and legal definition of *genocide*, but the intimately related notion of *ecocide* that applies to nature and the environment is not yet formally accepted within the body of international law. In the context of this special issue reflecting on the development of green criminology, the article argues that the concept of ecocide provides a powerful tool.

This chapter explores the essence of European genocide and its consequences on the African indigenous people during their colonization and incorporation into the European-dominated racialized capitalist world system in the late 18th century. It uses multidimensional, comparative methods, and critical approaches to explain the dynamic interplay among social structures, human agency, and genocidal terror to explain the connection between genocide and the emergence of the capitalist world system or globalization. Raising complex moral, intellectual, philosophical, ethical, and political questions, this chapter explores the essence, roles, and impacts of colonial genocidal terrorism on the indigenous Africans. First, the chapter provides background historical and cultural information. Second, it conceptualizes and theorizes colonial genocidal terrorism as an integral part of the capitalist world system. Specifically, it links capitalist incorporation and colonialism and various forms of violence to genocidal terrorism. Third, it examines the structural aspects of colonial genocide by connecting it to some specific colonial policies and practices. Finally, it identifies and explains different kinds of ideological justifications that the European colonial settlers and their descendants used in committing crimes against humanity.

Having garnered immeasurable wealth and prestige from criminal colonial pursuits, it is scandalous that there has been a rigging of European history, a consensus of forgetting that facilitates the psychotic condition called *colonial amnesia*. This systematic suppression of colonial memory has disfigured the moral compass of the European Continent. I have often pondered the contradiction that Europeans pride themselves on being the champions of Christianity yet justified their terrorist practices. Despite all the morality that they set out to bestow on colonized African people, it is amazing that no-one was tapping anyone on their enslaving shoulders to remind and restrain each other in the name of said moral responsibility.

What is even more profound was that after the cantankerous enslavement system was routed by rebellious African resistors and their European and mixed race free allies, von Bismarck, then German Chancellor, hosted 14 European nations for six months (1884-85) to *scramble for Africa*. They all agreed to participate in the dastardly African underdevelopment (Rodney, 1973) with no one recorded as voicing any objection.

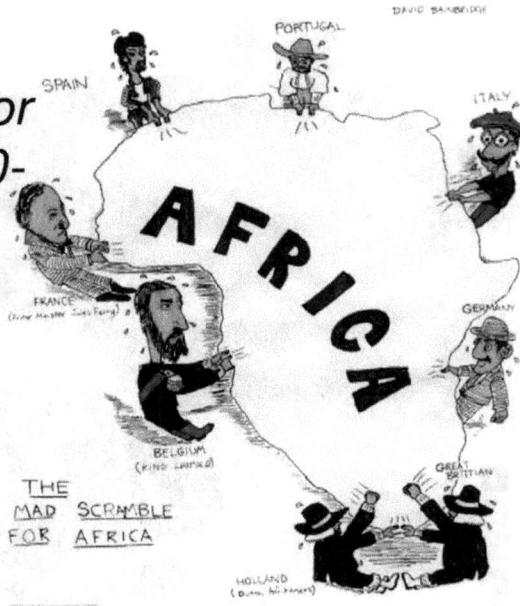

The Scramble for Africa 1880-1914

DAVID BAMBRIDGE

PORTUGAL

SPAIN

ITALY

AFRICA

FRANCE
(Prime Minister Jules Ferry)

GERMANY

BELGIUM
(King Leopold)

GREAT BRITAIN

THE
MAD SCRAMBLE
FOR AFRICA

HOLLAND
(Dutch Africaners)

Since being employed as an International Fellow at the Flensburg Maritime Museum in Germany to curate an exhibition and write a paper on Danish Colonial Legacy in Flensburg, the Virgin Islands and Ghana from an African Caribbean perspective, I have had to do some serious critical reflection on this psychosis of forgetting, a sort of self-hypnosis, which enables Danes and Germans alike, who have to be considered together because of their entangled histories, to convince themselves to this day, that their Empire days was a project of noble civilisation of backward Africans. The political economy of the carving up of the African Continent is conveniently forgotten.

Source: CIA Factbook
Simran Khosla/ GlobalPost

Even my consciousness that the European refusal to acknowledge the criminality of racist colonial terrorism is a ruse to refuse to recognize reparations responsibility had not prepared me for the bald double unconsciousness regarding colonial memory. This contrived amnesia is a pathology that demands a forensic audit. Such pervasive schizophrenia must mean of course, that there is collusion among all institutions of socialization – home, school, media, popular culture, church, musea, politics -in a word, society, to bury any evidence or remorse- they all put a blanket on the past.

The nineteenth century saw immense changes in Africa. Some were driven by famine and disease. Some changes were the result of the territorial ambitions of African rulers. As the century progressed alliances with merchants and missionaries from Europe began increasingly to have a bearing on how African leaders achieved their goals. At the beginning of the century, Europeans were still hugely ignorant of the continent. The systematic colonization of Africa, which gathered momentum in the 1880's, was not even on the horizon in the first half of the 19th century. Europeans had confined themselves to trading mainly along the coast. Inland the trade in slaves and commodities was handled by African and Arab merchants. With the British abolition of the slave trade in 1807, the British navy took to patrolling the coasts, intercepting other nations' slave ships. In the last two decades of the 19th century conflicts and rivalries in Europe began to affect people in Africa directly. In the 1880's European powers divided Africa up amongst themselves without the consent of people living there, and with limited knowledge of the land they had taken. In 1914 conflict in Europe came to a head and the First World War broke out. The contribution of African people to the war effort was crucial.

Imperialism, or the extension of one nation-state's domination or control over territory outside its own boundaries, peaked in the 19th century as European powers extended their holdings around the world. The huge African continent (three times the size of the continental United States) was particularly vulnerable to European conquest. The partition of Africa was a fast moving event. In 1875 less than one-tenth of Africa was under European control; by 1895 only one-tenth was independent. Between 1871 and 1900 Britain added 4.25 million square miles and 66 million people to its empire. British holdings were so far-flung that many boasted that the "sun never set on the British Empire." During the same time frame, France added over 3.5 million square miles of territory and 26 million people to its empire. Controlling the sparsely populated Sahara, the French did not rule over as many people as the British. By 1912 only Liberia and Ethiopia in Africa remained independent states, and Liberia was really a protectorate of U.S.-owned rubber companies, particularly the Firestone Company.

By the end of the 19th century, the map of Africa resembled a patchwork quilt of different colonial empires. France controlled much of North Africa, West Africa, and French Equatorial Africa (unified in 1910). The British held large sections of West Africa, the Nile Valley, and much of East and southern Africa. The Spanish ruled small parts of Morocco and coastal areas along the Atlantic Ocean. The Portuguese held Angola and Mozambique, and Belgium ruled the vast territories of the Congo. The Italians had secured Libya and parts of Somalia in East Africa. Germany had taken South-West Africa (present-day Namibia), Tanganyika (present-day Tanzania), and Cameroon. Britain had the largest empire and the French the second largest, followed by Spain, Portugal, and Belgium. Germany and Italy, among the last European nations to unify, came late to the scramble for Africa and had to content themselves with less desirable and lucrative territories.

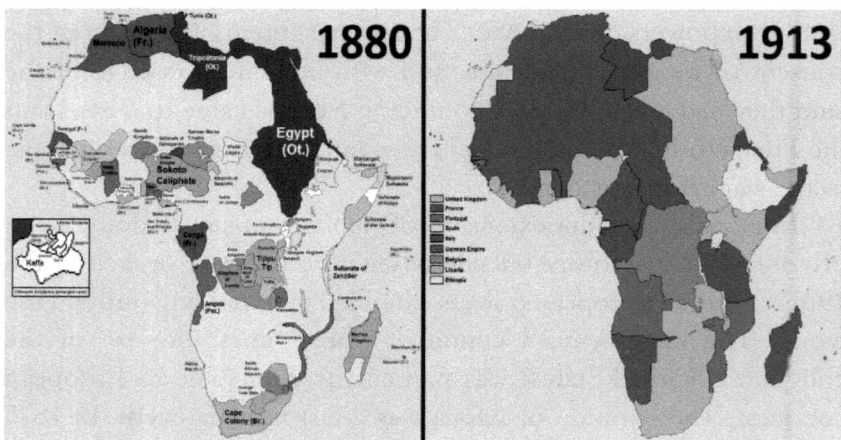

There were many different motivations for 19th century imperialism. Economics was a major motivating factor. Western industrial powers wanted new markets for their manufactured goods as well as cheap labour; they also needed raw materials. J. A. Hobson and Vladimir Lenin both attributed imperial expansion to new economic forces in industrial nations. Lenin went so far as to write that imperialism was an inevitable result of capitalism. As the vast mineral resources of Africa were exploited by European imperial powers, many Africans became labourers in mines or workers on agricultural plantations owned by Europeans. The harsh treatment or punishment of workers in the rubber plantations of the Belgian Congo resulted in millions of deaths. However, economics was not the only motivation for imperial takeovers. In some instances, for example the French takeover of landlocked Chad in northern Africa, imperial powers actually expended more to administer the territory than was gained from raw materials, labour, or markets. Nationalism fuelled imperialism as nations competed for bragging rights over having the largest empire. Nations also wanted control over strategic waterways such as the Suez Canal, ports, and naval bases. Christian missionaries travelled to Africa in hopes of gaining converts. When they were opposed or even attacked by Africans who resented the cultural incursions and denial of traditional religions, Western missionaries often called on their governments to provide military and political protection. Hence it was said that "the flag followed the Bible." The finding of the Scottish missionary David Livingstone by Henry Stanley, an American of English birth, was widely popularized in the Western press. Livingstone was not actually lost, but had merely lost contact with the Western world. Explorers, adventurers, and entrepreneurs such as Cecil Rhodes in Rhodesia and King Leopold II of Belgium, who owned all of the Congo as his personal estate, also supported imperial takeovers of territories. Richard Burton, Samuel and Florence Baker, and John Speke all became famous for their exploration of the Nile Valley in attempts to find the source of that great river. Their books and public lectures about their exploits fuelled Western imaginations and interest in Africa.

Cultural imperialism was another important aspect of 19th-century imperialism. Most Westerners believed they lived in the best possible world and that they had a monopoly on technological advances. In their imperial holdings, European powers often built ports, transportation, communication systems, and schools, as well as improving health care, thereby bringing the benefits of modern science to less developed areas. Social Darwinists argued that Western civilization was the strongest and best and that it was the duty of the West to bring the benefits of its civilization to "lesser" peoples and cultures. Western ethnocentrism contributed to the idea of the "white man's burden," a term popularized by the poet Rudyard Kipling. Racism also played a role in Western justifications for imperial conquests. European nations devised a number of different approaches to avoid armed conflict with one another in the scramble for African territory. Sometimes nations declared a protectorate over a given African territory and exercised full political and military control over it. At other times they negotiated through diplomatic channels or held international conferences. At the Berlin Conference of 1884–85, 14 nations decided on the borders of the Congo that was under Belgian rule, and Portugal got Angola. The term spheres of influence, whereby a nation declared a monopoly over a territory to deter rival imperial powers from taking it, was first used at the Berlin Conference. However, disputes sometimes led European nations to the brink of war. Britain and France both had plans to build a north-south railway and east-west railway across Africa; although neither railway was ever completed, the two nations almost went to war during the Fashoda crisis over control of the Sudan, where the railways would have intersected. Britain was also eager to control the headwaters of the Nile to protect its interests in Egypt, which was dependent on the Nile waters for its existence. Following diplomatic negotiations the dispute was resolved in favour of the British, and the Sudan became part of the British Empire. Africa, imperialism and the partition of 13 War did break out between the British and Boers over control of South Africa in 1899. By 1902 the British had emerged victorious, and South Africa was added to their empire. In West Africa, European powers carved out long narrow states running north to south in order that each would have access to maritime trade routes and a port city. Since most Europeans knew little or nothing about the local geography or demographics of the region, these new states often separated similar ethnic groups or put traditional enemies together under one administration. The difficulties posed by these differences continue to plague present-day West African nations such as Nigeria.

The French and British adopted very different approaches to governance in their empires. The French believed in their "civilizing mission" and sought to assimilate the peoples of their empire by implanting French culture and language. The British adopted a policy of "indirect rule." They made no attempt to assimilate the peoples of their empire and educated only a small number of Africans to become civil servants. A relatively small number of British soldiers and bureaucrats ruled Ghana and Nigeria in West Africa. In East Africa, the British brought in Indians to take jobs as government clerks and in commerce. Otherwise, the British tried to avoid interfering with local rulers or ways of life. Although the British and French policies were radically different, both were based on the belief in the superiority of Western civilization. European colonists also settled in areas where the climate was favourable and the land was suitable for agriculture. Substantial numbers of French colons settled in the coastal areas of North Africa, especially in Algeria and Tunisia, while Italians settled in Tunisia and Libya. British settlers moved into what they named Rhodesia and Kenya. In Kenya, British farmers and ranchers moved into the highlands, supplanting Kenyan farmers and taking much of the best land. The Boers, Dutch farmers, fought the Zulus for control of rich agricultural land in South Africa. The Boers took part in a mass migration, or Great Trek, into the interior of South Africa from 1835–41 and established two independent republics, the Orange Free State and the Transvaal. Dutch farmers clashed with the British for control of South Africa in the Boer War. In Mozambique and Angola, Portuguese settlers (prazeros) established large feudal estates (prazos). Throughout Africa, European colonists held privileged positions politically, culturally, and economically. They opposed extending rights to native African populations. A few groups, such as the Igbos in Nigeria and the Baganda in Uganda, allied with the British and received favoured positions in the colonial administrations. However, most Africans resisted European takeovers. Muslim leaders, such as Abdul Kader in Algeria and the Mahdi in Sudan, mounted long and effective armed opposition to French and British domination. But both were ultimately defeated by superior Western military strength. The Ashante in Ghana and the Hereros in South- West Africa fought against European domination but were crushed in bloody confrontations. The Zulus led by Shaka Zulu used guerrilla warfare tactics to halt the expansion of the Boers into their territories, but after initial defeats the Boers triumphed. The Boers then used the hit-and-run tactics they had learned from the Zulus in their war against the British. The British defeated the Matabele and Mashona tribes in northern and southern Rhodesia. In the 20th century, a new generation of nationalist African leaders adopted a wide variety of political and economic means to oppose the occupation of their lands by European nations and settlers.

Lasting occupation of land, exploitation of human and material resources, and quelling resistance required the *erosion of social bonding, indigenous beliefs, values, identities*, and *indigenous knowledge*. Colonialists achieved this by using different agents including missionaries, anthropologists, physicians, and journalists. Since violence and outsiders' propaganda alone cannot sustain oppression, colonizers resorted to local agents to carry out the colonial mission. The most important of these were individuals educated in colonial schools or serving as subordinates in the colonial system. These so-called local elites inherited the colonial state whose function was not to serve the colonized but to exploit them. Classical colonialism ostensibly ended when these local collaborators demonstrated, through training and internalization of colonial values, their proclivity to serve as auxiliaries of neocolonialism.

The Philosophy of Colonialism: Civilization, Christianity, and Commerce

As the imperial powers of Europe set their sights on new geographic regions to expand their spheres of influence in the 19th century, Africa emerged as a prime location for colonization due to its wealth of natural resources and purportedly undeveloped economies ripe for exploitation. In reality, European colonization devastated traditional African societies and economies. However, the leaders spearheading the movement cited the "white man's burden," a term popularized in Rudyard Kipling's poem to morally justify imperialist expansion. The philosophy underpinning the "White Man's Burden" consisted of the "Three C's of Colonialism: Civilization, Christianity, and Commerce."

Map of Colonial Africa

http://www.lib.utexas.edu/maps/historical/africa_1890.jpg

Civilization

In 1884, the Berlin Conference marked the official beginning of colonialism in Africa. One of the justifying principles behind colonialism was the need to civilize the purportedly backward peoples of Africa. Fifteen years following the Berlin Conference, the supposed imperative of civilizing non-whites was expressed in Rudyard Kipling's poem published in 1899 in McClure's Magazine entitled "White Man's Burden":

> To seek another's profit
> And work another's gain

Take up the White Man's burden—
And reap his old reward:
The blame of those ye better
The hate of those ye guard—
The cry of hosts ye humour
(Ah slowly) to the light:
"Why brought ye us from bondage,
"Our loved Egyptian night?"

The idea of the White Man's Burden was to better ("seek another's profit") an ostensibly backward people (anyone who was not white). The lines following this initial declaration reveal the prevailing attitude in regards to how such a civilizing mission would proceed. Kipling bemoans that the African people will come "slowly to the light" and would lament their release from "bondage." In essence, Kipling believed that these non-white racial groups were so backward that they would be unable to comprehend the benefits of Europeanization. It was Kipling's belief that Africans must be pulled toward the "light" in order to see the error of their, in his view, savage nature.

The sentiments expressed in "White Man's Burden" were not uncommon during this time. Africans were considered culturally inferior, an idea that was supported by scientific racism. According to a lecture given the USA, 35 years before the official start of colonialism, the so-called inferiority of Africans was evident in the "deep-rooted intellectual and physical differences seen around us, in the White, Red, and Black Races, are too obvious and too important in their bearings, to be longer overlooked..."(Nott, 1851: 3) The speaker, Dr. Nott, a medical doctor, goes on to assert that the black, white, and "red" races are categorically different from one another and could not possibly be related. Dr. Nott gave this lecture in the United States 35 years before the official beginning of colonialism. However, the same ideas, the same ideological belief in the inferiority of Africans and call toward a European view of civilization remained, as white settlers began to claim swathes of Africa for their homeland's possession. Towards the end of his speech, Dr. Nott states that Africans are incapable of civilizing themselves: "There Africa stands with her fifty millions of blacks, and there she has stood for the last five thousand years, with this people occupying the same countries, without one step towards civilizations; and all the experiments in the United States, the West Indies, &e., have failed" (Nott: 19-20).

Ultimately, these mentalities led to a violent, forceful takeover (Conklin, 1997: 230-231). However, prior to this the idea existed that Europeans had a responsibility to colonize and therefore civilize Africans (12). The idea of civilization was "the triumph and development of reason, not only in the constitutional, political, and administrative domains, but in the moral, religious, and intellectual spheres... the essence of French achievements compared to the uncivilized world of savages, slaves, and barbarians" Ibid. :(14). In France, this idea was followed by a campaign to popularize ideas about Africans' lack of civilization through educational and media materials (Ibid.:13-14). Practically, this was carried out in the colonies through increasing infrastructure, public health campaigns, education, and political reform (38-39; 73-74). Unfortunately, the eventual result of this was the use of coercive measures, including forced labour and violence that would ultimately cripple the continent (Ibid.:230-231).

THE WHITE (?) MAN'S BURDEN.

Political Cartoon illustrating the Irony of Colonial Ideology
https://en.wikipedia.org/wiki/The_White_Man%27s_Burden#/media/File:The_white_mans_burden.gif

Christianity

Christianity was one justification that European powers used to colonize and exploit Africa. Through the dissemination of Christian doctrine, European nations such as Great Britain, France, and the Netherlands sought to educate and reform African culture. In his book *A History of Africa,* scholar J.D. Fage (1955) describes the racially based logic of European intellectuals and missionaries saying: "Mid- and late-nineteenth-century Europeans were generally convinced that their Christian, scientific and industrial society was intrinsically far superior to anything that Africa had produced"(Fage: 322). Unfamiliar with the diverse cultures on the continent of Africa, European explorers viewed practices unfamiliar to them as lesser and savage.

To many European nations, Christianity represented western civilization and the basis for Anglo-Saxon morality. Christianity served as a major force in the partition and eventual colonization of Africa (Boahen 12). During the late 19th century, European nations increasingly vied for global power. In an attempt to augment political and regional influence, nations like Great Britain and France needed a justification for expansion.

Essentially Christianity was a guise by which Western governments justified the exploitation and conquest of African nations. In the poem *The White Man's Burden,* poet Rudyard Kipling exclaims, "Take up the White Man's burden, the savage wars of peace—Fill full the mouth of Famine and bid the sickness cease". Originally denoted as a reference to United States imperialism in the Philippines, the Anglos-centric basis of the poem holds true to the root structure of imperialist ideology. Denouncing the religious practices of Africans as witchcraft and heathenism, European nations sought to convert, and then exploit the indigenous peoples of Africa.

In Kipling's poem, the lines, "Your new-caught sullen peoples, Half-devil and half-child" refer to the European belief that Africans were heathens, resigned to live a life of savagery. Furthermore European missionaries called upon the tenants of Christianity to spread what they believed was a just and compassionate doctrine. In practice they were used to degrade the culture and society of the African people. Under the pretence of humanitarian theology,

154

European powers strategically implemented Christianity as a divisive imperialistic tool.

In a missionary memoir written by monk named Daniel Kumler Flickinger, Flickinger describes the state of African culture, religion, and society in the nation of Ethiopia. In a chapter entitled Evangelization—Its Difficulties Flickinger states, "The only reason why our theological views are not as foolish and corrupting as theirs (Ethiopians), and that we are not believers in witchcraft, devil-worship, and a thousand other foolish things, is simply because the light of Heaven shines upon us"(1877: 84). Flickinger articulates an argument used by Christian missionaries to justify the exploitative and coercive tactics implemented by European nations.

Photo depicting early Christian missionaries and native Africans
http://www.christianitytoday.com/images/36056.jpg?w=640

Commerce

While European powers justified colonialism in Africa as a moral obligation to bestow modern civilization and Christianity on African societies, the potential for commerce and natural resources provided the true impetus for the colonization of Africa. Following the abolition of the British slave trade in 1807 and the decline of trade with the United States in the mid-1800s for the same reason, Africa represented to Europe a recently legitimized and untapped region for economic expansion (Lugard, 1893: 69-75). To further compound the potential for aggressive competition, the industrial revolution and mechanization of European industries ignited an unprecedented

155

demand for natural resources. The abundance of raw materials available Africa (such as rubber, minerals, and oil) thus emerged as a viable solution to fuel the burgeoning industry of European factories. This amalgamation of factors drove Europe, into a race to claim territory and obtain raw materials in what became known as the "Scramble for Africa" (Gain & Duigan, 1966).

While European and African merchants had established trade partnerships prior to colonialism, European trade companies, often funded by colonial governments, served as the initial primary agents for economic expansion. The untapped wealth of natural resources provided the incentive for these trade companies to aggressively establish economic control over African territories. These first attempts at establishing control were met with mixed success, but the individuals upon their return to Europe effectively employed nationalistic rhetoric to lobby for increased government support. Upon being expelled from the Ugandan kingdom of Bunyoro, the British explorer published *The Rise of our East African Empire*, in which he justifies the colonization of Africa as an imperialistic and economic obligation:

> "It is sufficient to reiterate here that, as long as our policy is one of free trade, we are compelled to seek new markets; To allow other nations to develop new fields, and to refuse to do so ourselves, is to go backward... We owe to the instincts of colonial expansion of our ancestors those vast and noble dependencies which are our pride and the outlets of our trade today; and we are accountable to posterity that opportunities which now present themselves of extending the sphere of our industrial enterprise are not neglected." (Lugard, 1893: 69-75)

The lobbying efforts and publications of memoirs successfully garnered national support for the establishment of colonies. Another equally important economic incentive drove the effort of colonial expansion. As the volume of factory goods skyrocketed with the development of industrialization, European demand could not match the rapid rate of production. Author Jules Ferry states, "the policy of colonial expansion, as seen from the perspective of a need, felt more and more urgently by the industrialized population of Europe and especially the people of our rich and hardworking country of France:

156

the need for outlets [for exports"(Ferry, "Speech Before the French Chamber of Deputies"). European powers responded by flooding their African colonies with European exported goods to match the volume of production, and as a result, the domestic African industries were driven out of competition (Gann and Duigan, 1966)).

While the administrative policies varied between the different colonies, the system of traditional African economies were completely uprooted and exploited by colonialism. In its most extreme form, such as the case of the Congo under the Belgium rule of King Leopold, the European powers erected "extractive states." In this notorious example, the population was stripped of all private property and forced into labour with the sole purpose of extracting and supplying as much of the colony's resources as possible to the colonizer. In addition to disrupting traditional African industries and forms of agriculture, the Europeans did little to foster the development of trade between African states. This exploitation produced far-reaching consequences, as African societies often remained economically dependent states long after their independence (Acemooglu, Simon, and Robinson, 2000).

Fight against genocidal colonialism and imperialism in Africa

After 1900, Europe began to introduce changes to colonial rule in an effort to increase revenues from the colonies. These changes included taking land from African people and giving it to the growing number of Europeans in the colonies. The other changes were the introduction of taxes like the hut tax and poll tax that forced Africans to work for European settlers. Africans were forced to work for Europeans in order to pay these taxes. This was because the new taxes had to be paid in cash and not as cattle or crops as was the practice before. Exploitation of African labourers by European employers added to the growing resentment among the local people.

Resistance movements began to rise in Africa. In colonies with a growing number of settlers, the demand for more land and labour increased tensions between colonial authorities and the white communities that had settled in the colonies. More land was taken from African people and given to Europeans for settlement. In response to these developments, some chiefs organized rebellions against colonial authorities.

Revolt: To rise against the government with the aim of removing it and replacing it with another government that is more acceptable. One of the chiefs who organized an armed rebellion against British colonial authority was Zulu Chief Bambatha. He was not happy with the loss of land his people suffered and the poll tax of one pound that they were forced to pay. His demand was that his people's land be returned and the poll tax lifted. The armed rebellion was finally crushed after lasting out a year. Chief Bambatha together with his 3000 followers was killed. There were similar **revolts** in Eastern Africa, South West Africa, and Zimbabwe. Like the Bambatha rebellions they were all crushed. In East Africa there was the Maji Maji revolt organised by Kinjigitile Ngwale in 1905. The revolt was against forced labour and tax policies forced upon the people by the German government, which was implementing a cotton scheme to increase her exports. To implement their scheme the Germans forced Africans to plant cotton instead of their traditional staple crops. And the Maji Maji revolted.

These Maji Maji revolts shared similar traits. In all of them there was a strong belief in African spirit mediums and a strong influence of Ethiopianism. This philosophy originated in Ethiopia. The aim of Ethiopianism was to restore African traditions and political structures. It rested on African faith in spirits to protect them. People believed that the spirits were capable of turning European bullets into water and that they would be immune to bullets by undertaking a cleansing ritual before battle. The initial success of the Maji Maji rebellions strengthened the people's belief in their spirit mediums. The African emphasis also managed to unite different ethnic groups to fight for the same purpose. However, pitted against European machine guns, the Africans were doomed to fail and they lost their faith in the protection of Maji Maji. About 26 000 people were killed by German forces. To avoid future rebellions the colonial government reduced its use of force and began to rely strongly on missionary education for implementing colonial policies.

An Uprising in Nyasaland (Malawi)

Not all uprisings in this period were influenced by African spirit mediums. In Nyasaland, now Malawi, the Christian church and the Seventh Day Adventist Church under the leadership of Priest John Chilembwe, played an important role organizing and carrying out an early uprising against colonial authority. John Chilembwe was the leader of this uprising to protest against the hut tax, which was increased by 8 shillings in 1909, and unfair labour practices on white owned estates. The First World War made matters even worse. John Chilembwe noticed that a large number of people who died while fighting against the Germans in September 1914 in Karonga were black people. He then wrote a letter to the Nyasaland Times newspaper challenging the idea that participation in the war would improve things for black people in Nyasaland.

John Chilembwe organized an armed rebellion against the colonial government. On the 23 January 1915, an armed group of men attacked the Livingstone Estate while another group attacked the Bruce Estate. A third group was sent to attack the Blantyre armoury in a bid to obtain weapons for an armed revolt on the capital, Zomba, to overthrow the colonial government. Although the first two attacks were successful, the attack on the Blantyre African Lakes Corporation Armoury was not and the final revolt failed. John Chilembwe was shot and killed while attempting to escape from Nyasaland. By the 4 February 1915, the uprising was over.

Though unsuccessful, the uprising prompted the government to reconsider the land and labour practices in Nyasaland. These were major causes of the uprising. They had been introduced mainly to exploit the colonies by extracting more labour from them and squeezing more productivity from the workers to lower the cost to the colony. At the same time taxation on black people was increased. The uprising had the effect of raising the awareness of black people to colonial rule and encouraged them to stand up for their rights and demand an end to colonial rule.

Herero Uprising

The rinderpest epidemic of 1896 to 1897 had destroyed the cattle of the Herero and Nama people of South West Africa, now Namibia. The Germans took advantage of the Herero's loss and occupied most of their good grazing land. At the same time, the German government adopted a policy of encouraging Germans to settle in the colonies. Because of this, more land was taken from the Herero people and given to German settlers.

In 1904 the Herero broke out in revolt and succeeded in regaining some of their land for a while. Hundreds of Germans were surrounded and killed by Herero fighters. The Herero tried to get the support of Nama people but failed to do so. The German government brought in reinforcements from Germany and was thus able to drive back the rebellions Herero.

Commander of the German forces, Lothar Von Trotha gave orders to shoot the Herero because, according to him, they no longer deserved German protection. Many Herero were killed and others fled to Botswana to hide. Because this was an attempt to wipe out all Hereros, it can be called genocide. The German victory resulted in more hardships for the Herero. All their remaining cattle were confiscated and their chiefs stripped of their authority.

The Formation of Political Parties

Another response to colonial transformation was the formation of political parties. These were formed by the small educated group of Africans mainly residing in developing colonial towns. These Africans were educated at missionary schools. At first, these parties did not seek to create a mass following, but to lobby their respective colonial governments to recognize the civil rights of Africans and protect and recognize the land rights of Africans in rural areas. The formation of political parties in this period reflected changes in African nationalism. It was now increasingly being influenced by western education and Christianity. This created a new educated social group in Africa, which was excluded from participating in colonial rule because they were Africans. Their aspirations were equality between Europeans and Africans and later they began to demand self-rule. From the beginning they worked closely with chiefs because they shared the same demands. But because colonial rule adopted chiefs into the administration of African people, the growing number of chiefs who were co-operating with colonial government strained the relationship between the new elite leaders and the chiefs. Furthermore, western educated leaders feared that because chiefs represent different ethnic groups, they would undermine the unity of African nationalism by causing ethnic rivalries in the colonies. Therefore they began to undermine chiefs in an attempt to overcome ethnic differences in the colonies.

In South Africa, the South African National Natives Congress (SANNC) was founded in 1912, becoming one of the earliest political parties. Following the 1913 Land Act that placed most of the land in white hands, the Congress sent a delegation to London to lobby the government to abolish the act. The delegation was not successful. Their approach to the government was in contrast to that of Chief Bambatha's. They did not call an all-outright British rebellion against colonial rule. Because of their western education the leaders of the SANNC were better placed to understand the politics of colonial rule. Unlike Chief Bambatha, their response appealed to all ethnic groups in South Africa. This made the SANNC response a national one against colonial injustices.

These new parties, like the SANNC were largely modelled on the American civil rights movement with the political independence cause playing a secondary role. Civil rights movements are mainly concerned with improving the human rights of followers. The aim was not to replace the form of government. The major political demand prior to the Second World War was for reforms and a more inclusive colonial government. These parties were Pan African in character. They did not recognize colonial borders. For example, in West Africa there was the National Congress of British West Africa (NCBWA) uniting political leaders in West African British Colonies.

The formation of political parties in South Africa was influenced by other developments in the country making it somewhat unique in the experience of colonialism in the continent. The development of the mining industry after the discovery of diamonds and gold rapidly transformed the South African economy.

The mining economy attracted labourers from both inside and outside South Africa. People came from as far as Nyasaland, Mozambique, and Zambia to South Africa as migrant labourers. Migration spread news and ideas about political, religious and other developments in the colonies. Out of this background, the Industrial and Commercial Union (ICU) representing Cape black dock-workers was formed. Its first President was Clements Kadalie from

Nyasaland, now Malawi. The Industrial and Commercial Union expanded to represent black farmers and sharecroppers who had been forced off their farms.

Following the Second World War, colonial governments began to introduce significant reforms to prepare Africans for self-government. At the same time this war also marked increasing control of Africans by colonial governments. The steps for self-government were often just a pretext for more centralized colonial authority. These 'preparations' meant that the government would increase control over chiefs and centralize power in the hands of colonial governors who would introduce sweeping changes, especially in the field of agriculture without consideration of the wishes of African people. This approach led to the black people and African political parties becoming increasingly radical. After the war, most of these demanded independence from colonial rule.

Britain and Europe's Conspicuous Silence on the Genocidal Legacy of Colonialism

Leading British politicians today share a negative assessment of the legacy of empire. Former Prime Minister Tony Blair, often himself accused of a kind of "neo-colonialism" regarding the former Yugoslavia and Iraq, dramatically condemned Britain's role in the slave trade as "one of the most inhuman enterprises in history." His successor, Gordon Brown, similarly offered his apologies for the sending of children of the poor to Australia and Canada in order to build up the dominions. And even Tory Prime Minister David Cameron, on a visit to Pakistan, when asked how Britain could help end the stalemate over Kashmir, insisted that it was not his place to intervene in the dispute, declaring, "I don't want to try to insert Britain in some leading role where, as with so many of the world's problems, we are responsible for the issue in the first place" (Smith, 2009). As The Economist 400 (Issue 8749), 3 September 2011) noted, with typical understatement, in 2011, "in modern Britain, it is bad form to speak too highly of the British Empire."

A dramatic change of public outlook has been fostered by, and in turn has encouraged, a scholarly re-evaluation of imperial rule over the past several decades, one that also encompasses the troubled history of the postcolonial era. Problems plaguing postcolonial states—religious and ethnic communalism, the easy eruption of violence, the weakness of democracy, the pervasiveness of corruption—are regularly traced to their legacy from colonialism. As the young historian Dara Price (2010), reviewing work on Indian history, has observed, "Sixty years after Britain's 'shameful flight' from the subcontinent, the reading and writing of modern South Asian history is still heavily influenced by the central question of British accountability for the contours of contemporary Indian society." This is even truer for the history of Africa, the Caribbean, and other former parts of the empire. The nature of the British "colonial legacy" to the postcolonial world remains a live issue a half-century after the empire's end.

While earlier British national self-satisfaction cried out for challenge and critique, and a highlighting of all the harms ignored in the earlier historiography, "critical" imperial history has in its turn become as conventional as its target once was. Having triumphed, the historiographical reaction against "imperial whiggism" now in its turn needs revision. The first step necessary is to contextualize this anti-imperial thought, just as the earlier positive historiography has been contextualized, and then take a careful look at the assumptions and fundamental values held by its exponents (Wormell, 2001). Just as "Whig-imperial" historiography was bound up in a specific situation and worldview, clearer to us now than it was to its exponents, the same holds true of anti-whig imperial historiography. It too has arisen out of specific problems facing scholars and intellectuals in the second half of the twentieth century, and has been developed in a particular intellectual and political climate, which needs to be explored as that surrounding its predecessor has been, so that we can arrive at a proper assessment of its strengths and weaknesses.

The origins of "critical imperial" historiography are to be found in more than simply a scholarly response to an earlier, egregiously one-sided body of historical work. More broadly, scholars as well as others were greatly disappointed in decolonization's aftermath. At first, independence was accompanied by euphoria, in the new states and among their sympathizers in the West. This heady atmosphere had been breathed in by many scholars, especially of the younger generation. In a presidential address to the African Studies Association in 1992, Martin Klein recalled the "excitement of watching the destruction of an oppressive colonial order and being involved in the creation of a new one" (1992:1). In this, Klein was speaking for most of his colleagues in those years. However, this excitement proved short-lived. After a few years in which the progress made in the last years of colonialism continued, newly independent states found themselves running into both political and economic trouble, some of which had been predicted by colonialists. The horrors of Partition in the Indian subcontinent, followed by continuing political turmoil in Pakistan, unending disputes over the status of Kashmir, military dictatorship in Burma, developmental frustrations in all the South Asian successor states, and the even greater political and economic disasters in Africa led in the course of the 1960s and 1970s to a general mood of disillusion.

Indeed, with regard to Pakistan, parts of the Caribbean, and most of all Africa, disillusion deepened into despair, as constitutional arrangements providing for multiple parties, individual rights, and the rule of law quickly succumbed to one-party rule, Caesarism, and corruption, broken only by coups and horrendous breakdowns of order. Eighteen of the twenty-one new states with parliamentary institutions in Africa failed to keep them, usually replacing them with "presidential" institutions that became a screen for dictatorship (Robinson and Torvik, 2008). The era of wars waged by European states against independence movements was succeeded by an even more calamitous era of postcolonial wars, some interstate but most civil, encompassing Nigeria, Angola, Sudan, and most of the other African states, as well as Pakistan, Burma, and India, which experienced several insurgencies. Almost nine million African and seven-and-a-half million Asian military personnel were killed in wars between 1960 and 1995, dwarfing the toll of decolonization wars—and this accounting leaves out the millions more civilian deaths in these conflicts (Sivard, 1996).

Similarly, the rapid economic gains that the ending of colonial "exploitation" had promised generally failed to materialize, and where there was initial strong growth, it slowed frustratingly after a few years. As early as 1967, the Deputy Secretary-General of the Commonwealth Secretariat, A.L. Adu, could remark in a public talk that "the political revolution that brought African leaders to power has undoubtedly failed to satisfy the economic and social needs of the people."[10] The rhetoric of nationalism and independence came to be increasingly employed in Orwellian fashion to support rulers who cared little for their people, and who outdid the former colonialists in repression, exploitation, and self-dealing. During the 1970s, prospects of economic development, political stability and democracy, individual freedom, and social justice all seemed to be receding out of sight, and a kind of "postcolonial melancholia" began to settle in. Even in India, where democracy and the rule of law had been maintained and some grounds for satisfaction existed, a slowdown in economic growth combined with a political deadlock leading to Indira Gandhi's resort to a state of emergency brought disappointment to the fore in the academic and even public mood. What, it was asked over and over throughout most of the former European empires, had gone wrong? Why had the end of colonialism not yielded better results?

One way out of the dilemma was to locate the source of these problems *outside the control* of the new states and their peoples. Decolonization, it was suggested, had brought not a clean slate, but one deeply scarred and pitted. As the preeminent Western scholar of Africa at the time, and a strong partisan of its nationalist movements, Basil Davidson, remarked in his admiring 1973 biography of Kwame Nkrumah, the "dish" the new leaders were handed on the day of independence "was old and cracked and little fit for any further use. Worse than that, it was not an empty dish. For it carried the junk and jumble of a century of colonial muddle and 'make do,' and this the new . . . ministers had to accept along with the dish itself. What shone upon its supposedly golden surface was not the reflection of new ideas and ways of liberation, but the shadows of old ideas and ways of servitude" (1973: 94).

But, as a matter of fact, colonization and its genocidal impact on the colonized Africans is rarely a topic of sustained public conversation in Britain. It is not even a tangential topic. It is simply ignored, elided with very infrequent and brief exceptions such as the one prompted now by the case of Kenyan survivors of torture and other human rights abuses of British rule in Kenya.

Mau Mau captives during the colonial era in Kenya

To be sure such evasions of honest national historical accounting are not unique to Britain.

One finds hardly any reflection in the US media on America's devastating interventions in Central American countries and collusion in egregious human rights violations that took place there under dictatorial regimes who engaged in crimes against humanity including mass murder on an enormous scale.

Nor do Americans know much about or discuss America's history of colonisation in the Philippines or its "Secret War" in Laos with its devastating bombing campaign that killed and injured thousands of Lao civilians.

So Britain is not unique in this wilful looking away; a looking away which is not an evasion of shame, for one can only experience emotions of shame when facing an honest accounting, rather, a looking away of studied moral evasion and denial. All nations, including and sometimes especially democracies, who wish to perceive themselves as paragons of moral virtue even if this virtue, however limited, almost never extends meaningfully beyond its borders to foreign affairs, disdain critical self-reflection. Nations are like individuals that way – egotistical, prone to self-rationalization and self-aggrandizement, uncomfortable with the hard work of self-examination, self-awareness, and self-criticism.

When speaking about nations one can only comment about tendencies and trends, as nations are complex, multi-dimensional, and vast, containing a diverse citizenship and made of individuals who may or may not share the attitudes and beliefs of many of their fellow co-citizens. Nevertheless, we can examine how nations function as collectives, and observe the attitudes and beliefs prevalent amongst citizens.

Certain nations cannot look away from the legacy of their own human rights violations because the legacy is inextricably linked with the people, culture, and very physical landscape of the nation.

Slavery happened in America and the former slaves eventually became US citizens. However deep the legacy of racism remains in America, America has also travelled far in confronting the legacy of slavery and segregation. How to address ongoing discrimination remains a frequent part of public discourse.

Such discrimination is an uncomfortable topic which undermines the common American self-perception of the United States offering equality and justice to all American citizens. Many would rather avoid the topic or claim that it is no longer salient. But racism still exists in many different forms and creates barriers to equal opportunity and justice. Structural racial injustices remain deeply rooted in American society. Conversation also does not necessarily lead to tangible policy outcomes to rectify injustices but it is a prerequisite for engaging the issue.

Still, the fact that social injustices happened within a nation's borders does not guarantee greater societal openness to addressing it. The Native American experience is barely ever acknowledged in the United States in any substantive way and American attitudes towards dispossession, discrimination, and persecution of Native Americans are as evasive as many European attitudes towards colonization.

Clearly then the American accounting with its past of slavery and segregation – however incomplete and imperfect – is not merely a mechanistic function of the location of where those crimes took place. The civil rights movement left a profound mark on American society and transformed it – forcing Americans to confront the brutal legacy of slavery, segregation, and ongoing formal and informal racism. The consequences of the movement are still felt in America today and its moral integrity and commitment to equality and justice are needed as much today as they were in the past. But there is no such similar movement which forced and forces Europeans to confront the human rights violations of colonization and their tenaciously enduring nature long after colonization officially came to a close.

Like slavery, segregation and structural and informal racism, the impact of colonization remain deeply felt and continue to violate the rights and welfare of those individuals, communities, and nations who were subject to it. Yet it has been relatively easy for Britain and other European countries to avoid confrontation of the legacy of violence, sectarian divisions, and human rights violations of their colonial pasts.

For Britons the legacy of colonization happened over there – far, far away. And the brutal consequences of colonization which are still felt today in India and Pakistan, in Iraq, and in Sudan – amongst other places – is rarely ever examined within a colonial and post-colonial context outside of rarefied academic contexts. In other words, the colonial legacy is evacuated such that Iraq and Sudan's sectarian conflicts are rarely attributed at least in part to Britain's ignorant and artificial borders created to protect British interests rather than the wellbeing of former colonial subjects and their social and political stability. Often these borders sowed the seeds of ethnic and political conflict, mass violence, and protracted wars.

Britain of course is not unique in Europe. Belgium has also done little to collectively examine the consequences of its colonization of parts of central Africa and yet perhaps no other colonizer in Africa played as direct and immediate a role in deliberately fomenting societal divisions that lay the groundwork for ethnic hatred and mass violence on a catastrophic scale. This would lead to massacres and genocide throughout the 20th century in Rwanda and Burundi. It also led to the largest scale crime against humanity in Africa under King Leopold's and then the Belgian government's control of Congo involving mass killings, torture, and gross violations of the most basic human rights. Belgium's king and later the Belgian government itself did not only foment ethnic and social tensions but organized and directed violence and killing with the purpose of economic exploitation of the Congolese.

The Netherlands is finally beginning to examine and provide some framework of restorative justice – however minimal – for human rights violations that took place in Indonesia as a result of Dutch colonization.

The Spanish have failed to address their role in Western Sahara and its consequences for the Saharawi people including their current lack of freedom. Nor have they accounted for colonial crimes in Central and South America that still impact peoples living there detrimentally and were massively violent and exploitative. The same holds true for Portugal regarding its colonies in Africa and its colonization of Brazil.

The French reckoning with massive human rights violations in Algeria is woefully incomplete.

After the Rwandan genocide in 1994, the French created a parliamentary commission whose aim was purportedly to examine France's role – a thoroughly neo-colonial one – in the Rwandan genocide of the Tutsi. Instead, it essentially exonerated France of wrongdoing, called for no criminal investigations, and denied the overwhelming evidence that France supported Rwanda's genocidal regime before, during, and after the genocide with training, finance, weaponry, and diplomatic support.

While Germany has confronted its Nazi past with relative candour and more introspection, contrition, and genuinely honourable and substantive efforts at reparation than any other nation with a similar history of massive human rights violations and genocide it has shown little of that moral maturity with regard to confronting its colonial legacy in Namibia.

Instead, it satisfied itself with an apology in 2004 for what it rightly termed as genocide but refused any legal claims against it with the argument that because no international laws protecting the rights of innocent civilians at the time existed it has no legal responsibility for those crimes. Such an argument might have legal legitimacy. But it is morally obtuse beyond measure and appallingly disrespectful to the memory of the victims and to their human rights – which existed – irrespective of whether they were legally codified. In this context the recent effort of Kenyans who were tortured during the Mau-Mau uprising to sue the British government is important not only for the pursuit of justice but also for the breaching of the largely informal but powerful societal silence over the violent legacy of colonization by Britain and other European states.

Conclusion

By way of a summary, the period of European colonization of Africa was a very brutal and destructive one. In the first place, colonial rule was often established through warfare. Throughout the continent Africans fought valiantly, but were ultimately unable to overcome the technological power of the European invaders. Africans were also unprepared for the brutal nature of the European colonizers. In South Africa, for example, the Xhosa people traditionally fought set-piece battles which rarely resulted in massive causalities and were fought away from civilian populations. When the British engaged in combat with the Xhosa people one of the tactics that they engaged in was to attack Xhosa villages, burning kraals and crops. Richard Meinertzhagen, a decorated British soldier, attacked a village in Kenya and "gave orders that every living thing except children should be killed without mercy." In 2012 three Kenyans were granted the ability to sue the British government over the tortures that they suffered during the colonial period. The tortures that they experienced included beatings, sexual assault, and even castration. In Namibia, which was known at the time as German Southwest Africa, the German colonialists carried out a horrific genocide that took the lives of about 100,000 people. The estimates of those killed in the Belgian dominated Congo range as high as 15 million. And these few examples do not even begin to describe the brutality of European rule.

The traumas that were inflicted by colonial violence continued to adversely impact Africa decades after the end of colonial rule. We see, for example, the dictatorship in Togo still carrying out the torture methods that were handed down by the French colonizers. In Rwanda the German and Belgian colonizers implemented divide and rule tactics that treated the Tutsi as a superior race to the Hutu. The oppressed Hutu population eventually came to resent the Tutsis. This resentment would later result in the genocide that took place in Rwanda in 1994. Nigeria also experienced tribal massacres that would result in a civil war that lasted from 1967 to 1970. Much like Rwanda, this conflict was largely the product of colonial divide and rule policies which favoured certain ethnic groups over others.

In conclusion, decades after the so-called winds of change blew away colonial rule, the impact of this colonial cartography lingers in profound sensitivities at the legacy of the outsiders' incursions into a continent that did not invite them to define its frontiers or impose their definitions of personhood and nationhood.

Bibliography

Adu Boahen, A. (1985). *Africa under Colonial Domination 1880–1935*. London: Heinemann.

Birmingham, David. (1995).The Decolonization of Africa. Athens: Ohio University Press.

Adu, A.L. (1967). "Post-Colonial Relationships: Some Factors in the Attitudes of African States," *African Affairs* 66 (1967): 295–309.

Acemoglu, Daron, Johnson, Simon, and Robinson, James A. (2000). "The Colonial Origins of Comparative Development: An Empirical Investigation." National Bureau of Economic Research. June 2000.

Adu Boahen. (1990).*General History of Africa VII: Africa under Colonial Domination 1880-1935*, University of California Press 2120 Berkeley Way, Berkley California.

Bond, Patrick. (2006). *Looting Africa: The Economics of Exploitation* London: Zed Books.

Calderisi R. (2006). *The Conference Board Review*, May/June 2006. 4. Quoted in John Pilger, "Iran may be the greatest crisis of modern times," *International Socialist Review* 53, May–June 2007.

Chandra, Bipan. (1981). "Karl Marx, His Theories of Asian Societies, and Colonial Rule," *Review* (Fernand Braudel Centre), *Vol. 5, No. 1* (summer, 1981): 31-47.

Chandra, Bipan. (2010). "Reinterpretation of Nineteenth-Century Economic History," *Nationalism and Colonialism in British India*. New Delhi: Orient Blackswan, 2010.

Collins, Robert. (1969).The Partition of Africa. New York: J. Wiley.

Conklin, Alice L. (1997). *A Mission to Civilize: The Republican Idea of Empire in France and West Africa, 1895-1930*. Stanford, Calif.: Stanford UP, 1997. Print.

Davidson, Basil. (1973). *Black Star: A View of the Life and Times of Kwame Nkrumah* (London: James Currey, 1973), 94.

Davis, Mike. (2001). *Late Victorian Holocausts: El Nino Famines and the Making of the Third World.* London/New York: Verso, 2001.

Depelchin, Jacques. (1992).From the Congo Free State to Zaire: How Belgium Provatized the Economy. Senegal: Codesria.

Doyle, Arthur C. (1909). The Crime of the Congo. London: Hutchinson & Co.

Duignan, Peter, and L.H. Gann. (1979). The Rulers of Belgian Africa. Princeton, Princeton University Press.

Durkheim, Émile. (1997). *The division of labour in society.* New York: Free Press.

Edgerton, Robert B. (2002). The Troubled Heart of Africa. New York: St. Martin's Press, 2002.

Emerson, Barbara. (1979).Leopold II of the Belgians. London: Weidenfeld and Nicolson.

Fage, J.D. (1955). *A History of Africa* Third Edition, 11 New Fetter Lane London.

Fieldhouse, D.K. (1961). "Imperialism: An Historiographical Revision," *The Economic History Review, Vol. 14 No. 2* (1961): 187-209.

Flickinger, Rev D.K (1877).Ethiopia; *Twenty Years of missionary Life in Western Africa.* Dayton Ohio: United Brethren Publish House 1877.

Fromm, E. (1955). *The Sane Society.* New York: Holt, Rinehart & Winston.

Fromm, E. (1961). *Marx's Concept of Man.* New York: Ungar.

Gann, Lewis H., and Peter Duignan. (1966). "Introduction." Colonialism in Africa, 1870-1960. London: Cambridge U.P., 1969. N. pag. Print.

Giddens, Anthony. (1971). *Capitalism and modern social theory: An analysis of the writings of Marx, Durkheim, Weber.* Cambridge, UK: Cambridge Univ. Press.

Henry Schwarz; Sangeeta Ray (2004). *A Companion to Postcolonial Studies. John Wiley & Sons.*

Hobson, J.A. (1965). *Imperialism: A Study.* Ann Arbor: The University of Michigan Press, 1965.

Hochschild, Adam. (1998). King Leopold's Ghost. New York: Houghton Mifflin Company, 1998.

Jules François Camille Ferry, "Speech before the French Chamber of Deputies, March 28, 1884," *Discours et Opinions de Jules Ferry.*

Kanza, Thomas. (1979). The Rise and Fall of Patrice Lumumba. Schenkham Publishing Company, Inc.

Kaplan. (1979). Urving Zaire. First Printing: 1979.

Keynes, John Maynard. (2007). *The general theory of employment, interest and money.* London: Macmillan.

Kipling, Rudyard (1899, 02). *The White Man's Burden.* McClure's Magazine (1893-1926), OL. XII., 2. Retrieved from http://search.proquest.com/docview/135628529?accountid=1 0747

Klein, Martin. (1992). "Back to Democracy," *African Studies Review* 35 (1992): 1.

Kroker, A. & Kroker, M. (1996). *Hacking the Future: Stories for the Flesh-Eating 90s.* Montréal: New World Perspectives.

Lenin, V.I. (1917). *Imperialism, the Highest Stage of Capitalism* (1917), https://www.marxists.org/archive/lenin/works/1916/imp-hsc/.

Marshall, Alfred. (2009). *Principles of economics.* New York: Cosimo.

Marx, Karl. (1992). *Capital: A critique of political economy, Volume 1.* Translated by Ben Fowkes. London: Penguin.

Marx, Karl. (1977). *Capital Vol. I* (New York: Vintage Books,

Morris, Morris D. (1963)."Towards a Reinterpretation of Nineteenth-Century Indian Economic History," *The Journal of Economic History, Vol. 23 No. 4* (December, 1963): 606-618.

Nott, J. C. (1851). *An Essay on the Natural History of Mankind.* Ann Arbor: ProQuest I&L Research Collections, Dade, Thompson & co. Retrieved from http://search.proquest.com/docview/88430679?accountid=10 747

Packham, Eric S. (1998). The U.N. Intervention in the Congo after Independence. Nova Science Publishers, Inc.

Pilger, J. 2007). "Iran may be the greatest crisis of modern times," *International Socialist Review* 53, May–June 2007.

Price, Dara. (2009). "Review of K.N. Panikkar, *Colonialism, Culture and Resistance,*" *English Historical Review* 124 (2009): 1192–94. For a

South Asian view, see Mashiur Rahman [Economic Adviser to the Prime Minister of Bangladesh], "Crippling Colonial Legacy: Epistemic and Economics," *Financial Express* (Dhaka, Bangladesh), 7 August 2010. For a similar complaint regarding Africa, see Uzodinma Iweala, "What is the legacy of colonialism in Africa?" podcast, http://bigthink.com/ideas/3412, January 16, 2008. ("I think what you have is a lack of acknowledgement [in Western media] that certain countries were responsible for the state of this place.")

Robinson, James A. and Ragnar Torvik. (2008). *Endogenous Presidentialism*, Working Paper 14603, National Bureau of Economic Research (December 2008), http://www.nber.org/papers/w14603.

Rodney, Walter. (1973*). How Europe Underdeveloped Africa. East African Publishers.*

Sartre, J-P. (1971), On Genocide. R. Falk, G. Kolko & R. Lifton, eds. *Crimes of War: A Legal, Political, Documentary and Psychological Inquiry into the Responsibility of Leaders, Citizens and Soldiers.* New York: Random House.

Silvard, Ruth L. (1996/2003) *World Military and Social Expenditures*, 16th ed. (Washington, D.C.: World Priorities, 1996). See also James D. Fearon and David D. Laitin, "Ethnicity, Insurgency, and Civil War," *American Political Science Review* 97 (2003): 75–90 (noting thirty-three civil wars in Asia and thirty-four in sub-Saharan Africa, 1945–2001).

Smith, Adam. (1977). *An inquiry into the nature and causes of the wealth of nations.* Chicago: Univ. of Chicago Press.

Smith, David (2006/2011) "Blair: Britain's 'sorrow' for shame of slave trade," *The Observer*, 26 November 2006; Peter Walker, "Brown to apologise to care home children sent to Australia and Canada," *The Guardian*, 16 November 2009; and anon., "David Cameron: Britain caused many of the world's problems," *Daily Telegraph*, 5 April 2011.

Sunga. L. S. (1997) *In the Emerging System of International Criminal Law: Developments and Codification*, Brill Publishers (1997) at page 90, Sunga traces the origin of the international movement against colonialism, and relates it to the rise of the right to self-determination in international law.

Weber, Max. (1978). *The Protestant ethic and the spirit of capitalism*. Los Angeles: Univ. of California Press.

Wormell, Deborah. (2001). *Sir John Seeley and the Uses of History* (Cambridge: Cambridge University Press, 1980); Robin Winks, ed., *Oxford History of the British Empire, Volume 5: Historiography* (Oxford and New York: Oxford University Press, 2001); Amanda Behn, "The Bisected Roots of Imperial History: settler world projects and the making of a field in modern Britain, 1883–1912," *Recherches Britanniques*, May 2011; her forthcoming Yale dissertation promises further enlightenment.

Chapter Five

Exemplifying German Colonial Genocide in South West Africa (Namibia)

Overview

The word genocide and its legal definition were coined after World War II (WWII) and in light of the obvious mass atrocities committed by the Nazi regime. Despite having a relatively new name the crime had existed for decades if not centuries before. Genocide had been committed long before WWII. However, at the time it was a nameless crime. There were no known words capable of capturing the severity of the act. The Herero genocide has commanded the attention of historians who study complex issues of continuity between the Herero genocide and the Holocaust. It is argued that the Herero genocide set a precedent in Imperial Germany that would later be followed by Nazi Germany's establishment of death camps The Herero and Nama genocide was a campaign of racial extermination and collective punishment that the German Empire undertook in German South West Africa (now Namibia) against the Ovaherero, the Nama, and the San. It is considered the first genocide of the 20th century. It took place between 1904 and 1908.

Introduction

In the last decade the long-term consequences of German colonial rule in Africa and the world as a whole have been becoming ever more apparent. Following on from the early work of historians like Horst Drechsler and Helmuth Bley in the early 1970s, a whole host of historians has sought to deal with the horrors of German colonial rule in the former German South West Africa (present day Namibia) in particular (1971). In a sense, the genocides perpetrated by the forces of Imperial Germany in Namibia have become mainstream, and General Lothar von Trotha's 'Vernichtungsbefehl' (extermination order) a further uncontested example of humankind's seemingly limitless ability to inflict pain and suffering upon fellow humans. In short, Germany's imperial past in Namibia is now comparatively well known. In addition, a fair number of people may be aware of the fact that Imperial Germany had a colonial role to play in the history of contemporary Tanzania, Togo, and Cameroon. However, it remains the case that in contrast to Namibia, the history of German colonial involvement on the West African coast is still comparatively understudied.

The debate over whether Germany's colonial policy toward the Herero and Nama constituted genocide suffers from two basic shortcomings: authors who are proficient in international criminal law (ICL) often have difficulties in getting the historical facts right, and historians with a good knowledge of primary sources lack knowledge about the evolving definition of genocide in ICL. As a result, the authors of many articles and books concerning the German atrocities committed against the Herero and Nama at the beginning of the 20th century either do not apply any precise definition of genocide at all or they quote the definition derived from the Convention for the Prevention and Punishment of Genocide, but without including the comprehensive jurisprudence about genocide that has emerged from international criminal tribunals. Because social science and history have not elaborated an undisputed and precise definition of genocide, this article proposes to apply the relatively narrow and precise ICL definition of genocide to the events in Germany's South-West African colony at the beginning of the 20th century. This method sheds new light on some neglected aspects of Germany's policy toward the Herero and Nama, which suddenly appear more important than those that until now have most frequently been regarded as genocidal. But, how did the phenomenon of genocide begin and what did the victims do?

In January 1904, the Herero people, led by Samuel Maharero, and the Nama people, led by Hendrik Witbooi, rebelled against the German colonial occupation. Their rebellion stood no chance of success against the oppressive German occupation of the region. In response, German General Lothar von Trotha ordered that 'within the German borders every Herero, with or without a gun, with or without cattle, will be shot.' Many were killed in combat, including during the Battle of Waterberg. Others died of dehydration in the desert. Those imprisoned in concentration camps died of disease and exhaustion. These various methods were used to respond to the failed Herero and Nama rebellion. They resulted in the annihilation of approximately 80% of the Herero people and 50% of the Nama.

Eight decades after the atrocities, the UN Whitaker Report determined that the atrocities constituted an attempt to exterminate the Herero and Nama people in German South West Africa. The report named the genocide of the Herero and Nama people as one of the biggest genocides of the 20th century (it stands among 'the Ottoman massacre of Armenians in 1915-1916, the Ukrainian pogrom of Jews in 1919, the Tutsi massacre of Hutu in Burundi in 1965 and 1972, the Paraguayan massacre of Ache Indians prior to 1974, the Khmer Rouge massacre in Kampuchea between 1975 and 1978, the contemporary Iranian killings of Baha'is, and the Holocaust).

Since the 1990s there has been a virtual academic consensus that a genocide was perpetuated by Germany during the Herero and Nama War. But the question of responsibility and continuity are still being debated. In the last decades, the Herero and the Nama have sought justice, recognition and reparations from the German government for the genocide they endured at the beginning of the 20th century. In 2004, the German government formally recognized the colonial atrocities perpetrated in German South West Africa and issued an apology. However, at the time, the German government ruled out any reparations for the survivors or their families. In 2015, the German government officially recognized the atrocities to constitute Völkermord (genocide) but again, ruled out any reparations.

The Namibians have taken their struggle to an American court, which started hearing their case. The German government officially referred to the 1904-1907 events as a "genocide" only recently (in 2016) and still refrains from dealing with who was responsibility and rejects calls for reparation. Instead, Germany has attempted reconciliation through other channels, such as providing aid to the Namibian government and returning victim remains that were stored in Germany after the genocide. The historiography of German colonialism and Namibian history has witnessed fierce debate regarding the events that took place in Southwest Africa between

1904-1907. Still today, some historical questions remain. This chapter will try to identify the main issues of this genocide and will highlight the most important ideas of the genocide.

In the late nineteenth and early twentieth centuries, European nations spanned the globe with overseas colonies in a belligerent quest for territory. These colonies were developed as commercial and strategic dependencies by the European states. The control extended through this colonialism reveals much about the European imperial state itself in its efforts to gain and maintain colonies. Colonialism is here defined as a desire for colonial possessions and imperialism is broadly termed a more fluid dynamic of dominance between collective societies encompassing much more than purely colonial relations. These two energies present a vivid image of Europe's extension of power over the non-European world. The following examination will focus upon the actual expansion of colonial control in the context of the late nineteenth-century acquisition of African colonies by Germany and their subsequent maintenance through to the early twentieth century. By examining the specific actions in the extension of German rule over African territory, the composite interactions of colonialism will be exposed. The study of German colonialism is significant because the dynamism and violence of colonialism make it more than just an anomaly of European history. Colonialism therefore represents a major theme of wider history because of its influence upon both the colonizer and the colonized. In addition, many of the elements that gave birth to colonialism are very much still in existence today, a reality that connects this historical excavation to the present. It is for these reasons that this analysis seeks to inquire into the power differentials of imperialism in general through study of German colonialism with the ultimate aim of interpreting the relationships underpinning German colonial expansion in Africa.

The historiography of imperialism is riddled with controversies and complexities. This inquiry unabashedly places itself against the older histories of imperialism that focused upon imperialism only in relation to broad issues within European economic and political history (Meritt, 1978: 97-116). More recent studies move beyond these topics in favour of research into specific social and cultural elements of colonialism (Ulrich van der Heyden and Joachim Zeller, eds. (002). This work hopes to combine elements of the old interpretations with new approaches so as to gain new insight when it seeks to consider the true breadth of imperialism in realms as diverse as culture, economics, society, and politics (Said, 1994). This analysis consequently accepts Johan Galtung's sage assertion that imperialism must be examined on a general level in order to most effectively render its structural character (Galtung, 1971: 81). To best understand the structure of imperialism, the more specific facts of German colonial expansion will be elaborated. This in turn will allow the extrapolation of the general dimensions of imperialism.

The primary motivating factor for colonialism is a pivotal historical question in the historiography of imperialism. Marxists in the early twentieth century saw colonialism as a consequence of the economic and social structures of capitalism that require ever-greater markets, labour and resources (Lenin, 1917). The Marxist economic argument has prompted a number of critical responses. Octave Mannoni stressed the psychological dimension of colonialism instead of relying upon causal references to economics or politics (1956: 18, 29, 202, 204). Arguing in 1961 specifically against Marxist mechanism, David Landes dismissed economic rationales and sees colonialism as not based in a mono-causal explanation (1961: 498-499). Others find European diplomatic imperatives responsible for the growth of colonialism. Ronald Robinson and John Gallagher (1961) contended that colonialism represents a cumulative process of European expansion without determining goals outside of strategic concerns.

Later leftist scholars like D.C.M. Platt and G.W.F. Hallgarten (1968) have refined the Marxist economic dimension to colonialism (296-306). Writing in 1966, Hannah Arendt believed that nationalistic mass political movements combined patriotism and national chauvinism to precipitate actions like colonialism (1980: 71). Inverting the traditional relationship between the metropolitan centre and the colonial periphery, David Fieldhouse (1966) declared that colonialism was encouraged by events in the colonies that required the European powers to safeguard their strategic interests. Alternately, Wolfgang Mommsen and Jean-Paul Sartre (2001: 30-31, 44) argue a systemic character to colonialism that rejects mono-causal explanation in favour of structural examination. Finally, there is another possible interpretation stressing the random and inchoate that sees no central internal logic to colonialism. Moving away from the inquiry into rationales, more recent studies of colonialism examine narrower aspects such as race, culture, society, gender and power relationships to seek justice. But, justice is a hard topic when it comes to genocide, but it can never be justified. This chapter reveals this atrocity, not as a "forgotten" genocide, but as the first genocide of the 20th century that will never be forgotten.

Colonial and Imperial Genocides

The global expansion of western Europe between the 1760s and the 1870s differed in several important ways from the expansionism and colonialism of previous centuries. Along with the rise of the Industrial Revolution, which economic historians generally trace to the 1760s, and the continuing spread of industrialization in the empire-building countries came a shift in the strategy of trade with the colonial world. Instead of being primarily buyers of colonial products (and frequently under strain to offer sufficient saleable goods to balance the exchange), as in the past, the industrializing nations increasingly became sellers in search of markets for the growing volume of their machine-produced goods. Furthermore, over the years there occurred a decided shift in the composition of demand for goods produced in the colonial areas. Spices, sugar, and slaves became relatively less important with the advance of industrialization, concomitant with a rising demand for raw materials for industry (*e.g.,* cotton, wool, vegetable oils, jute, dyestuffs) and food for the swelling industrial areas (wheat, tea, coffee, cocoa, meat, butter).

This shift in trading patterns entailed in the long run changes in colonial policy and practice as well as in the nature of colonial acquisitions. The urgency to create markets and the incessant pressure for new materials and food were eventually reflected in colonial practices, which sought to adapt the colonial areas to the new priorities of the industrializing nations. Such adaptation involved major disruptions of existing social systems over wide areas of the globe. Before the impact of the Industrial Revolution, European activities in the rest of the world were largely confined to:

(1) occupying areas that supplied precious metals, slaves, and tropical products then in large demand; (2) establishing white-settler colonies along the coast of North America; and (3) setting up trading posts and forts and applying superior military strength to achieve the transfer to European merchants of as much existing world trade as was feasible. However disruptive these changes may have been to the societies of Africa, South America, and the isolated plantation and white-settler colonies, the social systems over most of the Earth outside Europe nevertheless remained much the same as they had been for centuries (in some places for millennia). These societies, with their largely self-sufficient small communities based on subsistence agriculture and home industry, provided poor markets for the mass-produced goods flowing from the factories of the technologically advancing countries; nor were the existing social systems flexible enough to introduce and rapidly expand the commercial agriculture (and, later, mineral extraction) required to supply the food and raw material needs of the empire builders.

The adaptation of the non-industrialized parts of the world to become more profitable adjuncts of the industrializing nations embraced, among other things: (1) overhaul of existing land and property arrangements, including the introduction of private property in land where it did not previously exist, as well as the expropriation of land for use by white settlers or for plantation agriculture; (2) creation of a labour supply for commercial agriculture and mining by means of direct forced labour and indirect measures aimed at generating a body of wage-seeking labourers; (3) spread of the use of money and exchange of commodities by imposing money payments for taxes and land rent and by inducing a decline of home industry; and (4) where the precolonial society already had a developed industry, curtailment of production and exports by native producers.

The changing nature of the relations between centres of empire and their colonies, under the impact of the unfolding Industrial Revolution, was also reflected in new trends in colonial acquisitions. While in preceding centuries colonies, trading posts, and settlements were in the main, except for South America, located along the coastline or on smaller islands, the expansions of the late 18th century and especially of the 19th century were distinguished by the spread

183

of the colonizing powers, or of their emigrants, into the interior of continents. Such continental extensions, in general, took one of two forms, or some combination of the two: (1) the removal of the indigenous peoples by killing them off or forcing them into specially reserved areas, thus providing room for settlers from western Europe who then developed the agriculture and industry of these lands under the social system imported from the mother countries, or (2) the conquest of the indigenous peoples and the transformation of their existing societies to suit the changing needs of the more powerful militarily and technically advanced nations-genocide.

Historically, genocide occurred in the wake of both imperial expansion and disintegration. Even before the conquest of the Americas, the fate of the indigenous Guanches in the "Fortunate" (Canary) Islands anticipated a pattern of European expansion leading to cultural destruction, environmental collapse, and physical extermination (Crosby, 1986). Eliminationist policies in the colonies included a variety of collateral procedures such as the destruction of home or *domicide* (Porteous and Smith, 2001), the forced abduction of children from aboriginal peoples (Moses, 2004), the destruction of their environment as "ecocide" (Barsh, 1990; Stannard, 1992) or "eco-catastrophe" (Ehrlich 1971), the systematic wreckage of vital supplies, provisions, and goods (Adelstein and Pival, 1971), and the devastation of the entire ecosystem. This is still occurring throughout the world, for instance in the oil-rich Niger Delta region under the control of international corporations (Human Rights Watch Africa, 1999).

Colonial genocide outlasted the demise of empire. In the Americas, national independence allowed the new postcolonial elites to pursue eliminationist campaigns unrestrained, while maintaining slavery. Vast regions were entirely "cleansed" of their indigenous elements. Southern Argentina became *terra nullius* after white settlers pursued a *tabula rasa* policy (Andermann, 2002; Rock, 2002). Chile nearly succeeded in the same goal, bar surviving exceptions like the Mapuches (Ray, 2007). The complete annihilation of Tasmania's Aborigines was allegedly pursued out of the sight of imperial authorities (Mann, 2005:70–110), but official knowledge and "inaction despite clear warnings and high mortality rates suggests that population decline was government policy" (Madley, 2004:176; Moses, 2004; 2008B). According to David Stannard, "the destruction of the Indians of the Americas was, far and away, the most massive act of genocide in the history of the world" (1992:x). Because of imperial rivalries, indigenous peoples were not the only victims of colonial rule. French-speaking Acadians in Nova Scotia were deported en masse by the British, while the genocide of the native Mi'kmaq could proceed (Plank, 2001). A similar fate befell other preexisting settler communities displaced by new immigrants who enjoyed the protection or complicity of central authorities.

Environmentally, British rule was marked by cyclical "holocausts" (Davis, 2001), during which settlers and the imperial core saw an opportunity to weaken the indigenous peasantry while increasing the latter's dependence on empire. Rubenstein (1983) shows how demographic pressure and overpopulation became primary reasons behind the targeting of unwanted "surplus" populations, focusing on the Irish Famine, the Nazi Holocaust and, on a class basis, Tudor England's enclosure movement. For Rubenstein, the process originates neither in the state's homogenizing impulse, nor in its attempts to redefine boundaries along ethnic lines. It rather commences with "benign" expulsion schemes or "encouragement to emigrate" as implemented in early nineteenth century England, when several parishes sent their paupers and "undesirables" to North America. Australia's colonization followed a similar logic. More recently, the extermination of nearly four-fifths of the Herero and Namaqua in German South West Africa (present-day Namibia, 1904–7) has been recognized as a late colonial genocide (Silvester and Gewald, 2003; Gewald, 2004).

An exclusive focus on the state could miss the "unintended" consequences of events like environmental destruction. Thus, *ecocide* and "ecological genocide" can refer to forms of environmental damage leading to the degradation and elimination of vulnerable communities. Some of these resulted in unprecedented forms of genocide, as with the American and Australian native populations. Tragic examples of eco-genocide included the extinction of the Guanches in the Canary Islands following Spain's "ecological imperialism" (Crosby, 1986), and the radical extermination of Tasmanians (Madley, 2004; Curthoys, 2007). In the age of modern imperial expansion, acts of genocide and mass murder were ostensibly carried out beyond direct state control through laissez-faire politics. Global liberalization, environmental depredation, droughts, floods, and imperial expansions resulted in mass famines, the advance of diseases, and regional climate change (Davis, 2001).

After the Chinese invasion and the exile of the Dalai Lama in 1959, Tibet epitomizes the link between policies of cultural homogenization, demographic engineering, and physical elimination (Shakya, 1999). The final invasion of Tibet coincided with the notorious "Great Leap Forward" (1959–62), the Stalin-inspired plan for massive industrialization during which up to 43 million Chinese perished and hundreds of millions were compelled to flee, some to Tibet. The Tibetan case also has elements of colonial and settler genocide (Jones, 2006A:94–8).

On the other hand, withdrawing or shrinking empires spawned genocides as forms of "securitization" and "preemptive" removal of supposedly disloyal populations (Levene, 2005:277–335; Lieberman, 2006). With its indiscriminate use of torture, France's war against Algeria (1954–62) led to 1.5 million dead, the "*regroupement*" of over 2 million Algerians and 1.4 million refugees flowing into France (Branche, 2004). Most famously, the demise of the Turkish/Ottoman Empire brought historically unprecedented genocidal waves against most of its ethnic, religious, and linguistic minorities (Melson, 1992; 1996). In turn, these were preceded by massive displacement and the large-scale ethnic cleansing of Turks and other Muslims fleeing Greece, Bulgaria, Serbia, and various countries whose new elites were bent on "homogenizing" their subjects (McCarthy, 1983; 1996; 2001; Lieberman 2006). Decades later, the final days of the British Raj evidenced massive atrocities against the Kikuyus and other tribes in Kenya (Elkins, 2005), while the entire population of Diego Garcia (Chagos islands) was secretly deported and their land given to the US Air Force in 1968 (Curtis, 2003:414–30).

The link between imperial genocides and cultural homogenization can be found throughout the history of Western colonial expansion, but it becomes clearer once colonies achieve independence. Thus, while the genocide of Native Americans proceeded, a systematic policy of destruction of indigenous culture or "Americanization" was applied through the introduction of compulsory education (Hoxie, 1984), so that the boarding school experience has been defined as "education for extinction" (Adams, 1995). The demographic displacement and cultural assimilation of Hawaiians has sometime been defined as "genocidal" (Bushnell, 1993; Kinzer, 2007).

In terms of mass murder and social engineering, the demise of empires can hardly compare with the more brutal and all-pervasive advent of the modern centralizing state. Its legitimizing ideology was both ethnically predicated and anchored in the notion of "unlimited progress," which included the eradication of various opponents and minorities. In its totalitarian version, this meant the promise of a new society inhabited by a "new man" and permeated by the "sense of a new beginning" (Griffin, 2007). The more rapidly modernization was imposed by ruling elites upon their constituencies, the more genocidal its tendencies.

Historical Background to German Colonial Genocide in Namibia

German history of the nineteenth and twentieth centuries has often been considered an exception, at times even a Sonderweg, or 'special path'. Some scholars are tempted to consider German colonialism in the same light. Germany was a colonial 'latecomer' and did not begin to acquire colonies until the mid-1880s. Its formal colonial reign lasted a 'mere' 30 years and covered such diverse territories as Southwest Africa (Namibia), East Africa (Tanzania), Togo and Kamerun (Cameroon), as well as Samoa, German New Guinea and the leased territory of Kiaochow (Jiaozhou Bay). Moreover, Germany was the first modern European imperial nation to become post-colonial, having been forcibly decolonized following the First World War.

Genocide has two phases: one, destruction of the national pattern of the oppressed group: the other, the imposition of the national pattern of the oppressor. This imposition, in turn, may be made upon the oppressed population which is allowed to remain, or upon the territory alone, after removal of the population and the colonization of the area by the oppressor's own nationals.

The German expansion of control in Africa between the years 1884 and 1914 is significant in several ways to the broader study of colonialism. The German conquest of what are now the countries of Togo, Cameroon, Namibia and Tanzania is a relatively under-explored area in colonial historiography when compared to histories of the colonies of Portugal, Britain and France. While other countries had successful colonies for the most part outside of Africa, Germany's territories in the Pacific and China were unusually pale shadows of its African colonies. The late and intense entry of Germany into colonialism also holds particular interest for the scholar of colonialism. Moreover, German colonialism represents a fascinating subject because of its telescoped time frame; the acquisition, extension and loss of the colonies all happened within three decades. Germany is additionally remarkable in that its colonialism began on a different track than the other colonial powers because of the perceived significance of commerce in the expansion. Finally, Germany presents an interesting paradigm of colonialism in relation to later events in the twentieth century.

It is the actions of Germany in the First and Second World Wars that have led to the *Sonderweg* thesis of Germany's "special path" of development. The *Sonderweg* argument is one of the reasons why many explanations have been sought for German colonialism and the subsequent heated debate that has surrounded the discussion of motivations. The dispute has been particularly contentious between ideologically opposed historians in divided post-war Germany (Fricke, (1961: 538-576). The German colonial experience is frequently cited by scholars as a precursor to the later events of the twentieth century by fitting the abuses of the colonial period into the *Sonderweg* thesis of purportedly Germanic exceptionalism (Berman, 1999: 37-68). The Versailles Treaty's judgment of Germany's unique colonial brutality drew on acts of violence in the colonies like the 1904-1906 war against the Herero tribe of Southwest Africa. But the question must be asked, without engaging in a comparative discussion of colonialisms, was the German conquest of colonial territory inordinately brutal? To answer this question, analysis must look beyond the *Sonderweg* thesis to consider all of the economic, social, political and cultural motivations for German colonialism. It is the particular circumstances of these elements within German colonialism that provide the rationales for this project.

A frequent argument in the thesis of German exceptionalism is the economic one, an especially significant controversy in the historiography of German colonialism. This is because the German colonies had a large number of business monopolies which have long been used as an explanation for the economic dimension of German colonialism. Marxist scholars like Jürgen Kuczynski, Fritz Müller and Helmuth Stoecker advocate the pivotal supporting role of monopoly capital in this colonialism (1948: 285, 318). Non-Marxist scholars like Mary Townsend, H.P. Jaeck and Horst Drechsler also declare that economic necessities and merchant capital propelled the colonial expansion (1943: 124-126). These arguments remain strong within studies of German colonialism, though their applicability is increasingly questioned. Calculated government policy for reasons related to international diplomacy is seen as another major cause of German colonialism. For instance, Werner Frauendienst argues that colonialism can only be seen as one minor component of the *Weltpolitik* or "world policy" of international involvement (Werner, 1959). Similarly, some historians like Landes (Op.cit. 504), Hallgarten (1914), Townsend and A.J.P. Taylor (1969: 816) contend that colonial expansion was designed to serve German strategic interests. A final argument contends that Germany acquired and developed a network of colonies solely to provide a backing for its claims to great power status (Pierard, 1964: 4, 258).

Supporting the domestic explanation of colonialism, Hans-Ulrich Wehler finds that domestic peace was sought as a by-product of a strong imperial policy by the "pragmatic expansionist" Chancellor Otto von Bismarck (1969: 113-193). This so-called "social imperialism" argument asserts that German imperialism was a wholly endogenous phenomenon created to pacify the German population, rather than a creation of external stimuli (Pogge von Strandmann, 1969: 142-144). Wehler's contention specifically works against the centre-periphery interpretations of Gallagher, Robinson, and Fieldhouse as well as the Marxist argument for the primacy of commercial expansion. Yet even within social imperialism, Mommsen argues for some reconsideration of the role of external forces (1969: 371). The social imperialism argument also contests

Thaddeus Sunseri's belief that historians have traditionally ignored the linkages between German colonial policies and German society as a whole (2001: 32). For this reason, discussion of Germany's colonies needs to address the quantity and quality of support for colonial expansion in the German populace.

The domestic argument is significant, for despite their relatively miniscule economic contribution, the four African colonies were quite important to Germany because of their effect upon national pride. This is a major facet of social imperialism; the colonies were supposed to galvanize the population, consequently bringing Germany together. Linking the leftist and social imperialism interpretations, Hans-Christoph Schröder connects colonialism intrinsically with supra-nationalism and social relations (1968: 7-9). This inquiry will consider contemporary society because the propaganda efforts of the government and the various social organizations propounding colonial expansion had an important effect upon the German public. Looking at society in this manner renders a vision of colonialism from a bottom-up perspective and allows a realistic portrayal of the role of popular sentiment in colonial expansion.

All of these different explanations of German colonial expansion may appear complex but they are further complicated by Landes' suggestion that many colonial acquisitions may have been the result of a fait accompli or unforeseen circumstances (Op.cit. 505). It is also possible that German colonial expansion was established by one motive and carried further by another. Similarly, it is likely that the extension of control over the colonies was established by the means considered most applicable to the time and context, as Gallagher and Robinson assert (1953: 12). It is also eminently possible that colonialism is a matter of scale where a steady escalation of degree results in further increases in territory, brutality and control.

Alongside these issues, a considerable lacuna exists in the discussion of the actual inhabitants of the regions that Germany annexed. These African peoples were very important in determining the actual course of the colonial expansion in Africa. For example, parallel to the expansion of German rule was the growth in native resistance to this expansion in various manifestations, from passive opposition to taxes and laws, to covert resistance and outright revolt against German authority. It is the extension of colonialism and the opposition to it that constitutes the essential form of colonialism. However, this inquiry acknowledges the considerable difficulty which exists in capturing the suppressed native voice since few histories have been written from the perspective of the original inhabitants in the German colonies.

Comprehending these diverse issues requires more than empirical data; a theory is needed to link the dominant themes. Histories of colonialism come from very disparate perspectives, and can therefore be very difficult to understand holistically. Winfried Baumgart and Wehler once called upon historians to forge new paths in German colonial history to further understand the historical past through the application of new theoretical models of interpretation (1971: 469, 481). Since Baumgart and Wehler, new research into gender, race and power relations has broadened the field, but wider use of theoretical models has not been manifest. In addition, newer approaches have moved away from necessary discussions of motivations for the expansion. The implications of the uncertainties elaborated above, as well as developments in the field of German colonial history, inevitably lead to the question of which interpretative framework to utilize in order to most accurately interpret the expansion of German control over Africa.

The Enabling German Domestic Determinants of Colonial Policy

The growth of Germany's colonies must be viewed in relation to contemporary German history. Germany came to strength in Europe through wars with Denmark, Austria and France, finally leading to unification in 1871. The unification of the German states was brought about largely through the diplomacy and the power politics of "blood and iron" championed by Chancellor Bismarck (Geiss, 1976). Strategically, the new European nation was the epitome of Mitteleuropa vulnerability, hemmed in by the French and Russian powers on both sides. Politically, Germany was ruled by the autocratic Kaiser and his Chancellor. Although Germany possessed an elected Reichstag and universal male suffrage, the governing elites maintained considerable independence of action. Beneath the Kaiser, a leadership cadre of aristocrats occupied the crucial seats of power

(Berghahn, 1994: 190-191. Under Kaiser Wilhelm I, the stoutly conservative Bismarck worked to restrain the press, outlaw socialist organizations and repress Catholics through his quasi-autocratic power. With the accession of Kaiser Wilhelm II to the throne in 1888, Bismarck's power declined until he was finally removed from office in 1890. In contrast to Bismarck's term, domestic and foreign policy under Wilhelm II proceeded along a much more random and inchoate path (Röhl, 1967: 160-166, 272). Ruling above a succession of weak Chancellors in a society simultaneously traditionalist and modernizing, Wilhelm II also was both more liberal and much more inconsistent than Bismarck.

Germany was subject to these tensions because of modernizing impulses in economics and politics. In economic matters, Germany was developing into the industrial power-house of Europe as traditional agriculture fuelled the growth of heavy industry. The newly-centralized state also fostered the expansion of German international trade. However, in 1873 Germany was struck by a debilitating recession that was to last until the last years of the nineteenth century (Berghahn, Op.cit. 12-17).

Germany was hit particularly hard because of problems caused by over-production and declining prices. Bismarck tried to solve these through the imposition of tariffs in 1879 and in 1884 during the fiscal restraints of the "door-closing panic" where German business perceived the doors of free trade commerce closing to their products and causing an economic downturn (Helmut Böhme, 1967: 223, 227, 236). The perceived disappointments of free-market liberalism provoked a reevaluation of liberal economics and politics. Popular desires for political reform and internal divisions with regard to class, status, religion and region also continued to plague the government (Berghahn, Op.cit. 123-130). One policy designed to preserve domestic peace was the 1879 "politics of rallying-together" which united the Prussian agricultural Junker elites with the Ruhr industrialists to create the Alliance of Iron and Rye Behnewn, 1970). The collective-policy was also revisited from 1897 to 1904 to unite the traditional elites of Germany against growing social fractures.

These circumstances were to provide fertile ground for the development of colonial policy. Bismarck indicated as early as 1881 his total rejection of a colonial policy. But in 1884, his paradigm shift in foreign policy towards colonialism was to initiate storms of debate, both at the time and in subsequent historiography. The transition from a middle European nation obsessed with the balance of power in European diplomacy to a country involving itself in territories thousands of miles away in Africa was a surprise then and continues to challenge scholars to explain Bismarck's volte face in international affairs. Bismarck's perennial willingness to change tactics in order to achieve his goals means that his change of course needs explication, but also indicates that the colonial expansion was not necessarily a departure from Bismarck's opportunistic approach to foreign and domestic politics.

Given Germany's recent consolidation as a nation-state and the recent recession, it is at first glance very strange that in early 1884 Bismarck would suddenly agree to establish a protectorate over the tiny hamlet of Angra Pequeña on the southwest coast of Africa (Berghahn, Op.cit.: 266). One reason Bismarck's move is odd is that German taxpayers were reluctant to fund overseas expenditures. Furthermore, German public opinion on the colonial issue was an unknown variable and could potentially have problematized the expansion greatly. Similarly, the impact of a colonial policy in European diplomacy could also have been negative if the great powers took exception to Germany participating in the "scramble for Africa" (Taylor, Op.cit: 3). Logistical problems such as the question of whether or not the German bureaucracy could expand to administer the colonies also cast doubts upon the viability of the acquisitions. Finally, the protection and control of African colonies with Germany's hitherto continental army and inconsequential navy seemed to indicate intractable difficulties.

The reconciliation of these problems reveals much about contemporary Germany. For as much as Germany did not appear ready to accept a colonial policy, there were signs in 1884 that a colonial expansion was both desirable and possible. In 1884 the circumstances in Europe seemed to favour a German land-grab since European diplomacy was placid (Geiss, Op.cit. 49-50). Additionally, fears of repeated recessions fostered the idea that colonies could provide a way out of cyclical depressions and economic isolationism. In this respect, the Young Historical School of economics and its demands for foreign markets found resonance in the economic policies of the government. The Young Historical School of economics included thinkers like Gustav von Schmoller, Werner Sombart and Max Weber. Government was also pressed by the private sector to acquire colonies to guarantee raw materials and additional markets. Furthermore, Bismarck saw the colonies as a tool for European diplomatic wrangling and an outlet for German emigration.

While the government began to see the benefits of colonies, the public became more aware of colonies through the work of the colonial propagandists. For example, the German Colonial Society or Deutsche Kolonialgesellschaft (hereafter DKG), while small in membership, was loud in demanding the necessity of colonies. It is noteworthy that t The DKG was never a large group, counting only 41,000 members in 1912 (Pierard, Op.cit: 373). The public began to believe that a colonial policy could generate great profits, especially if conducted on the British model. The promises advanced by European colonial adventurers of an "El Dorado" in the far reaches of Africa soon reached the German populace. Consequently, the population, especially the middle class, began to identify the potential benefits of German colonies. This combination of diplomatic, commercial and nationalistic motivations proved enough to push Bismarck toward a policy of colonial expansion.

It is necessary to sketch the development of German colonial sentiment in order to provide some background to the entire history of the colonial expansion. Germany itself had not previously been a significant force in world trade though some of the Hanseatic cities had traded overseas. The first colonial enterprise was a trading post and transport hub established on the Gulf of Guinea by the Brandenburg trade federation in 1682. After the loss in 1717 of this territory, the only other initiative in the pre-history of colonial expansion was the installation of missionary outposts on the coasts of Africa such as the Bethany mission station in southwest Africa half a century before the government's acquisition. The rapid doubling of German territory after 1884 therefore raises questions about the motivations behind this expansion.

In 1883 the economic motives for colonialism achieved newfound prominence. The Foreign Office or Auswärtiges Amt (hereafter AA) bureaucrat Heinrich von Kusserow, the trading company Woermann's, and the banker and Bismarck-confidante Gerson von Bleichröder, all identified the beginning of a European rush for African colonies and wanted a place for Germany in this race (Stern, 1977: 396, 412-416, 435). The trading cities of Hamburg and Bremen begged for naval protection of their African trade and perpetual guarantees for the rights of German traders in the colonies. Bismarck, goaded by the purported ease and economy of the British charter-company administration model and Kusserow's urging, began to accept Germany's need to participate in colonialism. Soon after the acquisition of Angra Pequeña by the trader F.A.E. Lüderitz, German business interests and the government, particularly the AA, began their close association. Though Kusserow embodies Marxist assertions of conspiracies between the finance oligarchy and the government, Kusserow's later decline illustrates that the Marxist paradigm is not necessarily apt (Müller, 135. Schröder, 7-8). Although Bismarck called the early colonies "supply posts," he believed that the companies should be responsible for the administration of the territories (Esterhuyse, 1968: 46). With Lüderitz's claim accepted, Bismarck bestowed imperial charters "*Freibriefe*," thereby sanctioning the claims of Woermann's and other companies in Cameroon and Togo. Yet, after the initial extension of German control, it was not long before the charter companies like Woermann's politely declined to administer the new German colonies under imperial charters. There was a dawning awareness that the colonies were not the new El Dorado. Germans began to realize that their colonies were not like Britain's India, but were in Africa, where consistent profits could not be assured.

In addition to these complex economic motivations, there were several international political considerations that indicated the potential advantages of a colonial policy. While the other European powers had earlier grasped pieces of Africa, Germany stood idly by. But in 1884, with a favourable economic and political climate, it was Germany's chance to acquire colonies. Bismarck realized that no other powers desired Angra Pequeña; consequently he decided to extend German protection over Lüderitz's trading post. If no other European nations desired the colonies, Bismarck could avoid antagonizing the other European powers while simultaneously acquiring potential bargaining chips for future European negotiations. But was this the dominant motivation? The thesis that Bismarck was a covert colonialist from the beginning for international reasons is advanced by Townsend and Taylor. However, these arguments have subsequently been effectively challenged by William Aydelotte (1974). Alternately, H.P. Merritt argues that Germany's expanding interest in Africa was largely a product of Bismarck's own beliefs in the protection of commerce (Merrit, Op.cit. 115). Nevertheless, the possession of the protectorates did establish a place for Germany in the new global diplomacy. European relations were also strengthened by the British support for German concessions since the German territory acted as a hedge against French claims.

Though the benefits of colonial expansion were present in international politics, they were even more clearly evident in domestic politics. H. Pogge von Strandmann (Op.cit. 142,159) and Wehler (Op.cit.20) assert that domestic political elements motivated the acquisition. Many then, as now, believed Bismarck's colonial plans were solely aimed at domestic concerns: even Bismarck's Senior Councillor Friedrich von Holstein quoted Bismarck as saying: "[a]ll this colonial business is a sham, but we need it for elections" (1955-1963, 161). Public opposition to European competitors' exclusionary treaties and the restriction of free trade led the Chancellor to conclude that the public mood was in favour of acquiring commercial rights for Germany in Africa. Even though Germany was markedly undemocratic, this public support was important to Bismarck. For instance, the Kartell-Politik compromise of 1887-1890 depended upon the consensus gained in the initial colonial expansion.

However, the 1884 elections manifested increased support for the Social Democrats, whose cautious imperialism spoke to working class acceptance of colonial policy. Another possible domestic goal within Bismarck's policy of colonial expansion has been identified in Bismarck's attempt to isolate the pro-British Nationalliberale Partei and its supporter, the reform-minded Crown Prince Friedrich. By providing a colonial competitor for the German population, Bismarck likely saw an opportunity to concurrently vilify the British, the Nationalliberales and the popular Crown Prince.

In addition to domestic politics, concerns about the population also contributed to the domestic argument. The colonies were hoped to serve as a domestic safety-valve by pushing discontent from Germany to the colonial periphery. In addition, many Germans, like the historian Heinrich Treitschke and the economist Arnold Wagner (1929), believed the contemporary over-population myth and, even worse, that Germany was being overpopulated by the lowest social orders. (1929: 670). It was hoped that the colonies would provide a place to settle this "excess" German population that would not be a loss to Germany as was immigration to other countries. Colonial expansion would therefore be a domestic palliative for the supposed threats of over-population, over-production and under consumption by providing new space and new markets for Germans.

This short introduction to the main motivations of colonial expansion has provided some context for the following brief survey of the history of German expansion in Africa. After the extension of German protection over Lüderitz's claim, German traders travelled throughout the newly-German territories of Southwest Africa, Togo and Cameroon signing treaties with local chieftains. In these treaties, German "commercial houses on the coast" were often specifically mentioned as having economic rights to territory (Esterhuyse, Op.cit.67, 88). Finally, rights to the East African territory were initially gained in 1885 but German rule was finally cemented in 1890 for four million marks. As with Southwest Africa, the borders of all of the colonies were further extended throughout the colonial period. After the first 835,000 square kilometres of coastal territories had been agreed upon, Bismarck justified his right to further expansion with the statement: "[*e*]*ine genaure Abgrenzung auch nach dem Innern zu, behält die Regierung seiner Majestät späten Festsetzungen nach Maßgabe der Entwicklung der Ansiedlungen und ihres Verkehrs vor*" In other words, Bismarck justified further expansion inland with the statement that Germany reserved the right to fix additional boundaries into the interior as settlements and traffic developed.

Further territory was important to Bismarck's plans for huge, centralized conglomerates to administer the early colonies, but the trading houses refused to merge. As mentioned above, the four colonies soon devolved into crown colonies when the companies could no longer manage their administration. The consolidation of German territory ended with the outbreak of war in 1914 and the loss of German territory in Africa (Baumgart, "Die Deutsche Kolonialherrschaft in Afrika," 469-470).

Yet before this there was a long period of expansion, from four small charter colonies to much larger territories. However, there were also incidents of stymied German colonialism. Germany held the Witu district of East Africa until 1890 when it was relinquished to Britain in exchange for the Heligoland territory. Significant German interest in 1888 in acquiring a colonial possession on the Niger River, renowned for its mineral wealth and transport links, coupled with British acquiescence, very nearly gained another colony for the Reich. Germany also tried to acquire parts of northeast Africa and South Africa with no success.

This continued desire for territory was one of the few unifying characteristics between the four very different German colonies. The largest of the colonies, Southwest Africa, was established primarily as a settler colony because of its much-publicized grasslands that seemed to offer a bountiful prairie for German colonists. In Southwest Africa land became critical to colonialism as ranching was the colony's most profitable business. Nonetheless, the barren steppes of the colony never proved a success for either companies or settlers. Unlike Southwest Africa, the large German East African colony was blessed with verdant soil and forests. The colony became a plantation colony because of the difficulties involved in settling and farming the available land. The two small West African colonies of Togo and Cameroon were more successful because of their fertile climate that nurtured desirable products for the German market. In fact, Togo's productive tropical agriculture meant the colony was the sole German African dependency that could turn a profit. These local differences and the links between the colonies mandate an approach to their history that contrasts much existing historiography by conceiving all the colonies as situated within a variegated yet interconnected system.

Additional variation is present diachronically, for whenever one speaks of colonial expansion, one cannot ignore the phases of rule, since differing themes were dominant in different times. Baumgart identifies three phases: annexation euphoria, anticlimax, and revolt. Germany wanted to expand the Togo colony by annexing the contiguous areas. As well, Germany acquired further territory in East

Africa in 1900 by annexing a northern province. Germany also had designs on South African territory. C.D. Penner, "Germany and the Transvaal before 1896," *Journal of Modern History* 12 (March 1940): 51-53, 57. But the colonial period can conversely be seen as developing from a period of thorough ambivalence to guarded acceptance and finally considerable enthusiasm in the new colonies. In the broader German population, the colonies remained peripheral issues until the shock of the colonial uprisings in the early twentieth century. After the revolts and the massive expenditures on their repression, the African colonies definitively entered German society. The subsequent reforms to the colonial system instigated by the Deutsche Zentrumspartei (hereafter Zentrum) and Sozialdemokratische Partei Deutschlands (hereafter SPD) established a new direction in colonial policy. In the aftermath of the disclosure of a range of scandals over the administration of the colonies and the "Hottentot" election of 1907, the governing parties maintained their hold on power, but with significant changes to the colonial system. The reforms were led by State Secretary Bernhard Dernburg, who immediately restructured the colonial economies and improved the treatment of indigenous peoples. The reforms to the colonial system persisted until the beginning of the world war.

Along with diversity and change, the theme of continual expansion stands out. While the initial colonies were acquired between 1884 and 1890, there was a recurrent momentum of expansion into the African interior and further along the coast. Though the boundaries of the respective European spheres of influence had been established at the 1884 Berlin Conference, the expansion of German control into further areas of the African hinterland was to continue for the following three decades. Both the Colonial Department or Kolonial-Abteilung (hereafter K-A) and its 1907 successor, the Imperial Colonial Office or Reichskolonialamt (hereafter RKA), worked to increase the size of its colonies by annexing contiguous territory. Germany also expressed significant interest in acquiring more land in the Niger district from either France or Britain from 1889 to 1908. There were also plans to connect Southwest Africa, Cameroon and areas of West Africa into a vast German Mittelafrika trading bloc. As seen above, the German government always retained its rights to further expansion. After the initial acquisition of territory, the consolidation of existing territory and conquest of further territory continued throughout the three decades. This expansion highlights the forces driving German colonialism as a whole, leading this study to focus upon colonial expansion as indicative of the general character of colonialism.

One final theme, inseparable from this continual expansion, was contestation between German and African, ranging from passive negotiation to active rebellion. Colonial discord was always based on the expansion of territory into foreign dominions or the consolidation of German control over existing territory. The actions of German administrators, soldiers and traders frequently caused unrest as indigenous societies fought the expansive energies of the Germans. For example, the most severe example of violence, the wars of 1904-1906 against the pastoralist Herero and Nama tribes, present colonial resistance and repression in their cruellest shape. Over seventy thousand Herero were killed in what can now be easily termed genocide (Hull, 2003: 147-148). Almost concurrently a peasant uprising in East Africa known as the Maji Maji War lasted from 1905 until 1907. The history of German colonial conflict, from major actions in 1888-1890, 1889-1894 and 1904-1907 to the many smaller struggles, reveals both the ability of Africans to resist German rule, and the ends to which Germany was prepared to go to dominate Africa.

Why Remember the Namibian Genocide?

Why is it so important to commemorate genocidal atrocities such as those committed in Namibia early in the 20th century today? There are a number of reasons, which may be understood if grouped with two interrelated trajectories. The first of these trajectories is that, despite the ongoing tendency towards denialism, the Namibian genocide is an integral part of the development of political society and culture in Germany. The second trajectory concerns the overall dynamic and logic of genocide as it unfolded during the entire course of the 20th century. The distinction between these two trajectories also relates to the hotly debated issue of the exceptionality of the Holocaust perpetrated by Nazi Germany against European Jewry as well as against groups such as the Sinti and the Roma. This also leads to the further issue, whether the wars and mass crimes emanating from the German state during the first half of the 20th century are rooted in some specifically German path of historic development, fundamentally different from the West.

In brief, it may be said that the Namibian genocide contributed towards establishing a specific routine among the German military and also amongst civilians and the way they looked at war and specific acts of war. This meant, in particular, seeing the enemy not as another human being but as a member of an alien, inferior race, that is best annihilated, like 'vermin', in the language of the Nazis. Or, in more recent terminology, like 'cockroaches' or 'rats'. Dehumanizing whole groups or categories of humans in this way is widely considered an important precondition for actors to perpetrate mass killings, be it in direct personal confrontation with the victims or in the seemingly abstract settings of saturation bombing and even more in today's cyber wars where soldiers no longer have to face or see those they are killing. In very different ways, all those situations are structured to shield the perpetrators from fully confronting the implications of their murderous acts.

In a colonial situation as it prevailed in Namibia in the early 20th century, the negation of the full human worth of the persons of the colonized is predicated in the structurally racist set-up of colonialism. This is even more the case when the aim of colonial rule is not simply control and exploitation of the country, its resources and inhabitants, but rather, settlement by members of the colonizing society. The inherent racism of settler colonialism has worked to lower the threshold of mass killings in appalling ways in many cases and is to be found particularly in the Americas, Australia and southern Africa. In the Namibian case, this links up with the more specifically German trajectory, when we observe continuities of this in accounts and novels read by a mass readership, of military practice as well as in the activities of specific persons, and in military doctrines and routines that link strategic ideas of decisive battles to the concept of final solution and extinction of the enemy.

Such concepts of brute force had an incubation period in the German colonies. While use is made here of the example of German South West Africa, the extermination strategy used in German East Africa in response to the Maji Maji rebellion, triggered in 1905, where the policy of scorched earth was applied, should not be forgotten. Famine was used as a deliberately created weapon, as a result of which an estimated 100,000 to 300,000 people were starved to death. In 1905 one of the leaders of German troops in the colony, Captain Wangenheim, wrote: 'Only hunger and want can bring about a final submission. Military actions alone will remain more or less a drop in the ocean.' Such a mindset was fertiliser, if not the seed, for the reactionary ideology of selection based on the claim of the superiority of the Aryan race emerging during the Weimar Republic among those who constituted the Nazi regime, and which culminated in the Holocaust perpetrated in the 1940s.

It has to suffice here merely to mention these problems. Another dimension concerns active remembrance. Here again, it is appropriate to refer to the German case where a specific form of public repentance and remembrance may be said, at least in retrospect, even to have been incorporated into the founding myth of the second German republic. Even though anti-Semitism unfortunately even today is not a thing of the past, also in Germany, and despite the initial post-war tendency of denialism, the insistence by a younger generation since the 1960s has borne fruit: the Holocaust is the object of regular remembrance on the part of officialdom as well as civil society, bordering on a cult of mea culpa, denying any critical engagement with radical Zionism and the Israeli policy of occupation and Apartheid, which is all too easily accused of and stigmatized as anti-Semitism.

It should be noted, however, that such late but eager remembrance and repentance, along with the – always and necessarily completely inadequate – material redress associated with it, has been halting and highly selective. Former forced labourers from Eastern Europe have been indemnified, on a rather paltry scale, more than 50 years after the end of World War II, and this could only be achieved by a combination of persistent civil society action in Germany and the German corporation's fear of incurring law suits in the United States. Other victim groups managed to secure some kind of compensation even later.

In the case of the Namibian genocide, consecutive German governments, regardless of their political hue, have consistently evaded a formal, official apology. This has been declined on the grounds that this might constitute an argument for the descendants of the survivors to sue for damages. In ignominious ways, state visits to independent Namibia have contrasted a cordial relationship with German-speaking Namibians (among them many who continue to consider themselves as 'South Westers') but dealing short shrift when called upon to respond to the consequences of colonial genocide. It must be said that the former minister of economic cooperation and development, social democrat Heidemarie Wieczorek-Zeul, stands out strongly by actually offering an apology in her speech at the central commemoration of the centennial of the battle at Ohamakari on 14 August 2004. However, subsequent experience has shown that this was a somewhat personal rather than an official act – even though today German officials sometimes claim that Wieczorek-Zeul has apologized and that thereby the chapter could be conveniently considered as closed. The contrary is borne out generally, by the so far unsuccessful quest of Namibian victim groups to reach a dialogue with German officials, and of course more specifically by the way the German government (mis)treated the Namibian delegation who had come to Berlin for the repatriation of the skulls in September 2011.

There are powerful symbolic ways for the admission of (historical) guilt, devoid of any glamour and pompous ceremonial rituals. They can be public and dignified at the same time, and have a lasting wider impact. The bent knees and bowed head of the then German Chancellor Willy Brandt in front of the Warsaw War Memorial certainly was such an act. There are other ways of making less public gestures of reconciliation, followed by practical policies.

One central demand, which the German government's behaviour in the genocide question has demonstrated by default, is first and foremost to listen to the victim groups, instead of decreeing what must be done. The exact modalities of remembrance and redress may be subject to debate but there is a responsibility and obligation to stand up, also through scholarly endeavour, against the clamorous calls for doing away with the past by a final stroke, thus repressing and, in the words of Theodor Adorno, 'defrauding' those murdered even of that only gift with which we, powerless, are able to provide them: remembrance'.

The Unforgotten German Genocide in Namibia

When one hears the word genocide, the mind may immediately go to the Holocaust by the Nazis during the Second World War. Very few know that the first genocide of the 20th century that almost led to the extinction of two nations of Southwest Africa – Herero and Namaqua – and this one was also done by the Germans. But let's take things from the beginning. The German South-West Africa was a colony of the German Empire between 1884 and 1915. It included a land of 835,100 square kilometres, which was one and a half times the size of Germany.

The areas of German South West Africa (now Namibia) were formally colonized by Germany between 1884–90. The semiarid territory was more than twice as large as Germany, yet it had only a fraction of the population—approximately 250,000 people. In contrast to Germany's other African possessions, it offered little promise for large-scale mineral or agricultural extractions. Instead, South West Africa became Germany's only real settler colony. By 1903 some 3,000 Germans had settled in the colony, primarily on the central high grounds. The launch of this new settler society, albeit still small, disrupted the socioeconomic balance of the territory and resulted in conflict. Apart from overarching anticolonial concerns, the primary points of friction were access to scarce resources such as land, water, and cattle. The largest conflict involved the Herero nation, a mainly pastoral people who over the preceding decades had adopted various traits of modernity, including use of horses and guns.

The fighting began on Jan. 12, 1904, in the small town of Okahandja, the seat of the Herero chieftaincy under paramount leader Samuel Maharero. It is still unclear who fired the first shots, but by noon that day Herero fighters had laid siege to the German fort. In the following weeks, fighting rippled out across the central high grounds. Seeking to gain control of the situation, Maharero issued specific rules of engagement that precluded violence against women and children. Nevertheless, 123 settlers and soldiers were killed in these attacks, including at least four women.

Maj. Theodor Leutwein, military commander and governor of the colony, was in charge of the German response. Since the Herero were well armed and, moreover, significantly outnumbered the

German colonial garrison, he favoured a negotiated settlement of the conflict. He was, however, overruled by the General Staff in Berlin who demanded a military solution. On April 13 Leutwein's troops were forced into an embarrassing retreat, and the governor was consequently relieved of his military command. In his place the German emperor, William II, appointed Lieut. Gen. Lothar von Trotha as the new commander in chief. He was a colonial veteran of the wars in German East Africa and of the Boxer Rebellion in China.

Von Trotha arrived on June 11, 1904. At that point there had not been any major combat for two months. The Herero had fled to the remote Waterberg plateau at the edge of the Kalahari (desert) to distance themselves from the German troops and supply lines, in an attempt to avoid additional battles and safely await a possible negotiation for peace or, if necessary, be well positioned to escape into British Bechuanaland (now Botswana). Von Trotha used this lull to gradually encircle the Herero. Moving his troops to the Waterberg plateau was a large undertaking, considering that the German maps of this area were incomplete and because water had to be hauled across the rugged terrain, along with the heavy artillery that would be vital for a successful attack. The general's expressed strategy was to "annihilate these masses with a simultaneous blow."

In the early morning of Aug. 11, 1904, von Trotha ordered his 1,500 troops to attack. Standing against an estimated 40,000 Herero, of whom only some 5,000 carried arms, the Germans relied on the element of surprise as well as their modern weaponry. The strategy worked. Continuous shelling by the artillery sent Herero combatants into a desperate offensive, awaited by the German machine guns. By late afternoon the Herero were defeated. However, a weak German flank to the southeast allowed the majority of the Herero nation to make a desperate escape into the Kalahari. In this exodus to British Bechuanaland, many thousands of men, women, and children eventually died of thirst.

In subsequent months von Trotha continued to pursue the Herero into the desert. Those who surrendered or were captured by the Germans were often executed summarily. By early October, however, von Trotha was forced to abandon the pursuit, due to exhaustion and lack of supplies.

In 1915, during the First World War, British and South African forces entered German Southwest Africa to conquer it. After the war, the area was commanded by the Union of South Africa (part of the British Empire) and was named Southwest Africa, after a directive by the Union of Nations. Herero and Namaqua were nations of animal breeders. The German colonizers tried to modernize them by converting them to farmers and workers for their land and businesses. However, the most important issues that led the tribes to rebel against their German colonizers were the ownership rights and the way the Germans used it. Herero gave more than ¼ of the 130,000 sq. km. of land that belonged to them, for the completion of the railway Otavi, which was built, according to the Germans, to help the 'development' of the area. However, in reality it was going to ignite the invasion of more colonizers that would exploit the land and the riches of the country as well as the people. According to the German historian Horst Drechsler , the Germans were planning – always with the purpose of 'developing' the country, the relocation of Herero to special designated areas (native reservations), confiscating their land without compensation and using the people of Herero and Namaqua as workers on their own land. And this was because Germans considered that the land belonged to them.

Many of the Herero people had, of course, already been used as workers/slaves at the businesses of the Germans. The annihilation order against the Herero and Nama people was issued at the end of the war after the Germans defeated the Herero on October 2, 1904. The genocide order, *Schiessbefehl*, issued by Lieutenant General Lothar von Trotha stated:

> I, the great General of the German troops, send this letter to the Herero people. The Herero people are no longer German subjects . . . The Herero people must leave the country. If the nation doesn't do this I will force them with the Groot Rohr [cannon]. Within the German borders, every Herero, with or without gun, with or without cattle, will be shot. I will no longer accept women or children, I will drive them back to their people or I will let them be shot at (Lemarchand, 2011).

Von Trotha's proclamation affirmed policies of terrorism and force resulting in an almost extinction of the Herero people by way of starvation, concentration camps, and other genocidal tactics. Germany's colonization of South West Africa, present day Namibia, ended in what many claim as the first genocide of the 20th century, killing tens of thousands of Herero people including men, women and children. This project seeks to discuss the way in which the German colonial forces committed genocide against the Herero and Nama people and the purpose of trade cards and other advertisements detailing accounts of Herero people, I will show the differences between what these portrayed and reality of how the Hereros were treated by the German settlers.

Dating back to April of 1884, Germany became a protectorate of the South-West African lands, the land would be known as the German South-West Africa (GSWA). Germany's aim for GSWA was to build its reputation as a main political power in the world at the expense of the Herero people. The systematic establishment and construction of German rule began with the arrival of Theodor Leutwein. Theodor Leutwein was a colonial administrator of GSWA until 1904. His agenda was to push the German administration agenda and secure political power by way of 'chieftain policies.' These policies allowed for African leaders to remain in their positions and create working relationships with them that gained him support of the most important Herero and Nama leaders such Hendrik Witbooi and Samuel Maharero.

When German colonizers first came to settle on the lands of present day Namibia, the relations between the Herero and the Germans can be summed up as a tense situation. The increase of German settlers to the land caused increasing problems with the Herero and Nama population. One major principle that rose conflict was that White Germans were not subject to African law where they were taken to German courts. Capital crimes as defined in African laws such as rape and murder were hardly ever punished. On the other hand, all Africans were subjected to German laws.

Events beginning in the early months of 1904 transformed the relations between the Herero and Germans in German South West Africa. Murders and mutilation of hundreds of women, men, and children ignited the war. In the beginning attacks, the Herero, sparing women, children and missionaries, killed 123 Germans. In this attack, the Hereros attacked those who raped their women and were not persecuted, and the Herero housekeepers killed their German employers while they were asleep. Chief Samuel Maharero ordered the Hereros that this war was only against the Germans, not all white, he did not want this to become a race war.

After a devastating defeat by the Herero people against Leutwein's army, General von Trotha designated himself as the supreme commander. Under his orders, Herero workers were imprisoned and lynched even those who sided with Kaiser were attacked. Three gallows were constructed in Windhoek, which displayed captured Hereros hanging like a public spectacle, which were left for days to instil fear among the Hereros. The picture below depicts what is described of the gallows where Hereros hung with the German soldiers overseeing the process. The small print on the left corner reads "German So. W. Africa Hanging Party. 312 Negroes Hanged." This photo of the lynching of Herero people was taken by White settlers, which showed the beaten bodies hanging from the gallows at Windhoek.

The atrocities against the Herero and Nama people are what are considered the first genocide of the 20th century. 60,000 to 100,000 Herero and Nama people were exterminated from their lands in South West Africa, which constitutes to about 85% of their population. Germans not only exiled the Hereros from their land, but also poisoned the water wells, driving them to the Omaheke desert. Under the orders of General von Trotha, was the annihilation order against the Nama and Herero people issued.

Let us note here that viewed from the prism of eugenics, the fittest (Aryan race) survived while black people were born to be mastered by the fittest. The Kaiser's race engineers used callipers and craniometry charts to measure the severed heads of Nama tribesmen; their ears and feet were considered "apish" telltale atavisms. Zoologist Leopard Schultze noted that taking *"body parts from fresh native corpses was a welcome addition."* An estimated 300 skulls were sent to Germany for experimentation; many from concentration camp prisoners. Historians emphasize the fact that while other colonial occupiers were brutal, German racism was extreme; in 1905, it entered German legal terminology — *Rassenschande* (racial defilement) — when marriage between German colonists in South Africa and Africans was banned. The eminent British historian, Richard Evans noted that:

"Only the Germans introduced concentration camps, named them as such and deliberately created conditions so harsh that their purpose was clearly as much to exterminate their inmates as it was to force them to work. (It would be left to the Nazis to devise the chilling term 'extermination through labour'.)

Only the Nazis mounted an explicit attempt to exterminate an entire colonized people on racial grounds. Only the Germans legally banned intermarriage in their colonies. Only Germans subsequently mounted a campaign of racial extermination on a global scale which encompassed not only Europe's Jews but also, potentially, the Jewish inhabitants of the rest of the world. Was there a connection between the two?" (Evans, The Third Reich in History and Memory, 2015).

In an article by Benjamin Madley in *European History Quarterly* (2005) examined how genocidal rhetoric, war of annihilation, and the use of concentration camps were transmitted across time and adopted by the Nazis. He examines Germany's colonial *Lebensraum* and *Vernichtung* (annihilation) policies within the context of equally brutal European colonial actions, but notes distinguishing features.

What distinguishes the German South West African genocide from most other colonial mass murders is the fact that the Germans in colonial Namibia articulated and implemented a policy of Vernichtung, or annihilation...German South West African colonists pioneered the implementation of a Weltanschauung, later adopted by the Nazis, in which superior Germans ruled over sub-human non-Germans with brutality and slavery. This paradigm provided new ideas and methods for Nazi colonialism that were transferred to Germany and to future Nazis ... Hermann Göring, Eugen Fischer, and Franz Ritter von Epp served as human conduits for the flow of ideas and methods between the colony and Nazi Germany.

German South West African race laws provided legal concepts later applied by Nazi lawmakers. As in the colony, "Mischlinge' became a topic of concern in the Nazi Justice Ministry while both the 1935 Defence Law prohibiting soldiers from marrying 'persons of non-Aryan origin' and the Nuremberg Laws criminalizing marriage and sex between Jews and 'Aryan' Germans were simply variants of German

South West African laws against interracial marriage and cohabitation. (Madley. "From Africa to Auschwitz: How German South West Africa Incubated Ideas and Methods Adopted and Developed by the Nazis in Eastern Europe" *European History Quarterly*, 2005)

British author, John Lewis-Stempel, also views the Namibian genocide as prefiguring the Holocaust:

> After beating the Herero in the battle of Waterberg, Trotha drove the survivors into the pitiless Omaheke desert with the intention they should die from thirst and starvation. Waterholes were poisoned by "cleansing patrols" of the Schutztruppe, the colonial army, to prevent the Herero from using them.
>
> In Berlin the German general staff publicly lauded Trotha for his "extermination" measures. By 1905 Herero fugitives still alive in the Omaheke were too weak to do anything but surrender. They were rounded up, put into cattle wagons and sent by train to concentration camps, where they became slave labour for the colony's new railways.
>
> Women were systematically raped by Schutztruppen, the incidents turned into photographs by the new-fangled Kodak roll-fill camera. The pictures were then sent as pornographic postcards to Germany... (*Daily Express*, Jan. 2014)

It is perhaps for reasons of claimed racial superiority that during the time of casualties in GSWA, many German people collected trade cards depicting false realities of the Hereros in South West Africa. The usage of these cards was to increase German propaganda and increase the support of the treatment of the Hereros in GERMAN SOUTH WEST AFRICA. In reality, the Herero and Nama people were executed in the most extreme ways, under the worst conditions. Although the policies to exterminate the Herero was impractically, both logical and militarily, the cruelty still burned in the eyes of von Trotha. Kaiser Wilhelm applauded von Trotha's action and energy, as he wrote to the General:

> You have entirely fulfilled my expectations when I named you commander of the colonial troops, and I take pleasure in expressing, once again, my utter gratitude for your accomplishments so far (Erichsen, 2010).

The cruelty by the Germans in South West Africa under Kaiser Wilhelm, directed controlled by General von Trotha. These accounts of atrocities were written in the 'Blue Book', which documented the genocide to be used to prevent Germany from ever regaining control over its colonies. Later this book was destroyed, in the interests of white settlers, stating that it was a propaganda tactic, not to be used for reparations, but to be used to ensure that German would lose all of its colonies.

The Herero people demanded reparations of one billion dollars for their ancestor's robbed land, possessions, and treatment. 100 years after the genocide, Germany's Minister for Economic Cooperation and Development Heidemarie Wieczorek-Zeul visited Namibia in 2004, asking for forgiveness of the atrocities dating back to 1904. An apology was also issued in 2007 from von Trotha's descendants, to Chief Alfons Maharero, the grandchild of Samuel Maharero for the atrocities that were inflicted upon the Herero people by von Trotha and his military. Although the Hereros were denied reparations for the ancestors, Germany has made strides in offering millions of euros to present-day Namibia through German development aid, but this act should not be mistaken with justice for the Herero people (Jones, 2012).

Why German Genocide in Namibia?

Scholar Jeremy Sarkin (2010) proposes two main reasons for the genocide and harsh treatment of the Hereros: punishment for rebelling against German rule during the uprising of 1904; secondly, the occupancy of the Herero's land and possession of their cattle. Jurgen Zimmerer (2003) discusses the way in which it is erroneous to call the attack on the Germans by the Herero people as an 'uprising' or 'rebellion' because of the differences between perception of colonial powers: the land was in possession of the Herero people so it was theirs, and the European conferences that gave Germany the colonial power which complicated matters.

> Genocide 'is never a sudden or unplanned act…It is a deliberate, pre-meditated and carefully orchestrated orgy of mass murder for political purposes…a well organised campaign of carnage…

The Herero people were in desperate situations, being driven out of their land to the Omaheke desert where they were left to perish. Many Herero cut the throats of their cattle in order to drink the blood, squeezing the last drops of dampness from the stomachs of the dying cattle. Many still died since these measures helped very little. It is the premeditated killings of women and children and deliberate extermination of the whole Nama and Herero people, which made this an act of genocide. Under the rule of General Adrian Dietrich Lothar von Trotha, a veteran of the German army of 10 years, the annihilation order against the Hereros was declared. Lothar von Trotha was a commander in Germany East Africa during the Wahehe uprising between 1894 and 1897. His reputation was summed up in just a word: ruthlessness. Von Trotha stated:

> I know enough tribes in Africa. They all have the same mentality insofar as they yield only to force. It was and remains my policy to apply this force by absolute terrorism and even cruelty. I shall destroy the rebellious tribes by shedding rivers of blood and money. Only then will it be possible to sow the seeds of something new that will endure (Johnson, 2003).

This statement was released in 1904. In 1905, von Trotha declared a state of martial law, making him the commander of the military and civil affairs. After an attempt of the Herero chiefs to negotiate peace, von Trotha dismissed it and in early August issued the 'Directives for the Attack on the Hereros'. On August 16th and 26th he ordered his troops to cut off waterholes and patrol along the Omaheke desert to prevent the Herero people from moving back to the colony. The main killer of the Hereros was through dehydration.

German Genocide Propaganda

During the genocide of the Herero people, many trade cards and other advertisements were being promoted at the time. "Some scholars have pointed to a broad-based escalation of racist rhetoric and racism in German culture as a result of the Herero War. Others have argued that older discourses of race and colonialism structured the terms around which the conflict was discussed and debated." Trade cards (*Sammelbilder*) were popularized when given away with the purchase of commodities such as soup powder or chocolate which posed as propaganda for Germans, as many German people, specifically children collected them (Ciarlo,2011). The majority of the trade cards displayed Herero women as lewd images and some even portrayed the Herero people as rebellious, and dangerous. These trade cards attempted to legitimize the treatment that Hereros had to endure at the hand of the Germans in GSWA by showing the Herero people in a negative light. "On one hand, some visions of the uprising (as opposed to textual and rhetorical invocations of race in newspapers and parliamentary debates) were not merely illustrative devices but broadcast and sold as commodities in and of themselves" (Ibid.). Ciarlo discusses the way in which criticisms broke out over how the Germans were handling the war in GSWA, bringing to light the colonial budget in order to attack the government's actions.

The most widely circulated images were on collectible trading cards of companies such as Aecht Frank coffee, Erkel soap, Theodor Hildebrand cocoa, Walser & Schwarz, and Hartwig & Vogel's chocolate. The card series began with scenes showing Hereros murdering and plundering, at times they showed the German women scared, implying the threat of sexual harassment (Ibid.).

This image shown above is of typical trading cards, this one of some Herero men stealing cattle. The words on the postcard says 'Herero uprising in German South Africa, by cattle consuming Hereros.' Aecht Frank was a coffee producing company now owned by Nestle that was founded in Germany issued trade cards of the Herero uprising in GSWA. While the Herero people are displayed in these actions, it was usually the Germans that stole cattle. Trade cards such as this one helped to insinuate the racial theories about Africans such as them being savages, dangerous and needing to be tamed. On the right of the trade card is a Herero woman creating pottery.

The trade card above displays a map of German South West Africa, and of a Herero woman, and children outside of Windhoek camp. Hartwig & Vogel's Chocolate Company produced this trade card instead of Aecht Franck. This projection can be contrasted with an original photo of Windhoek, a concentration camp that Hereros were placed in after the war of 1904.

This is a photo of the concentration camp of Windhoek. It can be seen how this photo, and the German propaganda trade card contrasts. While the trade card seeks to imply that ordinary, peaceful things are going on in the German South West Africa, when in reality there is a stark difference. Herero people were being killed, starved and worked to death in concentration camps.

The colonial war was always framed as a race war. This trade card displays the Herero people as rioting and rebelling against the German colonizers. This card depicts them as dangerous, showing the Herero looting a home of a German man, the house burning and a German dead in a pool of blood. The Herero are seen as carrying bundles of valuables, a visual proof of theft. The words on the card are translated from Google Translation as 'The Herero riot in German South West Africa, looting Mr. Gamisch's farm. This trade card can be interpreted as the Herero people are not only violent, but they need to be controlled. Cards such as these allowed for Germans to accept what Germany was doing to the Herero people in Africa, these types of depictions increased the thoughts of racial superiority of the German people over Africans. According to this political propaganda, Germans needed protection from inferior animals. Trade cards such as these went mainstream in 1905. Throughout the German genocide of the Herero people, collections of trading cards and photographs were offered in order to not only portray the

Herero people as savagery, but to also gain backing support from German citizens, especially those that disagreed with the colonizing of Africa.

The photo above shows the Hereros men with guns shooting at perhaps German men. This photo depicts how Germans attempted to depict the Herero people as dangerous. The bottle of the trade card, translated through Google Translations, says the colonial struggle in South West African: Hereros in combat.

The war in South West Africa shifted the German consumer imagery in three ways: first, the acceleration of the tendency to deploy images of African natives in advertising, the Herero conflict became a modern media event which increased interests on both the advertiser and public's side. Secondly, to attract purchasers advertisers and third, the African imagery came with a shift in pictorial styles used to illustrate African figures (Ibid.). The trade cards were not only used to increase support of Germany's colonialism in South West Africa, but to justify the brutal cruelty that Germans placed upon the Herero people. The images meant to imprint on the minds of children, who largely collected these trade cards, to increase German propaganda through false depictions.

In sum, the atrocities against the Herero and Nama people are what are considered the first genocide of the 20th century. 60,000 to 100,000 Herero and Nama people were exterminated from their lands in South West Africa, which constitutes to about 85% of their population. Germans not only exiled the Hereros from their land, but also poisoned the water wells, driving them to the Omaheke desert. Under the orders of General von Trotha, was the annihilation order against the Nama and Herero people issued.

During the time of casualties in GSWA, many German people collected trade cards depicting false realities of the Hereros in South West Africa. The usage of these cards was to increase German propaganda and increase the support of the treatment of the Hereros in GSWA. In reality, the Herero and Nama people were executed in the most extreme ways, under the worst conditions. Although the policies to exterminate the Herero was impractically, both logical and militarily, the cruelty still burned in the eyes of von Trotha. Kaiser Wilhelm applauded von Trotha's action and energy, as he wrote to the General:

> You have entirely fulfilled my expectations when I named you commander of the colonial troops, and I take pleasure in expressing, once again, my utter gratitude for your accomplishments so far (Erichsen, 2010).

The cruelty by the Germans in South West Africa under Kaiser Wilhelm, directed controlled by General von Trotha. These accounts of atrocities were written in the 'Blue Book', which documented the genocide to be used to prevent Germany from ever regaining control over its colonies. Later this book was destroyed, in the interests of white settlers, stating that it was a propaganda tactic, not to be used for reparations, but to be used to ensure that German would lose all of its colonies.

The Herero people demanded reparations of one billion dollars for their ancestor's robbed land, possessions, and treatment. 100 years after the genocide, Germany's Minister for Economic Cooperation and Development Heidemarie Wieczorek-Zeul visited Namibia in 2004, asking for forgiveness of the atrocities dating back to 1904. An apology was also issued in 2007 from von Trotha's descendants, to Chief Alfons Maharero, the grandchild of Samuel Maharero for the atrocities that were inflicted upon the Herero people by von Trotha and his military. Although the Hereros were denied reparations for the ancestors, Germany has made strides in offering millions of euros to present-day Namibia through German development aid, but this act should not be mistaken with justice for the Herero people (Jones, 2012).

German Colonial Genocide and Namibian Resistance

From January 1904 the German colony of South West Africa (since 1990 the sovereign state of Namibia) seethed with the repercussions of the greatest resistance movement against colonial rule the country had yet witnessed. The colonial administration had been gradually implanted after the Berlin conference in 1884 which had sealed the partition of Africa among the European powers. A new brand of German radical nationalism began to echo the proverbial quest by the young Emperor William II for a 'place in the sun', calling for Germany's establishment as a world power on a par with Britain, with a powerful fleet and an array of overseas colonies. But Germany managed to grab only a few colonies in Africa and Oceania after 1884, which turned out to be dismal and costly commercial failures. Yet in nationalist circles, colonies appeared indispensable to prove the country's status as a world power. Amongst the colonies acquired, Namibia was the only territory considered suitable for extensive settlement by Europeans. Settler ideology envisaged the creation of a 'New Germany'. Under such circumstances, any challenge to colonial rule was tantamount to disparaging national honour and grandeur. At the same time, the quest for settlement translated into a sustained drive to expropriate Africans from their lands and from their livestock.

After the formal establishment of colonial rule in 1884, it took years to assert full or proper control. Only in 1895 did the Khowesin (part of the Khoikhoi or Nama, referred to as 'Hottentots' in discriminating colonial jargon), under the leadership of Hendrik Witbooi, succumb to the colonial troops. The charismatic chief had clairvoyantly, but in vain, tried to unite the leaders of the different local communities threatened by colonialism. The decade that followed was marked by Governor Leutwein's strategy to advance the settlement project and, in his own words, to 'gradually get the natives accustomed to the new dispensation. Of their former independence, nothing but memories will be left.' Leutwein pursued this by a policy of divide and rule and almost constant warfare, pitting different African groups against each other. Since he had at his disposal only a very limited armed contingent, Leutwein relied on treaties with the indigenous chiefs to supply auxiliaries when the need arose to quell uprisings against the fledgling colonial power.

The Herero–German war that began in early 1904 was the most formidable challenge to colonial control once the formal subjugation of the country had been completed. The Ovaherero had largely been able to keep colonial encroachment at bay but the combined effects of the huge losses of their herds through the rinderpest, a locust invasion, a malaria epidemic and, above all, the consequences of the fraudulent practices of traders which led to the sequestration of cattle and alienation of land, plunged the Herero communities into crisis. Progressively, alienated land was appropriated by settler farmers. Complaints were rife about the Ovaherero, women in particular, being mistreated by the colonists. Further encroachment loomed with the proposed railway, which was to cut through the Herero heartland to reach the copper mines of Tsumeb at its far north-eastern fringe. On either side of the railway, a strip of European settlement was envisaged, thus to speed up further land alienation and European settlement.

At the very beginning of the war, Paramount Chief Samuel Maharero (ironically promoted to such an invented new position by the colonial administration in return for earlier collaboration) gave strict orders to his followers not to attack women, children, missionaries, non-German Europeans or members of other indigenous groups. In January 1904 fighting spread rapidly (catching the authorities and settlers by total surprise), but Ovaherero fighters observed their leader's instructions. While male farmers were frequently killed when their farms were attacked, as a rule, women, children and missionaries were escorted to the German forts. This did not prevent the spread of propaganda about horrendous atrocities committed by the Ovaherero. In their campaign, the Ovaherero initially succeeded in securing control of most of central Namibia, with only the German forts resisting the onslaught.

The colonial power started to pour in reinforcements, along with a new commander-in-chief, General Lothar von Trotha. He had earned his credentials as a member of the international expeditionary force that ravaged North China in retaliation for the Ihetuan ('Boxer') uprising in 1901 and, prior to that, by breaking African resistance, in particular that of the Wahehe, in then German East Africa, now Tanzania. From the beginning, von Trotha was quite outspoken about his mission. He considered the confrontation as a 'war of races'. He claimed superior knowledge that 'African tribes ... will only succumb to violent force. It has been and remains my policy to exercise this violence with gross terrorism and even with cruelty. I annihilate the African tribes by floods of money and floods of blood. It is only by such sowings that something new will arise which will be there to stay' – meaning of course, German settlement of the country, thus devoid of competitors. This strategy was, despite the opposition of Leutwein, approved and endorsed by the army headquarters (General Staff) in Berlin. Under von Trotha's command it was implemented faithfully.

Based on a mindset guided by a 'total war mentality' and extermination strategy, von Trotha was looking for a decisive battle. The military actions marking a turning point took place at Ohamakari (Waterberg) on 11 August 1904. The Ovaherero had assembled there as a people, men, women and children, with their herds of cattle. After the military encounters, the majority of Ovaherero broke through the German encirclement in an easterly direction, going into the waterless Omaheke – a vast dry land with no surface water, bordering on Bechuanaland (today Botswana). To this day, historians are not agreed whether this was actually a military victory for the German colonial army. In any case, to secure a final and decisive victory, units of German soldiers followed the fleeing Herero in hot pursuit, cutting off access to waterholes and poisoning those they came across. More than seven weeks later, on 2 October, von Trotha proclaimed his infamous extermination proclamation and publically called on his troops to ensure that the Herero would perish in the semi-desert: 'Within the German borders,' the proclamation stated (meaning the borders of German South West Africa), 'every Herero, with or without a gun, with or without cattle, will be shot.'

The proclamation also stressed that neither women nor children would be spared; they would be denied refuge. While colonial apologists are eager to point out that an 'internal' order by von Trotha instructed the soldiers to shoot above the heads of women and children to force them to flee, they ignore that this command served the purpose, namely to chase them back into the waterless Omaheke to die of thirst and exhaustion. Their fickle indicator, intended to water down the extermination order and thus the intent to destroy, makes the actions an even more gruesome way of 'exterminating the brutes' (a phrase coined by Emperor William II in his speech when dispatching the soldiers to North China to mercilessly suppress the insurrection in 1901).

By today's standards and in accordance with the UN Convention on the Prevention and Punishment of the Crime of Genocide of 1948, von Trotha's proclamation was a purposeful order for genocide, as part of an overall strategy to secure the country for European, in particular German, settlement. The numbers of those who died a horrible death as a consequence of that order may never be fully ascertained. It is generally accepted that the various Herero groups might have numbered up to 100,000, of whom, according to some estimates, as few as 20,000 survived the ordeal. The concept of genocide, however, is not predicated on such number crunching. According to the UN convention of 1948, genocide is not defined by numerical dimensions but as 'acts committed with intent to destroy, in whole or in part, a national, ethnical, racial or religious group, as such'. That this was the imminent aim and character of the warfare conducted by the German colonial troops is borne out amply by the pronouncements of von Trotha and his superiors.

When the extermination order was eventually rescinded by the emperor, the genocide had already been perpetrated. Moreover, the official military account of the 'Great General Staff' in its concluding paragraphs summarized it as a major achievement of the war that the Herero nation was annihilated and had ceased to exist. It celebrated the prowess of the German troops. The late change of policy may be seen as the fruit of representations by missionaries who witnessed the carnage but also of heated public debate in Germany. Thus, August Bebel, founder and parliamentary leader of the Social Democratic Party, worked strenuously to oppose budget appropriations for the colonial war and castigated von Trotha's strategy as that of 'a vile butcher'. Bebel reminded his audience of the emperor's infamous farewell speech (as already quoted above) to the expeditionary corps sent to China when he called on the troops to act in ways to make a name for themselves in the same way the Huns did in Europe 1,500 years earlier. Bebel surmised that there might have been a similar order given in private, 'otherwise it would be wholly inconceivable for me that a general could issue such an order which contravenes all principles of martial law, civilization, culture and Christianity'. The Catholic Centrist Party also questioned colonial policy at the time. On the government's side, there were considerations of expediency: the genocidal strategy was cutting the ground from beneath the settlers' feet by killing off potential labour power as well as the better part of the cattle herds of the Ovaherero which the settlers meant to appropriate for themselves. Paul Rohrbach, the commissioner for settlement affairs in German South West Africa, bemoaned after the war that the workforce, urgently required as the most important asset for building the colonial economy, had short-sightedly been destroyed.

Nama Resistance and Consequences

On 4 October 1904, things took a new turn with the start of the Nama-German war in southern Namibia. This was probably occasioned by witnessing the fate meted out to the Herero. The various Nama groups avoided a large-scale battle and managed to hold out much longer than the Ovaherero. General von Trotha responded by transferring his strategy of genocidal suppression to this region as well. His proclamation to the Nama explicitly cited the Herero experience. Larger Nama groups capitulated after Hendrik Witbooi, by now an octogenarian, died in action more than a year after the commencement of the uprising, but some carried on until 1908.

Those who gave themselves up to the Germans met a similar fate to the surviving Herero. Contrary to earlier promises, they were made prisoners. Men, women, children and elderly people, indiscriminately, were detained in concentration camps. They shared this fate with the surviving Ovaherero. These concentration camps were located largely in the relatively cold and moist climate of the two port towns of Swakopmund and Lüderitz. Unaccustomed to these conditions, underfed, ill-clothed and badly accommodated, thousands of prisoners died from sheer neglect, or from their exertions as forced labour. Even after the war had officially been terminated, groups of Nama were transported to other German colonies in Africa, Togo and Cameroon. Of these groups of deportees, many also died before they were repatriated shortly before the beginning of World War I. It is estimated that of more than 20,000 Nama who lived in southern Namibia before the uprising, less than 10,000 survived these various forms of savage repression.

One of the more appalling features of this mass destruction of human lives is the kind of open publicity the perpetrators may be said almost to have revelled in. Picture postcards were produced displaying in particular the concentration camps. The term concentration camp emerged shortly before the turn of the century during the Spanish-American war on Cuba and got wider currency in the course of the Anglo-Boer war in South Africa, when British strategy employed such guarded camps to defeat settlers of Dutch origin. While the term did not carry quite the same meaning it acquired through the Nazi Holocaust some 40 years later, the element of destruction both in South Africa and Namibia was quite obvious and undeniable. The postcards from the German colony show an appalling disregard for human suffering, which could be conveyed, as it were, as a greeting to one's loved ones at home. The same is true of colour pictures showing scenes of prisoners being hanged, or of forced labour scenes representing 'native life' as though this was a quasi-normal feature in the lives of the so-called natives—as if it were natural for Africans to be subjected to inhuman treatment and the regular application of brute force.

The recent repatriation of human skulls has focused attention on the ways in which the German public of the early 20th century was informed, including about the transportation of human remains from the colony to the metropole. One image, reproduced on postcards and in book illustrations, shows soldiers packing a crate with human skulls with the caption that these had been cleaned of their flesh by Ovaherero women using shards of glass. Participants in the Namibian delegation who went to Berlin in September 2011 to receive the skulls also recalled stories they had heard from their parents and grandparents who had gone through these ordeals. In Germany, these skulls became the material upon which academic careers were built. Such racial science became a mainstay of Nazi ideology and discriminatory practices.

In other respects as well, this first genocide of the 20th century may arguably be considered to be one of the most publicised by the perpetrators themselves. There were popular novels, books of reminiscences and literature filled with colonial propaganda, all of which extolled the exploits of the German troops. In line with sentiments that recent research has traced amongst German soldiers involved in the mass murders during World War II, this literature conveys praise for the hardship valiantly endured whilst killing not only opponent fighters, but old people, women and children. The experience of the colonial genocide in Namibia, therefore not surprisingly, eventually fed into Nazi ideology and propaganda. The most popular novel on the 'civilising mission' of exterminating the Herero, originally published in 1906, was 'Peter Moors Fahrt nach Südwest' by Gustav Frenssen. It attained a print run of over 400,000 copies and was reprinted for the last time in Germany by the German army headquarters for distribution in the trenches on the 'Eastern Front' in 1944, when it was referred to as Schützengrabenliteratur (Trench literature). In Namibia, stalwarts put out a new edition very recently.

The nationalist and colonial hysteria came to a head when incumbent Chancellor von Bülow used this atmosphere to engineer a grand political realignment ('Bülow-Block') and to organize an election campaign in 1907, still known in history as 'Hottentot Elections'. By this means, Bülow managed to break the former majority of the Social Democrats and the Centre, and a centre-right majority was returned which ensured the passing of the budgets needed to further pursue the quest for world power.

Officially the military authorities declared the war terminated in March 1907, a timely move in the run-up to the elections mentioned above. But Ovaherero prisoners of war were released only at the end of May 1908, while Nama prisoners were never set free during German rule. In fact, deportation of Nama communities to Cameroon took place even after the formal end of the war. Moreover, the colonial administration pursued a grand design to further uproot the populations of central and southern Namibia, shifting Herero to the south, while transporting Nama to the centre, the northern portion of the white settlement zone.

Those survivors who were released found themselves in dramatically changed circumstances. Above all, they were expropriated of their land and their livestock. This meant the clearing of their land for settlement by white farmers and the appropriation of their herds in so far as they still existed. Moreover, Africans were legally barred from owning land and large livestock. In this way, Africans were systematically prevented from reconstructing a basis for an independent life for themselves, and Ovaherero in particular were prevented from resuming the symbolic rebuilding of their communities, which largely hinged on cattle herds. In terms of the UN genocide convention, measures to break up and destroy the communal life of the target group or, as in this case, to systematically prevent its reconstruction, also amount to an act of genocide. Furthermore, Africans were forbidden to settle in large groups, even when employed on a settler farm, and above all, they were subjected to a strict obligation to enter into waged labour which was subjected to comprehensive administrative control. To ensure the smooth and comprehensive working of this system and to foreclose any new attempt at rebellion, all Africans over seven years of age were subjected to a labour obligation, registered and required to carry a token, the so-called pass mark (Passmarke) around their necks. This token has turned into a much sought after collector's item, a dubious modern kind of 'memory culture'. In its time, the token served as the means by which any white person could check to make sure that the African was entitled to be in any particular place and otherwise could be turned over to the police. To this was added a system of strict racial segregation. The systematic discrimination was linked to harnessing the labour power of dispossessed Africans in the interests of the new colonial economy, centred on white settlements. The Native Ordinances, strictly regulated and ruthlessly enforced after 1905, in many ways presaged what four decades later would be called Apartheid.

In sum, what distinguishes the German South West African genocide from most other colonial mass murders is the fact that the Germans in colonial Namibia articulated and implemented a policy of Vernichtung, or annihilation. German South West African colonists pioneered the implementation of a Weltanschauung, later adopted by the Nazis, in which superior Germans ruled over sub-human non-Germans with brutality and slavery. This paradigm provided new ideas and methods for Nazi colonialism that were transferred to Germany and to future Nazis.

Bibliography

Adams, D. (1995) *Education for Extinction: American Indians and the Boarding School Experience, 1875–1928*. Lawrence, KA: University Press of Kansas.

Adelstein, M., and Pival, J. (eds.) (1971) *Ecocide and Population*. New York: St. Martin's Press.

Arendt, Hannah. (1980). The Origins of Totalitarianism (New York: Harcourt, Brace and World, 1966). Wolfgang J. Mommsen, ed. Theories of Imperialism (London: Weidenfeld and Nicolson, 1980), 71.

Barsh, R. (1990) Ecocide, Nutrition, and the "Vanishing Indian." In P.L. van den Berghe (ed.) *State Violence and Ethnicity*. Boulder: University Press of Colorado, pp. 221–51.

Andermann, J. (2002) Argentine Literature and the "Conquest of the Desert," 1872–1896. Birkbeck College, University of London. At **www.bbk.ac.uk/ibamuseum/texts/Andermann02.htm**, accessed July 2009.

Berghahn, Volker R. (1994). Imperial Germany, 1871-1914: Economy, Society, Culture, and Politics (Providence, RI: Berghahn Books, 1994), 190-191.

Branche, R. (2004) Torture and Other Violations of the Law by the French Army during the Algerian War. In A. Jones (ed.) *Genocide, War Crimes and the West: History and Complicity*. London: Zed Books, ch. 6.

Bushnell, O. (1993) *The Gifts of Civilization: Germs and Genocide in Hawai'i*. Honolulu: University of Hawaii Press.

Ciarlo, David. (2011) *Advertising Empire: Race and War Visual Culture in Imperial Germany*. London, England: Harvard University Press.

Crosby, A. (1986) The Fortunate Isles. In *Ecological Imperialism: The Biological Expansion of Europe, 900–1900*. Cambridge: Cambridge University Press.

Curthoys, A. (2007) Raphaël Lemkin's Tasmania: An Introduction. In D. Moses and D. Stone (eds.) *Colonialism and Genocide*. London: Routledge.

Curtis, M. (2003) *Web of Deceit: Britain's Real Role in the World*. London: Vintage.

Davis, M. (2001) *Late Victorian Holocausts: El Niño Famines and the Making of the Third World*. London: Verso.

Elkins, C. (2005) *Britain's Gulag: The Brutal End of Empire in Kenya*. London.

Erichsen, Casper and David Olusoga. (2010) *The Kaiser's Holocaust*. London: Faber and Faber.

Esterhuyse, J.H. (1968). South West Africa, 1880-1894: The Establishment of German Authority in South West Africa (Cape Town: C. Struik, 1968), 46. Wehler, Bismarck und Imperialismus, 258. Bismarck called the colonies "*Versorgungsposten.*"

Fieldhouse, David (1966). The Colonial Empires: A Comparative Survey from the Eighteenth Century (London: Weidenfeld and Nicolson, 1966).

Friedrich von Holstein, The Holstein Papers. Second Volume. eds. Norman Rich and M.H. Fisher. (Cambridge: Cambridge University Press, 1955-1963), 161. This specific entry is from 19 September 1884. Bismarck was reported to have used the word *Schwindel* which was translated into the English "sham."

Galtung, Johan "A Structural Theory of Imperialism," Journal of Peace Research 8 (1971): 81.

Geiss, Imanuel. (1976). German Foreign Policy, 1871-1914 (London: Routledge, 1976).

Gewald, J. (2004) Namibia (German South West Africa and South West Africa). In D.L. Shelton (ed.) *Encyclopaedia of Genocide and Crimes against Humanity*. 3 vols, New York: Macmillan, pp. 721–5.

Griffin, R. (2007) *Modernism and Fascism: The Sense of a Beginning under Mussolini and Hitler*. London: Palgrave.

Hans-Christoph Schröder, Sozialismus und Imperialismus: Die Auseinandersetzung der deutschen Sozialdemokratie mit dem Imperialismusproblem und der "Weltpolitik" vor 1914

(Hannover: Verlag für Literature und Zeitgeschehen, 1968), 7-9. Klotz.

Hans-Ulrich Wehler, Bismarck und Imperialismus (Köln: Kiepenheuer und Witsch, 1969), 113-193. Hans-Ulrich Wehler, "Bismarck's Imperialism 1862-1890," Past and Present 48 (August 1970): 120.

Helmut Böhme, "Big-Business Pressure Groups and Bismarck's Turn to Protectionism, 1873-79," Historical Journal 10, no. 2 (1967): 223, 227, 236. "Door-closing panic" is translated from *Torschlußpanik*. Unless otherwise indicated, all translations are mine.

Horst Drechsler. (1971). Let Us Die Fighting: The Struggle of the Herero and Nama against German Imperialism (1884 – 1915) (London 1980) & Bley, Helmut, Namibia under German rule, 1894 – 1914 (London 1971).

Hoxie, F. (1984) *A Final Promise: The Campaign to Assimilate the Indians, 1880–1920.* Lincoln: University of Nebraska Press.

Human Rights Watch Africa (1999) *The Price of Oil: Corporate Responsibility and Human Rights Violations in Nigeria's Oil Producing Communities.* New York: Human Rights Watch.

Hull, Isabel V. (2003). "Military Culture and the Production of 'Final Solutions' in the

Colonies: The Example of Wilhelminian Germany," in The Spectre of Genocide: Mass Murder in Historical Perspective eds. Robert Gellately and Ben Kiernan, (Cambridge, Cambridge University Press, 2003), 147-148. Phillipp Prein, "Guns and Top Hats: African Resistance in German South West Africa, 1907-1915," The International Journal of African Historical Studies 20, no. 1 (1994): 102, 107.

Johnson. S. (2003) *Peace without justice: Hegemonic instability or international criminal law?* London: Ashgate Publishing.

Jones, A. (2006a) *Genocide: A Comprehensive Introduction.* London: Routledge.

Jones, Adam. (2012) *Genocide: A Comprehensive Introduction.* London: Routledge.

Jürgen Kuczynski, Studien zur Geschichte des deutschen Imperialismus. Band I: Monopole und Unternehmerverbände

(Berlin: Dietz, 1948), 285, 318. Müller. Jürgen Kuczynski, Studien zur Geschichte des deutschen Imperialismus. Band II: Propagandaorganisationen des Monopolkapitals (Berlin: Dietz, 1950), 36, 258, 311. Helmuth Stoecker, Drang nach Afrika: Die koloniale Expansionspolitik und Herrschaft des deutschen Imperialismus in Afrika von den Anfängen bis zum Ende des zweiten Weltkrieges (Berlin: Akademie Verlag, 1977).

Kinzer, S. (2007) *Overthrow: America's Century of Regime Change from Hawaii to Iraq*. New York: Times Books.

Landes, David S. (1961). "Some Thoughts on the Nature of Economic Imperialism," Journal of Economic History 21, no. 4 (1961): 498-499.

Lemarchand, René. (2011) *Forgotten Genocides: Oblivion Denial, and Memory*. Philadelphia: University of Pennsylvania Press.

Levene, M. (2005) *Genocide in the Age of Nation State*, vol. 2: *The Rise of the West and the Coming of Genocide*. London: I.B. Tauris.

Lieberman, B. (2006) *Terrible Fate: Ethnic Cleansing in the Making of Modern Europe*. Chicago: Ivan R. Dee

Madley, B. (2004) Patterns of Frontier Genocide, 1803–1910: The Aboriginal Tasmanians, the Yuki of California, and the Herero of Namibia. *Journal of Genocide Research* 6 (2), 167–92.Find this resource:

Mann, M. (2005) *The Dark Side of Democracy: Explaining Ethnic Cleansing*. Cambridge: Cambridge University Press.

Mannoni, Octave. (1956). Prospero and Caliban: The Psychology of Colonization (New York: Praeger, 1956), 18, 29, 202, 204.

Melson, R. (1992) *Revolution and Genocide: On the Origins of the Armenian Genocide and the Holocaust*. Chicago: University of Chicago Press.

Melson, R. (1996) The Armenian Genocide as Precursor and Prototype of Twentieth Century Genocide. In A.S. Rosenbaum (ed.) *Is the Holocaust Unique?* Boulder: Westview, pp. 87–100.

McCarthy, J. (1983) *Muslims and Minorities: Population of Ottoman Anatolia and the End of the Empire*. New York: New York University Press. Find this resource:

Melson, R. (1992) *Revolution and Genocide: On the Origins of the Armenian Genocide and the Holocaust*. Chicago: University of Chicago Press. Find this resource:

Melson, R. (1996) The Armenian Genocide as Precursor and Prototype of Twentieth Century Genocide. In A.S. Rosenbaum (ed.) *Is the Holocaust Unique?* Boulder: Westview, pp. 87–100.

Meritt, H.P. (1978). "Bismarck and the German Interest in East Africa, 1884-1885," Historical Journal 21, no. 1 (1978): 97-116. C.D. Penner, "Germany and the Transvaal before 1896," Journal of Modern History 12 (March 1940): 31-59. G.N. Sanderson, "The Anglo-G 2012) German Agreement of 1890 and the Upper Nile," English Historical Review 78, no. 306, (1963): 49-72. A.J.P. Taylor, Germany's First Bid for Colonies. 1884-1885: A Move in Bismarck's European Policy (London: Macmillan and Co., 1938).

Mommsen, Theories of Imperialism, 149. Jean-Paul Sartre, Colonialism and NeoColonialism (New York: Routledge, 2001), 30-31, 44.

Moses, A. (ed.) (2004) *Genocide and Settler Society: Frontier Violence and Stolen Indigenous Children in Australian History.* Oxford: Berghahn.

Moses, A. (ed.) (2004) *Genocide and Settler Society: Frontier Violence and Stolen Indigenous Children in Australian History.* Oxford: Berghahn. Find this resource:

Moses, A. (2008a) Genocide and Modernity. In D. Stone (ed.) *The Historiography of Genocide.* Houndmills: Palgrave Macmillan, pp. 156–93.Find this resource:

Moses, A. (ed.) (2008b) *Empire, Colony, Genocide. Conquest, Occupation, and Subaltern Resistance in World History.* Oxford: Berghahn. Find this resource:

Moses, D., and Stone, D. (eds.) (2007) *Colonialism and Genocide.* London: Routledge.

Plank, G. (2001) *An Unsettled Conquest: The British Campaign against the Peoples of Acadia.* Cambridge: Cambridge University Press.

Platt, D.C.M. (1968). "The Imperialism of Free Trade: Some Reservations," Economic History Review 21, no. 2 (August 1968): 296-306. Hallgarten identifies the cause of imperialism in human psychology as well as capitalist economic forces. George Wolfgang Felix Hallgarten, Imperialismus vor 1914: die soziologischen Grundlagen der Aussenpolitik europäischer Grossmächte vor dem Ersten Weltkrieg (München: Beck, 1963).

Pierard, Richard Victor. (1964)."The German Colonial Society, 1882-1914" (Ph.D. diss., State University of Iowa, 1964), 4, 258. Klotz, 47.

Pogge von Strandmann, H. (1969). "Domestic Origins of Germany's Colonial Expansion," Past and Present 42 (1969): 142-144.

Porteous, J., and Smith, S. (2001) *Domicide: The Global Destruction of Home.* Montreal: McGill-Queen's University Press.

Ronald Robinson and John Gallagher, Africa and the Victorians: The Official Mind of Imperialism (London: Macmillan, 1961).

Shakya, T. (1999) *The Dragon in the Land of Snows: A History of Modern Tibet since 1947.* London: Pimlico.

Stannard, D. (1992) *American Holocaust: The Conquest of the New World.* Oxford: Oxford University Press.

Ray, L. (2007) *Language of the Land: The Mapuche in Argentina and Chile.* Copenhagen: International Work Group for Indigenous Affairs (IWGIA).Find this resource:

Rock, D. (2002) *State Building and Political Movements in Argentina, 1860–1916.* Stanford: Stanford University Press.

Röhl, John C. G. (1967). Germany without Bismarck: The Crisis of Government in the Second Reich, 1890-1900 (Berkeley: University of California Press, 1967), 160-166, 272.

Ronald Robinson and John Gallagher, "The Imperialism of Free Trade," Economic History Review 6 (1953): 12.

Rubinstein, W. (2004) *Genocide: A History.* Harlow, UK: Pearson-Longman.

Said, Edward W. (1994). Culture and Imperialism (New York: Vintage, 1993). Nicholas Thomas, Colonialism's Culture: Anthropology, Travel and Government (Princeton, NJ: Princeton University Press, 1994).

Sarkin, Jeremy. (2010) *Germany's Genocide of the Herero: Kaiser Wilhelm II, His General, His Settlers, His Soldiers.* Cape Town, South Africa: UCT Press.

Silvester, J., and Gewald, J. (2003) *Words Cannot Be Found: German Colonial Rule in Namibia: An Annotated Reprint of the 1918 Blue Book.* Leiden: Brill.

Townsend, Mary Evelyn. (1943)."The Economic Impact of Imperial German Commercial and Colonial Policies," Journal of Economic History 3 (December 1943): 124-126. Penner, 57.

Prosser Gifford and William Roger Louis. eds. Britain and Germany in Africa: Imperial Rivalry and Colonial Rule (New Haven: Yale University Press, 1967), 716,719.

Müller. Horst Drechsler, Aufstände in Südwestafrika: der Kampfe der Herero und

Nama, 1904-1907, gegen die deutsche Kolonialherrschaft (Berlin: Dietz, 1984), 17, 146148. Horst Drechsler, "Let Us Die Fighting:" The Struggle of the Herero and Nama against German Imperialism (1884-1915) (London: Zed Press, 1980), 3.

Sunseri, Thaddeus. (2001). "*Baumwollfrage*: Colonialism and the Wool Trade," Central European History 34, no. 1 (2001): 32.

Ulrich van der Heyden and Joachim Zeller, eds. Kolonialmetropole Berlin: Eine

Spurensuche (Berlin: Berlin Edition, 2002). Birthe Kundrus, ed. Phantasiereiche: Zur Kulturegeschichte des deutschen Kolonialismus (Frankfurt: Campus Verlag, 2003).

Pascale Grosse, Kolonialismus, Eugenik und bürgerliche Gesellschaft in Deutschland

1850-1918 (Frankfurt am Main: Campus Verlag, 2000). Marianne Bechhaus-Gerst and

Reinhard Klein-Arendt, eds. Die (koloniale) Begegnung: AfrikanerInnen in Deutschland 1880-1945, Deutsche in Afrika 1880-1918 (Frankfurt am Main: Peter Lang, 2003). Sara Friedrichsmeyer, Sara Lennox and Susanne Zantop, eds. The Imperialist Imagination:

German Colonialism and Its Legacy (Ann Arbor: University of Michigan Press, 1998).

Vladimir Lenin's 1917 *Imperialism, The Highest Stage of Capitalism* and Rosa Luxemburg's 1913 *The Accumulation of Capital*. Kenneth J. Tarbuck, ed. Imperialism and the Accumulation of Capital by Rosa Luxemburg and Nikolai Bukharin, (London: Penguin Press, 1972).

Werner Frauendienst, Das deutsche Reich von 1890 bis 1914 (Konstanz: Akademische Verlagsgesellschaft Athenaion, 1959).

Winfried Baumgart, "Die Deutsche Kolonialherrschaft in Afrika: Neue Wege derForschung," Vierteljahrsschrift für Sozial und Wirtschaftsgeschichte 58 (1971): 469, 481. Wehler, "Bismarck's Imperialism," 119.

Wolfgang J. Mommsen, Review of Bismarck und der Imperialismus by Hans-Ulrich Wehler Central European History 2 (1969): 371.

Zimmerer, Jürgen. (2003) *Genocide in German South-West Africa: The Colonial War of 1904-1908 and Its Aftermath.* Monmouth, Wales: Merlin Press.

Chapter Six

Theoretical Reprise, Summary, Conclusion and Way Forward

Theoretical Reprise: On War and Genocide in General

If it is not "war" itself that is the cause of genocide, nevertheless, *ideas* of war are important in the production of that genocide itself. In other words, genocide occurs when an organized, armed collective actor comes to define a social group or population as an *enemy*, not merely in a political but in an essentially military sense, i.e. as an enemy *to be destroyed*. This statement vividly explains why there is consensus that interstate wars provide an ideal circumstance for carrying out atrocities, which would be unthinkable otherwise (see Melson, 1992; Bartrop, 2002; Fettweis, 2003; Shaw 2003; Levene, 2005). Bartov's (1996) work on Hitler's war in the East anticipated much of this war-centred approach. Under the aegis of total war, pressures toward ethnic and cultural homogenization reach their peak. Yet homogenizing practices can persist long after wars end. They were pursued under Soviet rule to the late 1980s, and continue in subtler ways in several liberal democratic regimes till today. Although extreme measures became less common, assimilationist policies persist.

When the Anglo-French allied forces landed at Gallipoli in 1915, Turkey's military authorities began a "securitization" campaign against the entire Armenian population, whom they perceived as the West's "fifth column." "What turned a war crime into a genocidal act was the context of total war [...] that translated deportation swiftly into the mass slaughter, abuse, and starvation of an entire ethnic group potentially troublesome to an authoritarian regime at war" (Winter, 2003:208). Under siege by the "West," Turkey's elites ended up imitating the West. As a consequence, their military nationalism bred a "culture of hatred" that demonized Christians and non-Turks. The Shoah was also carried out during the peak of war.

Might indiscriminate aerial bombing during wartime be classified as a genocidal act as well? Some authors regard the intentional bombing of civilian populations just short of genocide (i.e. Shaw, 2003). Examples include Saddam Hussein's chemical strikes on Iraqi Kurds (Jones, 2003), the US attack on neutral Cambodia (Owen and Kiernan, 2006), the Luftwaffe's carpet bombing of the Basque market town of Guernica (Conversi 1997), the Italian army's use of mustard gas against Libyan and Ethiopian civilians in the years prior to World War II (Walston, 1997; Del Boca, 2005; Conversi, 2009) and, controversially, the Anglo-American bombing of Dresden and other German cities during World War II, which nevertheless followed the Nazis' carpet bombings of cities like Coventry, London, Warsaw, and Rotterdam (Langenbacher, 2004). Some authors warn against confusing war crimes with organized plans of extermination as "a political and intellectual mistake, symptomatic of our culture of sensationalism" (Hatzfeld, 2005:105–6). However, most approaches recognize that the inhumanity of war and the unaccountability of wartime leaders provide the key to understanding both genocides and related tragedies. Hiroshima and Nagasaki have been called the first instances of a "nuclear holocaust" (Alperovitz, 1995). The long-term impact of both international war and local wars on defenceless civilians remains difficult to assess. As Ghobarah et al. (2003) remind us, "civil wars kill and maim people long after the shooting stops." Indeed, in Afghanistan and Cambodia the devastating legacy of land-mines has led to massive human displacement, especially in the countryside.

Summary

"We Germans acknowledge our historical, political, moral and ethical responsibility and the guilt that Germans brought upon themselves", said Heidemarie Wieczorek-Zeul during a visit to Namibia back in 2004. Speaking at the Waterberg, where Emperor Wilhelm II's troops had mercilessly put down a rebellion against German colonial rule a hundred years earlier, the then minister for development aid was close to tears.

For decades, Germany's colonial history was of no interest, as it was relatively short-lived (1884 –1919) and was viewed as unremarkable. Scholars ignored the influence that Social Darwinists and eugenicists had in late-19th-century; creating new values of totalitarian dominance modelled on Darwin's *On the Origin of Species*, with its brutal account of nature as a competitive violent struggle for survival. Germany applied these values brutally in the African colonies.

As a new generation of German historians began to examine the history of German colonialism in South West Africa (today Namibia), the genocide of the Herero people emerged out of oblivion. Germany's colonies in South West Africa were a testing ground for Darwinian racial science, & genocide.

In what is often called the twentieth century's first genocide, the German colonial authorities, from 1904 to 1906, set out systematically to exterminate two ethnic groups, the Herero and the Nama, following an uprising in what was then German South West Africa and what is now Namibia. The Namibian government is currently in talks with the German government to demand that Berlin officially acknowledge that the genocide took place, issue an apology, and pay reparations. While Germany has already acknowledged the genocide occurred, it rejects any legal responsibility. International law did not address genocide at the time, argue the Germans. According to the Wall Street Journal, a German diplomat said, "The German government uses this term (of genocide) in a historical-political sense, not in a legal sense." Germany also opposes reparations, which legally "implies liability."

In terms of historical hindsight, tens of thousands of Herero and Nama people were killed by the so-called "protective troops" or died in concentration camps in the years after the 1904 battle. It was the first genocide of the 20th century, historians say. Namibia had waited a long time for such words, but the German government of the time backed off, saying Wieczorek-Zeul had spoken as a private person. The backpedalling fitted a decades-old pattern: No matter what government happened to be in power, the country won international respect for coming to terms with the Holocaust, while at the same time its colonial past was ignored.

In 1904, Germany adopted a racist policy in its colony, issuing an edict that introduced a new German legal concept – *Rassenschande* (racial defilement). The edict banned intermarriage between German colonists and Africans. This policy was followed by a racial policy of annihilation —*Vernichtung* – a decade before World War I.

In 1904, about 150 German settlers were killed during the Herero uprising, though (as historian Peter Gay noted) *"gallantly enough, they spared women, children, and other foreigners."* The German response did not spare Herero women and children. General Lothar von Trotha, a hard-line Prussian army officer was in charge. He called the insurrection, *"the beginning of a racial struggle"* and led 10,000 to 14,000 troops; his stated goal was the extermination of the Herero nation:

> It was and is my policy to use force with terrorism and even brutality. I shall annihilate the revolting tribes with rivers of blood and rivers of gold. Only after a complete uprooting will something emerge." *(Rivers of Blood, Rivers of Gold* by Mark Coker, 2001) [Another translation: "I know that African tribes yield only to violence. To exercise this violence with crass terrorism and even with gruesomeness was and is my policy. (Richard Evans, *The Third Reich in History and Memory*, 2015).

After defeating the Herero force at Waterberg, Trotha announced that any Herero *"found inside the German frontier, with or without a gun or cattle would be executed."* Herero cattle-herders caught in the action were killed on the spot; women and children were driven into the desert to die of starvation; he even ordered their waterholes to be poisoned.

Protests from religious factions in Germany led to a change in policy; the natives were driven into 'concentration camps' — *Konzentrationslager* — where they were brutalized and starved as slave labourers. The estimated Herero population was reduced from 80,000 to 15,000; and of the 20,000 Nama tribe only 10,000 survived. There was a backlash and Trotha was recalled to Germany in 1905.

Notwithstanding the protests, the official German General Staff publication, *Der Kampf,* referred to Trotha's campaign of *"extermination of the Herero nation"* as a "brilliant" accomplishment. After the war, colonial rule imposed travel restrictions and all native peoples above the age of seven were required to wear a metal disc with a numbered identification. Bley documented this racially motivated genocidal massacre (1904-1907), noting that eugenics was invoked as its justification. He suggested that the Herero/Nama genocide was the prototype for the Holocaust.

The 1960s was an era bent on denial and forgetting; it has been described as "the Great Silence" a time when no German was interested in delving into atrocities committed by the German government– not the Jewish Holocaust, nor the one in the former African colony. So the question of comparisons remained unaddressed until the 1990s.

When interest in German colonial history was revived in the 1990s, colonial origins of racial science and the history of Germany's colonizing experience suddenly seemed irrelevant to historians of the Nazi era. German colonists imposed a totalitarian regime on the cattle-raising tribes, Herero and Nama, modelled on Darwin's *Origin of Species* and the belief that the natural order is a competitive violent struggle for survival of the fittest.

Between 1904-1908, the Herero and Nama tribes were slaughtered; thousands were shot and thousands more were herded into *Konzentrationslager*— *"concentration camps" (the first official German use of the term)* —where they were starved, brutalized, and worked to death. At Shark Island – known as a "death camp"– prisoners were used in gruesome scientific experiments. Their severed heads were measured and catalogued by German anatomists and physical anthropologists. Foremost among these was anthropologist/eugenicist Eugen Fischer, the director of the Kaiser Wilhelm Institute of Anthropology. He sought to prove the superiority of the Aryan race – both in SW Africa and later as the leading 'racial hygienist' under the Third Reich. At least 300 skulls were shipped to Germany for further research.

The Kaiser's race engineers used callipers and craniometry charts to measure the severed heads of Nama tribesmen; their ears and feet were considered "apish" telltale atavisms. Zoologist Leopard Schultze noted that taking *"body parts from fresh native corpses was a welcome addition."* An estimated 300 skulls were sent to Germany for experimentation; many from concentration camp prisoners.

Historians emphasize the fact that while other colonial occupiers were brutal, German racism was extreme; in 1905, it entered German legal terminology – *Rassenschande* (racial defilement) – when marriage between German colonists in South Africa and Africans was banned. The eminent British historian, Richard Evans noted that:

> Only the Germans introduced concentration camps, named them as such and deliberately created conditions so harsh that their purpose was clearly as much to exterminate their inmates as it was to force them to work. (It would be left to the Nazis to devise the chilling term 'extermination through labour'.)
>
> Only the Nazis mounted an explicit attempt to exterminate an entire colonized people on racial grounds. Only the Germans legally banned intermarriage in their colonies. Only Germans subsequently mounted a campaign of racial extermination on a global scale which encompassed not only Europe's Jews but also, potentially, the Jewish inhabitants of the rest of the world. Was there a connection between the two?" (Evans, *The Third Reich in History and Memory*, 2015).

In sum, the first genocide of the 20th century occurred not in Europe but in Southwest Africa, a colony that had been annexed by Germany in the early 1880s. Estimates suggest as many as 80 percent of the nomadic Herero tribe—believed to number around 100,000 a century ago— perished, either killed by German soldiers or left to die of thirst and starvation in the desert. The violence and indignity did not end there. Moved by the racist eugenics of the time, German authorities shipped thousands of skulls and other body parts of the aboriginal dead back to Europe. The specimens were subjected to studies that formed the basis for now-discredited theories of European racial superiority. Many of the skulls belonged to tribesmen left to die in squalid concentration camps in the desert; their bodies were beheaded. In some instances, according to a 2011 article in *Der Spiegel*, widows were ordered to use shards of glass to scrape the flesh off their husbands' heads so as to better prepare the skulls for transport.

Summary

The first genocide of the 20th century occurred not in Europe but in Southwest Africa, a colony that had been annexed by Germany in the early 1880s. Between August 1904 and 1907, the Germans attempted to exterminate the indigenous Ovaherero people, along with the groups of rebellious Khoikhoi.

Although most outsiders use the name "Herero", "Ovaherero" is more linguistically accurate. The disadvantage of both names is that they lump together the eastern Namibian Ovambanderu, who have never considered themselves unambiguously part of a uniform "Herero" nation, with the Otjiherero-speaking populations around Okahandja and Omaruru. The Southern African Khoikhoi were called "Hottentots" in colonial racist jargon. The Germans did not succeed in killing all of these insurgents, but their explicit intentional effort to do so qualifies their actions clearly as genocidal.

For years German leaders who visited Southwest Africa's postcolonial successor state of Namibia refused to meet with Ovaherero representatives. The German Democratic Republic took in refugees from Apartheid-era Namibia and helped South West African Peoples' Organization (SWAPO) in its struggle against the South African apartheid regime both financially and militarily. (See Ulrich van der Heyden, Ilona Schleicher, and Hans-Georg Schleicher, *Die DDR und Afrika* (Münster: Lit, 1993-1994). But this past summer, the German Minister for Economic Cooperation and Development, Heidemarie Wieczorek-Zeul, spoke to Ovaherero leaders at the Waterberg during the commemoration of the 1904 war and acknowledged "the violence inflicted by the German colonial powers on your ancestors, particularly the Herero and the Nama" and "the atrocities committed." Wieczorek-Zeul also admitted that "following the uprisings, the surviving Herero, Nama and Damara were interned in camps and put to forced labour of such brutality that many did not survive." More ambiguously, the German Minister concluded that "the atrocities committed at that time would *today* be termed genocide."

There are several reasons for this hedging around the word genocide even by a left-wing German government of Social Democrats and Greens. First, the Chief Hosea Kutako Foundation, headed by the Ovaherero Paramount Chief Kuaima Riruako, filed lawsuits against the German government and several firms (including the Deutsche Bank and SAFmarine) whose predecessors profited from the use of Ovaherero slave labour between 1904 and 1907. A second reason is that other former colonial powers would certainly

241

disapprove of a German admission of responsibility for colonial genocide, given the broad and varying definitions of that term. The definition in the United Nations "Convention on the Prevention and Punishment of the Crime of Genocide" includes "causing serious bodily or *mental* harm to members of the group." According to Raphael Lemkin (. (1944: 79), who first defined the term genocide, it does not necessarily mean the immediate destruction of a nation, except when accomplished by mass killings of all members of a nation. It is intended rather to signify a coordinated plan of different actions aiming at the destruction of essential foundations of the life of national groups, with the aim of annihilating the groups themselves. The objectives of such a plan would be disintegration of the political and social institutions, of culture, language, national feelings, religion, and the economic existence of national groups, and the destruction of the personal security, liberty, health, dignity, and even the lives of the individuals belonging to such groups.

All modern colonial governments starting with the Spanish conquistadors in America could easily be accused of promoting such "cultural disintegration" or of causing "mental harm", and hence, perhaps, of genocide. Third, *denial* of the Ovaherero genocide is widespread in Germany and among descendants of colonial settlers in present-day Namibia. The absence of exact figures on the size of the Ovaherero population before 1904 and on the number killed in 1904 is emphasized by the specialists in genocide denial, despite the fact that the decisive criterion for genocide is *intention*, not the degree of success. The Germans clearly intended to exterminate their Ovaherero subjects, and this goal was approved at the highest levels of the German metropolitan government in Berlin.

A final reason some Germans may be reluctant to acknowledge the character of the events of 1904 may be the desire not to be saddled with official responsibility for yet another case of genocide—especially one that some historians interpret as having laid part of the groundwork for the Nazi Holocaust. In Thomas Pynchon's novel *V*, Southwest Africa is described as setting the stage for Nazism, and in *Gravity's Rainbow* the Ovaherero resurface in Nazi Germany as the "Schwarzkommando" who worship a rocket program and are dressed in pieces "of old Wehrmacht and SS uniforms." This is of course entirely fictional, but it does gesture toward the widespread sense of continuity between "Southwest Africa" and Nazism, and toward Ovaherero survivors' adoption of many of the cultural attributes of their oppressors after 1904.

Ovaherero converted in great numbers to Christianity in the concentration camps after resisting missionary blandishments for more than a half century. Many Ovaherero men began to wear odd bits of German military uniforms. These practices emerged out of the post-1904 context of defeat, identification with the aggressor, and German "native polices" that emphasized an abject form of partial assimilation which turned Ovaherero survivors into isolated proletarians. Ovaherero were given German names or simply numbers, their land was seized and sold to German settlers, and their traditional authority structure was banned. Because Ovaherero culture and religion revolved centrally around livestock, they were forbidden from owning cattle. The *oturupa*, or "troop players" movement, was initially a degraded version of the enemy's culture. During the decade after WWI, *oturupa* organized themselves into districts, with regiments and ranking individuals taking the names and titles of their former German officers. They conducted German-style drills and sent each other notes written in German. The *oturupa* and the Evangelical church also became sites of mutual aid and anticolonial resistance after 1918 and continued to accumulate new meanings.

Genocide, Modernity, and Westernization

Story and fact are always in uneasy tension with each other. No matter how carefully we line up the historical data or how honestly we report the actual events through which we have lived, these do not by themselves tell the story of our lives. To tell all is not to tell a tale. Getting the facts straight is not enough to find the story to which they belong. In fact, getting the facts straight is a very different activity from that of finding a story that can be 'faithful' to the facts of genocidal Western imperialism.

Indeed, imperialism cannot be understood merely as an economic-military system of control and exploitation. Cultural domination is an integral dimension to any sustained system of global exploitation. In relation to the Third World, cultural imperialism can be defined as the systematic penetration and domination of the cultural life of the popular classes by the ruling class of the West in order to reorder the values, behaviour, institutions and identity of the oppressed peoples to conform with the interests of the imperial classes. Cultural imperialism has taken both 'traditional' and modern forms. In past centuries, the Church, educational system, and public authorities played a major role in inculcating native peoples with ideas of submission and loyalty in the name of divine or absolutist principles. While these 'traditional' mechanisms of cultural imperialism still operate, new modern instrumentalities rooted in contemporary institutions have become increasingly central to imperial domination.

Westernization is a pervasive modern phenomenon. Its impact is more pervasive and pernicious than many people are aware and/or willing to admit. The spread of the dominant Western culture has caused a gradual demise of many peripheral cultures. The incursion of Western agents into African soil, beginning with British military conquest and American missionary intrusion, has resulted in a significant influence and westernization of the continent and their culture and worldview. Consequently, it is almost a cliché to assert that since colonial contact the long-evolved African traditional values are being replaced by Western values. Today, the literal colonization of Africans by the imperial West has ended, but the process of westernization is continuing, thanks to the ongoing influence being exerted by modern media, technology and other trends of globalization. I am not highlighting the 'form' or 'material' aspect of the culture, such as clothing (although mimicry in this area is almost faultless among a large section of Africa. Rather, my goal has been to discuss the current state of mindset and fundamental cultural structures of the African that have resulted from the adjustments in the lives and minds of the people because of the imposition of westernization. In fact, it is more than merely a process of adjustment consequent upon conquest, it is an extensive overhauling of cultural institutions, values and practices.

Cultural standardization and genocide share a similarly modern trajectory. The correlation between nationalism and modernity depends on how the latter is defined. Whether we identify modernity entirely within the philosophical (Enlightenment and post-

Enlightenment), the political (French Revolution), the economic (ascent of the bourgeoisie), the scientific (Darwinism), or the technological (Industrial Revolution) sphere, we can find each of these senses well represented within radical nationalism, particularly Nazism. The latter was indeed inconceivable without, or outside, modernity as intended in any of the above senses. It can be associated with the spread of Jacobin-inspired centralism and state idolatry, the protection of bourgeois interests, the diffusion of "only the fittest survive" racialism, and, finally, massive industrialization.

Key members of the Frankfurt School, notably Max Horkheimer and Theodor Adorno, were among the first to identify genocide as an intrinsic feature of modernity (Kaye and Strath, 2000). Zygmunt Bauman described the Holocaust as "a rare, yet significant and reliable, test of the hidden possibilities of modern society" (1989:12). Hannah Arendt (1958) has similarly related the Holocaust to modernity, with its massive human dislocations. For Richard Rubenstein (1987:284), the Holocaust "bears witness to the *advance of civilization*" (as noted by Bauman 1989:9) and conveys some of "the dominant trends in contemporary civilization." The process leading to the Holocaust accompanied the rise of rapidly modernizing nation-states in the West and followed the demise of multiethnic empires (Lieberman 2006). It began "in the late Eighteenth century and [is] still continuing" (Bartov 1996:70). For Levene "the issue goes to the heart of the evolution and crystallization of the modern world as we know it and, not least, the current international system of nation-states which emanated from it" (2005:10). Indeed, it can be described as a "product of the most 'advanced' stage in the development of the modern state" (Naimark 2001:8). According to Edward Said, modernity's quest to dominate the planet was predicated on a drive "to divide, deploy, schematize, tabulate, index, and record everything in sight (and out of sight); to make out of every observable detail a generalization and out of every generalization an immutable law" (1995:86). This modern obsession with ordering, studying, documenting, measuring, and hierarchizing was first experimented on the West's colonial subjects. It was already discernible in the pre-Enlightenment methods by which Spanish elites had attempted to classify Native Americans between 1512 and 1724 (Pagden 1986). Later, fingerprinting technology was pioneered in the British Empire, as Britain was reluctant to apply these measures of surveillance and control at home (Sengoopta 2003).

According to Porter (2000), eliminationism is the way modernity was perceived by Poland's elites as they aspired to "tame" the masses via exclusionary nationalism. Poland's early romantic intellectuals espoused a voluntarist, "Renanian" concept of the nation, in which the "deed" (*czyn*) for the new Polish state played a central role (Porter 2000). This initially open project failed, turning into an authoritarian ethnicism just when literacy was expanding and linguistic Russification was identified as a major threat. Polish elites manipulated public opinion into hatred against "non-Poles." The subsequent destruction of the "Yiddish nation," mostly within Poland, has been the focus of a fresh wave of investigation (Weinstein 2001; Gottesman 2003; Kriwaczek 2005).

By most historical standards, the first modern *genocide* was perpetrated at the hands of westernizing Turkish nationalism during the final collapse of the Ottoman Empire (Alvarez 2001:11–14; Rae 2002:124–62; Power 2003:1–23; Weitz 2003:1–7; Mann 2005:111–78; Jones 2006A:101–23; Carmichael 2009). However, the Armenian genocide was preceded by massive episodes of ethnic cleansing throughout the Balkans. In Russia, pogroms against Jews and Muslims had been carried out with unprecedented ferocity. More Jews were killed in Russia between 1903 and 1906 than in Nazi Germany's *Kristallnacht* (in 1938). With a hint of revenge, the "lesson" was quickly learned in Turkey, where massive numbers of Chechen, Circassian, and Bosnian refugees from these areas had fled, uncovering horrific stories of ethnically based mass brutality. The entire post-1864 *Muhajir* (exodus) is a still neglected area of research (Levene and Roberts 1999; Shenfield 1999).

Many forms of ethnic cleansing accompany, or follow, waves of cultural Westernization. Israel's attacks on the Palestinians expanded in tandem with the country's self description as a bulwark of the West, particularly the US, and Serbia's ethnic cleansing of Muslims and other nationalities has been justified as an attempt to protect the West against the "Islamic threat."

The Young Turks' annihilation campaigns were the first of their genre and inspired other genocidal killers, most notoriously Adolf Hitler (see Hovannisian 1988; 1998; Dadrian 1996; Melson 1996;

Power 2003:23; Winter 2003; Jones 2006A:101). In turn, Lemkin's career as an international lawyer was deeply shaped by his youth years reading of the Armenian genocide (Power 2003). Armenian nationalists claim that these campaigns were part of a recurring pattern of persecution (see Dadrian 1996). However, a comparison between the pre-1915 anti-Armenian pogroms and the fully fledged genocide carried out once Turkish nationalists seized power shows a radical shift in strategy. The intent was to "solve" the Armenian question by eliminating the group as a whole. Bloxham (2003) identified the unfolding of events as resulting from a process of "cumulative radicalization," more than as a centrally planned and coordinated eradication effort. However, the responsibility of Turkey's military elites has been ascertained by international scholars beyond any realistic doubt (see Mann 2005; Üngor 2008; Carmichael 2009). Although it is difficult to identify any starting point for the Armenian genocide (Kaligian 2008), two "points of no return" can be identified. The first was the general arrests of April 1915, when the "secular" Ittihad ve Terakki Cemiyeti (Committee of Union and Progress) began to deport the bulk of the Armenian elite, including those who were assimilated and loyally serving the state. A second irreversible step was the general deportation order of May 1915 affecting all Armenians and leading directly to the death by torture, famine, and assassination of most deportees (Üngor 2006). Both events occurred in the midst of World War I and affected non-Armenians as well. In fact, over 100,000 Christians of all denominations became victims of the massacres (Schaller and Zimmerer 2008), along with hundreds of thousands of Arabs and Kurds. Government fears were largely unfounded, since until the very last moment even Armenian and Kurdish "nationalists" continued to envision themselves as loyal members of a multinational Ottoman Empire (Klein 2007), an outcome that became then impossible.

Because of Westernization, development has become a buzzword in recent decades. No longer do we have the 'first' and 'third' world. We have the 'developed' and the 'underdeveloped' world. Typically the developed world is understood to be Western countries, while the underdeveloped world comprises former colonies in the Global South in Asia, Africa and Latin America. We tend to consider development in purely Western and monetary terms, without consideration for local cultural norms and cultural differences. Development has become a doctrine that is aggressively spread by Western states and NGOs, often at the expense of local communities and their standard of living.

Developing states are presented in negative terms in the media and, at times, by NGOs themselves. They are presented as backward, inferior and in need of 'rescuing'. The assumption is that the developing world needs to be pulled into modernity, its 'tribal' culture banished. Poor countries should be made to resemble Western states with highways and sprawling cities. NGOs, of course, tend to take their agenda from Western governments and the transnational corporations that fund them.

White, Western-educated consultants trot across the globe, providing their 'expertise' on how best to develop a given community. The International Monetary Fund and World Bank set structural adjustment programs that swept across Africa in the Cold-War era. These programs served only to distort problems and in some circumstances contributed to political violence and unrest. The World Bank continues to contribute to the misery of those living in the 'underdeveloped' world.

The idea that everyone should be westernized and have access to Western goods, medicine, education and global capitalist markets means that local education systems, for example, are deemed to be redundant and outdated. The use of indigenous medicine is also undermined because it doesn't fit into 'modern' Western medicinal norms. Yet indigenous medicinal knowledge is often rooted in history and proven to be successful at curing ailments.

In Search of a World without Genocide

Genocide is now understood as a major type of collective violence, with a distinctive place in the spectrum of political violence, armed conflict, and war, of which it is usually seen as a part. However the idea of genocide dates only from the 1940s, when in the space of four years after its introduction (in a critique of Nazi occupation policies during the Second World War), it became the subject of a major international convention. The concept quickly become central to political and cultural discourses about violence, but the developed academic study of the phenomenon took some decades to develop, before finally taking off around the end of the Cold War. The rapidly expanding field is interdisciplinary, with major contributions from historians, sociologists, political scientists, anthropologists, legal scholars, and others. It has highly contested parameters, including the definition of the phenomenon, the universe of cases, the appropriate explanatory frameworks, and so on. It is also considerably politicized, with significant disagreements over how the academic study of genocide should be related to the development of international policies for its prevention. The field's growth came initially through the extension of understandings of the Nazi genocide of the Jews, which by the late 20th century was known as "the Holocaust," to other cases, both historic (such as the Ottoman extermination of the Armenians) and contemporary (such as the Cambodian and Rwandan genocides). However, it has since expanded to consider phenomena quite different from the Holocaust in scale and form, such as the diverse and long-drawn-out pattern of genocide during European colonization of the non-Western world. At the same time, the transformations of political violence and war in the post–Cold War world have led to new divergences over the applicability of the genocide idea to recent events. Recent cases, such as the former Yugoslavia, have raised questions about the relationships of population removal and sexual violence to genocide. Because of these tensions, the growth of the field has been accompanied by theoretical, paradigm, and political differences.

The text of the Convention for the Prevention and Punishment of the Crime of Genocide was adopted by the United Nations General Assembly on 9 December 1948. After obtaining the requisite twenty ratifications required by article XIII, the Convention entered into force on 12 January 1951. The term "genocide" was first used by Raphael Lemkin in his book *Axis Rule in Occupied Europe*, published in late 1944. Although the word appears in the drafting history of the Charter of the International Military Tribunal, the final text of that instrument uses the cognate term "crimes against humanity" to deal with the persecution and physical extermination of national, ethnic, racial and religious minorities. Prosecutors also used the term occasionally in their submissions to the Nuremberg Tribunal, but "genocide" does not appear in the final judgment, issued on 30 September - 1 October 1946.

The failure of the International Military Tribunal to condemn what some called "peacetime genocide" prompted immediate efforts within the United Nations General Assembly. In effect, the Tribunal had confined the scope of crimes against humanity to acts perpetrated after the outbreak of war, in September 1939. At the first session of the General Assembly, in late 1946, Cuba, Panama and India presented a draft resolution that had two objectives: a declaration that genocide was a crime that could be committed in peacetime as well as in time of war, and recognition that genocide was subject to universal jurisdiction (that is, it could be prosecuted by any State, even in the absence of a territorial or personal link). General Assembly resolution 96 (I), adopted on 11 December 1946, affirmed "that genocide is a crime under international law which the civilized world condemns" and mandated the preparation of a draft convention on the crime of genocide. It was silent as to whether the crime could be committed in peacetime, and although it described genocide as a crime "of international concern", it provided no clarification on the subject of jurisdiction.

Drafting of the Genocide Convention

Drafting of the Convention proceeded in three main stages. First, the United Nations Secretariat composed a draft text. Prepared with the assistance of three experts, Raphael Lemkin, Vespasian Pella and Henri Donnedieu de Vabres, it was actually a compendium of concepts meant to assist the General Assembly rather than any attempt to provide a workable instrument or to resolve major differences. Second, the Secretariat draft was reworked by an Ad Hoc Committee set up under the authority of the Economic and Social Council. Finally, the Ad Hoc Committee draft was the basis of negotiations in the Sixth Committee of the General Assembly, in late 1948, which agreed upon the final text of the Convention, submitting it for formal adoption to the plenary General Assembly.

Certain aspects of the drafting history of the Convention have figured in subsequent interpretation of some of its provisions. For example, the definition of genocide set out in article II is a much-reduced version of the text prepared by the Secretariat experts, who had divided genocide into three categories, physical, biological and cultural genocide. The Sixth Committee voted to exclude cultural genocide from the scope of the Convention, although it subsequently agreed to an exception to this general rule, allowing "forcible transfer of children from one group to another" as a punishable act. The drafters also voted down, by a very substantial margin, an amendment that sought to add a sixth punishable act to article II. It would have enabled prosecution for imposing "measures intended to oblige members of a group to abandon their homes in order to escape the threat of subsequent ill-treatment". References to these debates have bolstered judicial decisions that essentially exclude "ethnic cleansing" from the scope of the definition.

In addition, the drafters quite explicitly rejected universal jurisdiction for the crime. Article VI recognizes only territorial jurisdiction, as well as the jurisdiction of an international criminal tribunal. There was, of course, no international criminal tribunal at the time. But when it agreed to the Convention, the General Assembly also adopted a resolution directing that work begin on a draft statute for such a court. This was the beginning of sporadic work that would eventually lead, half a century later, to the adoption of the Rome Statute of the International Criminal Court.

Over the next fifty years, the two related but distinct concepts of genocide and crimes against humanity had an uneasy relationship. Not only was genocide recognized by treaty, it came with important ancillary obligations, including a duty to prevent the crime, an obligation to enact legislation and to punish the crime, and a requirement to cooperate in extradition. Article IX gave the International Court of Justice jurisdiction over disputes between States parties concerning the interpretation and application of the Convention. Crimes against humanity were also recognized in a treaty, the Charter of the International Military Tribunal, but one that was necessarily of limited scope and whose effective application concluded when the judgment of the first Nuremberg trial was issued. The only other obligations with regard to crimes against humanity at the time existed by virtue of customary international law.

Key Provisions of the Convention

The preamble makes reference to General Assembly resolution 96 (I), and re-affirms that "genocide is a crime under international law, contrary to the spirit and aims of the United Nations and condemned by the civilized world". It declares that genocide has inflicted great losses on humanity at all periods of history, and that international cooperation is required in order "to liberate mankind from such an odious scourge".

Article I provides the important clarification that genocide can be committed "in time of peace or in time of war", distinguishing it from crimes against humanity, about which there was still, in 1948, much doubt about its application absent an armed conflict. The provision also links the concepts of prevention and punishment. Noting the connection, the International Court of Justice, in the *Bosnia and Herzegovina* v. *Serbia and Montenegro* judgment of 26 February 2007 (*Application of the Convention on the Prevention and Punishment of the Crime of Genocide (Bosnia and Herzegovina* v. *Serbia and Montenegro)*, said that not only was genocide prevented because of the deterrent effects of punishment, the duty to prevent genocide had its own autonomous scope which was both "normative and compelling".

The crime of genocide is defined in article II, the provision that sits at the heart of the Convention. Genocide is a crime of intentional destruction of a national, ethnic, racial and religious group, in whole or in part. Article II lists five punishable acts of genocide. This definitional provision has stood the test of time, resisting calls for its expansion, and it is reproduced without change in such instruments as the statutes of the *ad hoc* tribunals for the former Yugoslavia and Rwanda and the Rome Statute of the International Criminal Court. The obstinate refusal to modify the definition is not explained by some innate conservativism in the international lawmaking process. Rather, the gaps left by the somewhat narrow definition of genocide in the 1948 Convention have been filled more or less satisfactorily by the dramatic enlargement of the ambit of crimes against humanity during the 1990s. The coverage of crimes against humanity expanded to include acts perpetrated in time of peace, and to a broad range of groups, not to mention an ever-growing list of punishable acts inspired by developments in international human rights law. For much the same reason, judicial interpretation of article II has remained relatively faithful to the intent of the drafters of the provision. Thus, it remains confined to the intentional physical destruction of the group, rather than attacks on its existence involving persecution of its culture or the phenomenon of "ethnic cleansing."

Article III lists four additional categories of the crime of genocide in addition to perpetration as such. One of these, complicity, is virtually implied in the concept of perpetration and derives from general principles of criminal law. The other three are incomplete or inchoate offences, in effect preliminary acts committed even where genocide itself does not take place. They enhance the preventive dimension of the Convention. The most controversial, "direct and public incitement", is restricted by two adjectives so as to limit conflicts with the protection of freedom of expression.

Reprising a principal established in the Charter of the International Military Tribunal, article IV denies the defence of official capacity to Heads of State and other leading political figures. Article V requires States to enact legislation to give effect to the Convention's provisions, and to ensure that effective penalties are provided. Many States have accordingly enacted the relevant texts of the Convention within their own penal codes, whereas others have deemed that the underlying crimes of murder and assault were already adequately addressed so that perpetrators of genocide committed on their own territory would not escape accountability.

One of the more controversial and difficult provisions says that genocide will be punished either by a competent tribunal of the territorial State, or by "such international penal tribunal as may have jurisdiction". Little more than a decade after article VI was adopted, the Israeli courts dismissed Adolf Eichmann's claim that the provision was an obstacle to the exercise of universal jurisdiction over genocide. It was held that despite the terms of the Convention, exercise of universal jurisdiction was authorized by customary international law.

Pursuant to article VII, States parties to the Convention are obliged to grant extradition "in accordance with their laws and treaties in force". There is some practice to suggest that this rather vague formulation is nevertheless taken seriously, and that States consider themselves obliged to facilitate extradition when genocide charges are involved, subject to recognized principles prohibiting *refoulement* where there is a real risk of flagrant human rights abuses in the receiving State.

Article VIII declares that a State party to the Convention may appeal to "competent organs" of the United Nations for them to take action pursuant to the Charter. This provision, which is largely superfluous because the right to seize the organs of the United Nations exists in any event, has apparently been invoked only once, by the United States of America in September 2004 (9 September 2004, Secretary Colin L. Powell, Testimony Before the Senate Foreign Relations Committee, United States of America).

The International Court of Justice is given jurisdiction over disputes "relating to the interpretation, application or fulfilment" of the Convention by article IX. In *Bosnia and Herzegovina* v. *Serbia and Montenegro*, the International Court of Justice confirmed that States could, in effect, commit genocide, and that the Court could adjudicate the issue pursuant to article IX. Several applications charging genocide have been filed before the Court, but only one, *Bosnia and Herzegovina* v. *Serbia and Montenegro*, has come to a final judgment.

The remaining provisions of the Convention are mainly technical in nature, and concern such issues as the authentic language versions, application to non-self-governing territories, entry into force, revision and denunciation. The Convention is silent on the subject of reservations. In its 1951 Advisory Opinion *(Reservations to the Genocide Convention, I.C.J. Reports 1951, p.15)*, the International Court of Justice confirmed that reservations to the Convention were not prohibited, to the extent that they were not incompatible with the instrument's object and purpose. Several reservations have been formulated, many of them without widespread objection. Most of the reservations have concerned the jurisdiction of the International Court of Justice set out in article IX.

Influence of the Genocide Convention

The Genocide Convention was the first human rights treaty adopted by the General Assembly of the United Nations. It focuses attention on the protection of national, racial, ethnic and religious minorities from threats to their very existence. In that sense, it sits four-square within the priorities of both the United Nations and the modern human rights movement, aimed at the eradication of racism and xenophobia. Furthermore, it stresses the role of criminal justice and accountability in the protection and promotion of human rights.

The Convention has been much criticized for its limited scope. This was really more a case of frustration with the inadequate reach of international law in dealing with mass atrocities. As history has shown, this difficulty would be addressed not by expanding the definition of genocide or by amending the Convention, but rather by an evolution in the closely related concept of crimes against humanity. Accordingly, the crime of genocide has been left alone, where it occupies a special place as "the crime of crimes".

Case law of the International Court of Justice and the International Criminal Tribunal for the former Yugoslavia has confirmed a restrictive approach to interpretation of the definition of genocide, resisting its extension to cases of ethnic cleansing and similar attacks upon groups aimed at their displacement rather than at their physical extermination. At the same time, in its 2007 ruling the Court found a robust concept of the prevention of genocide within the vague words of article I of the Convention. It spoke of a duty of "due diligence" imposed upon States, one that extended even to acts committed outside of their own borders by entities over which their influence may extend. This obligation to prevent genocide dovetails nicely with the responsibility to protect, recognized in 2005 by the United Nations General Assembly and endorsed the following year by the Security Council.

Unlike most of the other main human rights treaties, the Genocide Convention does not establish a monitoring mechanism. There have been periodic calls to set up a treaty body, possibly by an additional protocol to the Convention or perhaps simply by a resolution of the General Assembly. In 2004, the Secretary-General of the United Nations established the high-level position of Special Adviser on the Prevention of Genocide.

In its report to the United Nations Secretary-General in January 2005, the International Commission of Inquiry on Darfur insisted that crimes against humanity might, in some cases, be just as serious as genocide. Its comments highlighted what is often a sterile debate about whether to characterize acts as genocide or as "mere" crimes against humanity. Indeed, crimes against humanity was the label attached to the Nazi atrocities at Nuremberg, and it remains one of the "most serious crimes of concern to the international community as a whole" listed in the Rome Statute of the International Criminal Court. Nevertheless, alongside the legal definition of genocide, rooted in the 1948 Convention and confirmed in subsequent case law, there is a more popular or colloquial conception. In practice, this lay understanding of genocide is more akin to crimes against humanity, in that it comprises a broad range of mass atrocities.

The Genocide Convention places the burden on the state to ensure that genocide is not committed. The ICJ must therefore approach issues of state responsibility in this light. This is not to say that the ICJ should make it easy to hold a state responsible, but it must also not make it unattainable. The standards must be clear and coherent, appropriate to the type of liability, the legal elements involved, the evidence procurable, and the realities of genocidal situations. The ICJ should re-examine the appropriateness of the 'evidence fully conclusive' standard in accordance with the civil nature of state responsibility and its relationship with the obligation to prevent genocide. It must also define this standard, especially in relation to 'beyond reasonable doubt'. In determining *dolus specialis*, the ICJ must relax rather than exact stringent proof, considering that the state is an inanimate juridical personality. Similarly, the ICJ must loosen its standard for inferring specific intent from the general pattern of acts. State responsibility for rendering assistance should work to prevent states from giving *any* support to genocidal activities rather than draw a thin line which states need only take care not to cross. The concept of 'effective control' must also be revisited *vis-à-vis* the interpretation of this principle in command responsibility. The ICJ should strive to stabilize these legal principles, instead of having vague guidelines or avoiding setting precedents.

In sum, under the Genocide Convention, a state has the following obligations: (i) to prevent and punish genocide; (ii) to punish persons committing genocide; (iii) to enact the necessary legislation; (iv) to prosecute those charged with genocide; and (v) to extradite those charged with genocide. Breach of any obligation engages state responsibility. From this list, it may appear that state obligations arise only from another actor's commission of genocide. The words of the Convention leave uncertain whether a state has a primary obligation not to commit genocide.

Coming to the conclusion that responsibility for genocide should ultimately fall on the state, the *Bosnia-Herzegovina Genocide Case* can be viewed in two ways: as a wasted opportunity or as a lesson for the future. The first could be seen as wasting a rare chance to hold a state responsible for the crime of all crimes and give flesh to the underlying principles of the Genocide Convention, while the second could be seen as a legal – and political – stock-taking of the implications of and gaps in the Genocide Convention. The first view is as valid as the second, for indeed the ICJ could have made better use of this opportunity; but in terms of moving forward the latter view provides the tool for catching the reins of the state.

Toward a World without Genocide

It is hard to square the idea of millions of people being bought and sold, of systematic sexual violation, natal alienation, forced labour, extermination, and starvation with any sort of "humane" behaviour: these are the sorts of things that should never be done to human beings. By terming these actions "inhuman" and suggesting that they either relied upon or accomplished the "dehumanization" of enslaved people, however, we are participating in a sort of ideological exchange that is no less baleful for being so familiar. We are separating a normative and aspirational notion of humanity from the sorts of exploitation and violence that history suggests may well be *definitive* of human beings: we are separating ourselves from our own histories of perpetration. To say so is not to suggest that there is no difference between the past and the present; it is merely that we should not overwrite the complex determinations of history with simple-minded notions of moral progress.

More important, though, is the ideological work accomplished by holding on to a normative notion of "humanity"—one that can be held separate from the "inhuman" actions of so many humans. Historians sometimes argue that some aspects of slavery were so violent, so obscene, so "inhuman" that, in order to live with themselves, the perpetrators had to somehow "dehumanize" their victims. While that "somehow" remains a problem—for it is never really specified what combination of unconscious, cultural, and social factors make a "somehow"—I want to question the assumption that slaveholders had to first "dehumanize" their slaves before they could swing a baby by the feet into a post to silence its cries, or jam the broken handle of a hoe down the throat of a field hand, or refer to their property as "darkies" or "hands" or "wool."

What if we use the history of slavery as a standpoint from which to rethink our notion of justice today?

The apparent right-mindedness of such arguments notwithstanding, this language of "dehumanization" is misleading because slavery depended upon the human capacities of enslaved people. It depended upon their reproduction. It depended upon their labour. And it depended upon their sentience. Enslaved people could be taught: their intelligence made them valuable. They could be manipulated: their desires could make them pliable. They could be terrorized: their fears could make them controllable. And they could be tortured: beaten, starved, raped, humiliated, degraded. It is these last that are conventionally understood to be the most "inhuman" of slaveholders' actions and those that most "dehumanized" enslaved people. And yet these actions epitomize the failure of this set of terms to capture what was at stake in slaveholding violence: the extent to which slaveholders depended upon violated slaves to bear witness, to provide satisfaction, to provide a living, human register of slaveholders' power.

More than misleading, however, the notion that enslavement "dehumanized" enslaved people is harmful; it indelibly and categorically alters those with whom it supposedly sympathizes. *De*humanization suggests an alienation of enslaved people from their humanity. Who is the judge of when a person has suffered so much or been objectified so fundamentally that the person's humanity has been lost? How does the person regain that humanity? Can it even be regained? And who decides when it has been regained? The explicitly paternalist character of these questions suggests that a belief in the "dehumanization" of enslaved people is locked in an inextricable embrace with the very history of racial abjection it ostensibly confronts. All this while implicitly asserting the unimpeachable rectitude and "humanity" of latter-day observers.

It could be argued that my interpretation of the word "dehumanized" is grammatically fundamentalist and intellectually obtuse, that the point of saying that slavery "dehumanized" enslaved people is to draw attention to the immoral actions of *slaveholders*—*their* inhumanity—rather than to make a claim about the abjection of enslaved people. I would respond by citing Philip Morgan's *Slave Counterpoint*, a prizewinning history of slavery in eighteenth-century North America. In the introduction, Morgan emphasizes that African American slaves "strove . . . to preserve their humanity."

Even as many historians explicitly and insistently vindicate the notion that enslaved people were human beings, they also implicitly and unwittingly suggest that the case for enslaved humanity is in need of being proven again and again. By framing their "discovery" of the enduring humanity of enslaved people as a defining feature of their work, by casting their work as proof of black humanity—as if this were a question that should even be posed—historians ironically render black humanity intellectually probationary. Efforts to separate "human" from "inhuman" and "dehumanized" thus create an unanticipated set of intellectual and ethical overflows.

Elsewhere in the same introduction, Morgan writes:

Wherever and whenever masters, whether implicitly or explicitly, recognized the independent will and volition of their slaves, they acknowledged the humanity of their bond people. Extracting this admission was, in fact, a form of slave resistance, because slaves thereby opposed the dehumanization inherent in their status.

I want to emphasize that I am not quoting these sentences because they are exceptionally imperceptive. I quote them instead because they are emblematic: by counterpoising an emphasis on "independent will and volition" against the possibility of "dehumanization," they crystallize a set of intellectual impulses and ethical premises that undergirds much of the scholarship on slavery. They frame their account of humanity as an aspect of the problem of freedom, and freedom of a very particular sort: the freedom to make choices and take intended actions—in other words, the bourgeois freedoms of classical liberalism. In so doing, they point to the peculiar complications that result from positioning the history of slavery at the juncture of the terms "human" and "rights."

Several problems flow from the notion that every history of slavery is peopled by liberal subjects striving to be emancipated into the political condition of the twenty-first-century Western bourgeoisie. From a historiographic perspective, we could say that this perspective alienates enslaved people from the historical parameters and cultural determinants of their own actions. It takes their actions—from singing a spiritual to breaking a tool to fomenting a revolution to having a good idea about how to run a better sluiceway—and collapses them down to a single anachronistic and essentially liberal moral: enslaved people's "agency" proved their humanity.

For the purposes of this essay, I am less interested in the historiographic implications of this line of reasoning than I am in its ethical dimensions. The tension between the specific actions and idioms of enslaved life and the broadly comparative categories of "independent will and volition," "agency," and "humanity" seem analogically—and, indeed, historically and ethically—related to the tension that Karl Marx noted between the historical and material inequalities of nineteenth-century society and the abstract equality of rights-based human emancipation, of which he was critical. In his essay "On the Jewish Question," Marx wrote that the political citizen was "an imaginary member of an imaginary universality." For Marx the material salience of human existence—"distinctions of birth, social rank, education, occupation"—continued to guide and determine the course of history, even as the inauguration of a new sort of history, the history of political equality, was announced to the world. In a passage that captures both the terrific promises and bounded limits of a rights-based notion of human emancipation, Marx wrote:

Political emancipation is, of course, a big step forward. True, it is not the final form of human emancipation, but it is the final form of human emancipation within the hitherto existing world order. It goes without saying that we are speaking here of [something greater than that] real, practical emancipation.

It is through Marx's appreciation for and critique of the notion of citizenship—and, by extension, of the rights-based notion of the human being at the heart of the historiography of slavery—that I want to turn more directly to the question of human rights.

A good deal of recent scholarship has emphasized the importance of both vernacular and institutional antislavery to the intellectual history of human rights. Samuel Moyn's recent and influential account of the history of human rights, however, departs from this timeline to argue for a much later set of historical benchmarks. It was not until well into the twentieth century, Moyn argues, that the idea of "a new world" emerged, "in which the dignity of each individual will enjoy secure international protection." While many other scholars are critical of the way that Moyn's timeline sets the history of slavery and antislavery to the side of the history of human rights, I think Moyn is not without reason. The version of human rights that dominates contemporary super-sovereign rights claims, I would suggest, is not significantly inflected by the history of slavery, although it would be better if it were.

Our current notion of universal human rights has its origin in a particular historical experience: that of Europe in the twentieth century. Human-rights thinking has emphasized the universal rights of democratic self-determination, freedom of conscience and expression, protection from political violence and, above all, the anathematization of genocide. Paraphrasing Marx, I think it is fair to say that the emergence of a global movement in support of human rights is the summary accomplishment of "the hitherto existing world order." It is not, however—nor in my view should it be—"the final form of human emancipation" or of what a just world should look like. In Moyn's view, in fact, human-rights thinking has provided the intellectual architecture for a sort of liberal neo-imperialism, the justifying terms of continuing European and American intervention in the affairs of former colonies.

There is a quite different genealogy for discussions of human freedom—this one rooted in the experience of slavery rather than the question of the humanity of slaves. The Movement for Black Lives proposal, "A Vision for Black Lives," insists on a relationship between the history of slavery and contemporary struggles for social justice. At the heart of the proposal is a call for "reparations for the historic and continuing harms of colonialism and slavery." Indeed, the ambient as well as the activist discussion of justice in the United States today is inseparable from the history of slavery.

The idea that enslavement "dehumanized" enslaved people suggests that their humanity needs to be proven again and again.

With this in mind, we might return to the question of "human emancipation"—this time with the purpose of essaying a notion of justice that is rooted in the history of slavery and goes beyond liberal notions of human rights. Through this route, we can arrive at a history of the global political economy that is attentive to what, following Cedric Robinson, I term racial capitalism.

In *Black Marxism* (1983), Robinson argues that the historical developments of capitalism and racism were inseparable. Engaging with black nationalism and orthodox Marxism, he argues that the path toward the just and the good cannot be found in the "authoritarian" pronouncements of uninflected Marxism, with its single route to revolution, nor in the historical "implications" of black nationalism, which threatens to replicate white-dominated institutions but with black people in charge. Instead the path to justice is located in the black radical tradition: in the democratic practices and revolutionary thought of black people living under conditions of racial capitalism.

Black Marxism begins with a history of slavery in medieval Europe, in part to demonstrate the historically contingent character of the relationship between slavery and blackness. It then turns to the early modern period and the European enslavement of Africans. In the era of the Atlantic slave trade, new notions of difference—absolute, racial notions of difference—were used to define, describe, and justify the political economy of slavery.

For Robinson, W. E. B. Du Bois was the preeminent historian of the ways that racism had defined the history of capitalism and interrupted the universalist pretensions of Marxist orthodoxy. In a 1920 essay entitled "The Souls of White Folk," Du Bois suggests that both economic exploitation and domination justified by imagined difference have histories "as old as mankind." But their combination in European imperialism—the "discovery of personal whiteness" by those who claimed title to the world and the concomitant designation of the world's dark peoples as "beasts of burden"—is recent, a product of the slave trade. Gone in Du Bois are the orthodox markers that serve to keep the history of slavery separate from the history of capitalism. In their place Du Bois proposes a new milestone, the emergence of a sort of capitalism that relies upon the elaboration, reproduction, and exploitation of notions of racial difference: a global capitalism concomitant with the invention of what Robinson termed "the universal Negro." In short: racial capitalism.

In *Black Reconstruction in America*, published fifteen years later, Du Bois roots his account of racial capitalism in the history of slavery in the United States. "The giant forces of water and of steam were harnessed to do the world's work, and the black workers of America bent at the bottom of a growing pyramid of commerce and industry; and they not only could not be spared, if this new economic organization was to expand, but rather they became the cause of new political demands and alignments, of new dreams of power and visions of empire," he writes in the book's first pages.

Black labour became the foundation stone not only of the Southern social structure, but of Northern manufacture and commerce, of the English factory system, of European commerce, of buying and selling on a world-wide scale; new cities were built on the results of black labour, and a new labour problem, involving all white labour, arose in both Europe and America.

In a few sentences, Du Bois scuttles the orthodox separation of slavery and capitalism. He names his history of American slavery "The Black Worker"—a subject, at once, of capital and of white supremacy. This, Robinson writes, was "the beginning of the transformation of the historiography of American Civilization—the naming of things."

Rather than following Adam Smith or Karl Marx, each of whom viewed slavery as a residual form in the world of emergent capitalism, Du Bois treats the plantations of Mississippi, the counting houses of Manhattan, and the mills of Manchester as differentiated but concomitant components of a single system. Many scholars have expressed a fear that terming both what happened in Mississippi and what happened in Manchester "capitalism" will make it impossible to

263

see the trees for the forest—"obscuring," in the words of James Oakes, "fundamental differences between economies based on enslaved [and] free labour." But there is no obvious reason that should be the case. Arguing that the history of (racial) capitalism began with the slave trade rather than the factory system does not necessarily pose any greater threat to historical and analytical precision than arguing that both Harriet Tubman and John C. Calhoun were human beings.

Indeed, Du Bois draws attention to the very differences that Oakes worries will be elided. He simply sees the production of these differences as an aspect of the history he is trying to understand, rather than as an inevitable answer to which any historical account must aspire. The history of white working-class struggle, for example, cannot be understood separate from the privileges of whiteness, to which the white working classes of Britain and the United States laid claim in their demands for equal political rights. And it was the ever-expanding frontier of imperialism and racial capitalism that pacified the white working class with the threat of replacement and promise of a share of the spoils. The history of racial capitalism, it must be emphasized, is a history of wages as well as whips, of factories as well as plantations, of whiteness as well as blackness, of "freedom" as well as slavery.

Critically, there is nothing static or simple about this formulation. Du Bois does not argue that all whites benefit from capitalism while all blacks do not. But nor does he argue that blacks and whites are "workers" in the same way. He suggests instead a subtle and dynamic relationship between capitalist exploitation and white supremacy. Likewise, Du Bois insists on a coeval and dialectical relationship between metropole and colony: even as the economic spaces of the Global South were reconfigured in relation to northern capital, metropolitan class relationships were reconfigured around ideas of freedom and entitlement that emerged from imperialism and slavery.

Du Bois's famous invocation of the "wages of whiteness" can best be understood in the context of a global economy that entwined Mississippi, Manhattan, and Manchester together in a white-supremacist system of differential rights and entitlements. Under the dominion of cotton, metropolitan wage workers came to understand themselves as white and to measure their entitlement in terms of slavery and empire: as natural and just when they shared in the spoils; as insupportable and impious when they did not.

Far from obscuring the differences between the social relations of production in the various regions of the world, *Black Reconstruction* provides an account of their historical interconnection, their racial predication, and their functional differentiation. "The abolition of American slavery," Du Bois writes, "started the transportation of capital from white to black countries where slavery prevailed . . . and precipitated the modern economic degradation of the white farmer, while it put into the hands of the owners of the machine such a monopoly of raw material that their dominion of white labour was more and more complete." The end of slavery in the United States, according to Du Bois, marked not the liberation of the independent forces of capitalism and freedom from their archaic interconnection with slavery, but the generalization on a global scale of the racial and imperial vision of the "empire of cotton." The history of racial capitalism is a history of the interconnected process by which economic, geographic, and racial differences were seeded, took root, and finally grew up to such an extent that they obscured efforts to search out their common origin: a history, at once, of integrative connection and divisive particularization.

Perhaps the fullest expression of Du Bois's account of global racial capitalism is in his 1946 book *The World and Africa*. There he describes the process by which "slavery and the slave trade became transformed into anti-slavery and colonialism, and all with the same determination and demand to increase profit an investment." Although this meant that terms of European stewardship were transformed, even at times inverted, the racial pattern of extraction and exploitation nonetheless continued unabated.

It all became a characteristic drama of capitalist exploitation, where the right hand knew nothing of what the left hand did, yet rhymed its grip with uncanny timeliness; where the investor neither knew, nor inquired, nor greatly cared about the sources of his profits; where the enslaved or dead or half-paid worker never saw nor dreamed of the value of his work (now owned by others); where neither the society darling nor the great artist saw the blood on the piano keys; where the clubman, boasting of great game hunting, heard above the click of his smooth, lovely, resilient billiard balls no echo of the wild shrieks of pain from kindly, half-human beasts as fifty to seventy-five thousand each year were slaughtered in cold, cruel, lingering horror of living death; sending their teeth to adorn civilization on the bowed heads and chained feet of thirty thousand black slaves, leaving behind more than a hundred thousand corpses in broken, flaming homes.

As much as anything, this is an account of the spatial aspect of racial capitalism. It emphasizes both the intimate, violent proximities and the material and cognitive distances of region, race, and scale (global and imperial, intimate and proximate). Du Bois's account is particularly interested in the material culture of racial capital, of how the suffering of dead elephants and enslaved Africans was reassembled elsewhere as sensory pleasures for the parlours and pool halls of imperial London. It is an environmental history of the resource-extracting, race-differentiating, world-wasting race to the end of time. Uncannily, the most ambitious and perceptive examples of the "new history of capitalism" turn out to have been written over seventy years ago.

Implicit in the insight of racial capitalism is the claim that there is something fundamental and racial (or, more precisely, rac*ist*) that is elided by the conventional understanding of capitalism's origins. With this parallax in mind, the burden of proof rests on the notion's advocates to show what is gained by thinking outward from the history of slavery to an overarching idea of racial capitalism. A history of capitalism framed by categories derived from analysis of the mills of Manchester might have seemed to make sense in the era of the miners' strike in Great Britain or of George Meany and the AFL-CIO in the United States (although the murder of Vincent Chin, among countless other examples, suggests otherwise). The history of American slavery, however, seems a more apt starting point for the analysis of a world characterized by the global division of labour, the resurgence of slavery as mode of production, the emergence of personal services (and pornography) as leading sectors of the economy, and the effulgence of nativism and white nationalism as fundamental features of white working-class ideology. History has moved on, and in so doing it has reshuffled its own past.

Much of the scholarship on slavery has relied upon a pat liberal notion of human rights as its moral paradigm.

Indeed, the history of capitalism makes no sense separate from the history of the slave trade and its aftermath. There was no such thing as capitalism without slavery: the history of Manchester never happened without the history of Mississippi. In *Capitalism and Slavery* (1944), Eric Williams gives a detailed account of the supersession of British colonial interests by manufacturing ones and the replacement of sugar with cotton as the foundation of capitalist development. Williams argues that Great Britain freed its slaves, but did not free itself from slavery. British capitalists simply outsourced the production of the raw material upon which they principally depended to the United States. During the antebellum period, 85 percent of the cotton produced in the United States was exported to Great Britain. During the same period 85 percent of the cotton manufactured in Great Britain was imported in raw form from the United States. Raw cotton was thus the largest single export of the United States and the largest single import of Great Britain.

Trying to abstract the social relations of production that characterized British (or American) cotton mills from the rest of the economy that gave them life—and then identifying this as the paradigmatic example of "capitalism"—quite simply does not make sense. "Would Great Britain have industrialized without slavery, though perhaps at a different pace or in a different way?" James Oakes has recently written. What is being proposed is an adventitious, ahistorical definition of capitalism—a thing which might have happened even though it actually did not—that serves no purpose except to preserve, at whatever cost, the analytical precedence of Europe over Africa, the factory over the field, and the white working class over black slaves. Capitalism counterfactually emancipated from slavery. That is not social science; it is science fiction.

Rather than asking over and over what Marx said about slavery, we should follow Robinson in asking what slavery says about Marx. We should use the history of slavery and colonial genocide as the source rather than the subject of knowledge. Let us begin with the most basic distinction in political economy: the distinction between capital and labour. Enslaved people were both. Their double economic aspect could not be separated and graphed on the axes of a Cartesian grid; their interests could not be balanced against one another or subordinated to one another in an effort to secure social order. They were both.

And so, too, were their children: racial capitalism swung on a reproductive hinge. The entire "pyramid" of the Atlantic economy of the nineteenth century (the economy that has been treated as the paradigmatic example of capitalism) was founded upon the capacity of enslaved women's bodies: upon their ability to reproduce capital. As Deborah Gray White points out, sexual violation, reproductive invigilation, and natal alienation were elementary aspects of slavery, and thus of racial capitalism. The alternative, of course, was the slave trade. As the slaveholder J. D. B. DeBow stated in his 1858 argument for reopening the Atlantic slave trade to the United States (which had been outlawed in 1808), it was either that or "await with folded arms the coming of population and of labour which will be the result of natural increase." A commercial mode of social reproduction would make black women disposable.

The political economy of the nineteenth century was founded on these basic facts. Every year the cotton merchants of Great Britain made tremendous advances to the cotton planters of the South. The planters used the credit to purchase seeds and tools and slaves and the food to feed them, and they planned to use those slaves to plant and pick and pack and ship the cotton that would cover the money that had been advanced to them, and then some. As pro-slavery political economist Thomas Kettel wrote in 1860:

"The agriculturalists, who create the real wealth of the country, are not in daily receipt of money. Their produce is ready but once a year, whereas they buy supplies [on credit] year round. . . . The whole banking system of the country is based primarily on this bill movement against produce."

In case the cotton proved too scant or poor to cover the amount that had been advanced against its eventual sale, or in case the cotton market dipped in the time between when an advance was made and the time the crop came in, cotton merchants required some sort of security from the planters to whom they loaned money. That security was the value of the enslaved. Therefore, given that enslaved people were the collateral upon which the entire system depended, it seems absurd to persist in asking whether the political economy of slavery was or was not "capitalist." *Enslaved people were the capital.* Their value in 1860 was equal to all of the capital invested in American railroads, manufacturing, and agricultural land combined.

It is important to add that the land tells a different part of the story, one that resounds with Du Bois's emphasis on empire alongside enslavement as the primary categories of capitalist accumulation. The land that enslaved people planted in cotton and which their owners posted as collateral was Native American land: it had been expropriated from the Creek, the Cherokee, the Choctaw, the Chickasaw, and the Seminole. Indeed, if one traces the legal history of private property in the United States back, trying to find a legal foundation for determining why (legally rather than morally speaking) we own what we think we own, at the bottom lies the decision of the United States Supreme Court in the case of *Johnson v. McIntosh* (1823). At stake in the case was the question of whether white settlers could purchase land directly from native inhabitants, and the answer of the Supreme Court was "no." Native American lands, the court ruled, must be passed through the public domain of the United States before being converted into the private property of white inhabitants. In other words, the foundation of the law of property in the United States combines, at once, the imperial assertion of U.S. sovereignty and the identification of that project with continental racial governance.

The version of human rights that dominates contemporary discourse is not significantly inflected by the history of slavery, although it would be better if it were.

The racial capitalism of the nineteenth century was founded upon the racialization and instrumentalization, the commodification and securitization, the expropriation and forcible transportation, the sexual violation and reproductive alienation of Africans and Native Americans. It is here we must begin to reimagine the categories against which we stretch the past into historical meaning, to follow the lead of those who self-consciously work in the tradition of Du Bois and Robinson: scholars such as Ruth Wilson Gilmore, Adam Green, Cheryl Harris, Peter Hudson, Robin D. G. Kelley, George Lipsitz, Lisa Lowe, Gary Okihiro, Nell Irvin Painter, David Roediger, Alexander Saxton, and Stephanie Smallwood. And no longer should the "capitalism-slavery debate" proceed without a full and forthright acknowledgement of and engagement with the pioneering work and enduring insights of W. E. B. Du Bois, C. L. R. James, Eric Williams, Walter Rodney, Angela Davis, and Cedric Robinson.

Let me return to the relationship between the history of slavery and contemporary notions of justice. Tragically, the history of slavery is increasingly being written without enslaved people. By this, I mean that a field formerly defined by the dissident, bottom-up methodology of African American Studies and social history is increasingly dominated by work that does not ask questions about the experiences, ideas, or history of the enslaved (even while it teaches us many new things about slaveholders and their business partners). Let me be clear: it is not only nonsensical but also unethical to continue asking whether slavery was capitalist without asking what that meant to enslaved people—to investigate what Du Bois termed "the philosophy of life and action which slavery bred in the souls of black folk."

From the history of the enslaved, we might make our way back toward the question of rights. I began by suggesting that much of the scholarship on slavery has unwittingly relied upon a pat liberal notion of human rights as its moral paradigm—despite the clear contradiction between the universalization of a bourgeois liberal actor and the legal and experiential realities of American slavery. The culturally dominant notion of human rights is not only unreflective of the history of slavery; it is unresponsive to the specific patterns of injustice that follow from the history of slavery. In its place, I suggest the possibility of using the history of slavery as a standpoint from which to rethink our notion of justice. What is left is to delineate the usefulness of this history to an account of justice.

There are six principal virtues of an account of justice rooted in the history of slavery and racial capitalism:

> First, it mounts its critique of modern injustice from the standpoint of Africa and what has come to be called "the Global South," rather than from Europe and "the Global North."
>
> Second, it focuses on the extraction and distribution of resources between classes and areas of the world: on the relationship of African American history to Native American history, for example, or on the relationship of either or both of those to the history of the white workers (and merchants and bankers) in the financial and

manufacturing centres of the United States and Europe. So doing, it proposes the generalization of an account of historical wrong based in the experiences of the dark and dispossessed rather than in those of the metropolitan bourgeoisie.

Third, it emphasizes the ways in which present distributions of privilege and abjection are related to past patterns. It opens a pathway along which historically deep notions of restorative justice and reparations, rather than a synchronic focus on "rights," might be seen as the only adequate form of redress.

Fourth, it insists upon a notion of justice attentive to questions of gender and sexuality, on the ways that reproductive invigilation and natal alienation—the subordination of the social reproduction of one group of people to the purposes of another—were core features of the human wrongs of slavery.

Fifth, it asserts a direct relationship between—and indeed, the functional sameness of—what are conventionally separated as the politics of "race" and "class." It correlates both the entitlement and vulnerability of the white working class with the subjection of the "dark proletariat," and connects the insistent racialization of the global working class to the operations of capital.

Sixth, and finally, it suggests the possibility of relating a critique of the instrumentalization of human beings through slavery to the instrumentalization of nature in capitalist forms of extraction. Over and against many recent efforts which assert that a forthright treatment of global environmental history requires the elevation of the categories of the "human" and the "Anthropocene" over and against other historical categories—principally those of race, class, gender, and colonialism— it insists upon the intimate and dialectical relationship between domination and dominion.

The Genocide Convention was approved by the General Assembly of the United Nations on December 9, 1948 and came into force on January 12, 1951; after a long delay, it was ratified by the United States in 1986. Since genocide is now a technical term in international criminal law, the definition established by the convention has assumed prima-facie authority, and it is with this definition that we should begin in assessing the applicability of the concept of genocide to the events we have been considering.

According to Article II of the convention, the crime of genocide consists of a series of acts" committed with intent to destroy, in whole or in part, a national, ethnical, racial, or religious group as such" (emphases added). Practically all legal scholars accept the centrality of this clause. During the deliberations over the convention, some argued for a clear specification of the reasons, or motives, for the destruction of a group. In the end, instead of a list of such motives, the issue was resolved by adding the words "as such"—i.e., the motive or reason for the destruction must be the ending of the group as a national, ethnic, racial, or religious entity. Evidence of such a motive, as one legal scholar put it, "will constitute an integral part of the proof of a genocidal plan, and therefore of genocidal intent."

The crucial role played by intentionality in the Genocide Convention means that under its terms the huge number of Indian deaths from epidemics cannot be considered genocide. The lethal diseases were introduced inadvertently, and the Europeans cannot be blamed for their ignorance of what medical science would discover only centuries later. Similarly, military engagements that led to the death of noncombatants, like the battle of the Washita, cannot be seen as genocidal acts, for the loss of innocent life was not intended and the soldiers did not aim at the destruction of the Indians as a defined group. By contrast, some of the massacres in California, where both the perpetrators and their supporters openly acknowledged a desire to destroy the Indians as an ethnic entity, might indeed be regarded under the terms of the convention as exhibiting genocidal intent.

Even as it outlaws the destruction of a group "in whole or in part", the convention does not address the question of what percentage of a group must be affected in order to qualify as genocide. As a benchmark, the prosecutor of the International Criminal Tribunal for the Former Yugoslavia has suggested "a reasonably significant number, relative to the total of the group as a whole", adding that the actual or attempted destruction should also relate to "the factual opportunity of the accused to destroy a group in a specific geographic area within the sphere of his control, and not in relation to the entire population of the group in a wider geographic sense." If this principle were adopted, an atrocity like the Sand Creek massacre, limited to one group in a specific single locality, might also be considered an act of genocide.

Of course, it is far from easy to apply a legal concept developed in the middle of the 20th century to events taking place many decades if not hundreds of years earlier. Our knowledge of many of these occurrences is incomplete. Moreover, the malefactors, long since dead, cannot be tried in a court of law, where it would be possible to establish crucial factual details and to clarify relevant legal principles.

Applying today's standards to events of the past raises still other questions, legal and moral alike. While history has no statute of limitations, our legal system rejects the idea of retroactivity (ex post facto laws). Morally, even if we accept the idea of universal principles transcending particular cultures and periods, we must exercise caution in condemning, say, the conduct of war during America's colonial period, which for the most part conformed to then prevailing notions of right and wrong. To understand all is hardly to forgive all, but historical judgment, as the scholar Gordon Leff has correctly stressed, "must always be contextual: it is no more reprehensible for an age to have lacked our values than to have lacked forks."

Bibliography

Alvarez, A. (2001.) *Governments, Citizens, and Genocide: A Comparative and Interdisciplinary Approach*. Bloomington: Indiana University Press.

Arendt, H. (1958) *The Origins of Totalitarianism*. New York: Meridian.

Bartov, O. (1996). *Murder in Our Midst: The Holocaust, Industrial Killing, and Representation*. Oxford: Oxford University Press.

Bartrop, P. (2002). The Relationship between War and Genocide in the Twentieth Century: A Consideration. *Journal of Genocide Research* 4 (4), 519–32.

Bauman, Z. (1989) *Modernity and the Holocaust*. Cambridge: Polity.

Bloxham, D. (2003) The Armenian Genocide of 1915–1916: Cumulative Radicalization and the Development of a Destruction Policy. *Past and Present* 181 (1), 141–91. Find this resource:

Bond, B. (1998) *War and Society in Europe, 1870–1970*. Guernsey: Sutton and Sutton. Originally published 1984.

Conversi, D. (2007). Homogenisation, Nationalism and War: Should We Still Read Ernest Gellner? *Nations and Nationalism* 13 (3), 1–24.

Conversi, D. (2009). Art, Nationalism and War: Political Futurism in Italy (1909–1944). *Sociology Compass* 3 (1) (Jan.), 92–117.

Dadrian, V. (1996) *German Responsibility in the Armenian Genocide: A Review of the Historical Evidence of German Complicity*. Watertown, MA: Blue Crane. Find this resource:

Darwin, J. (2008) *After Tamerlane: The Global History of Empire since 1405*. London: Bloomsbury.

Del Boca, A. (2005) *Italiani, Brava Gente?* Vicenza: Neri Pozza Editore. Find this resource:

Dieckhoff, A., and Jaffrelot, C. (eds.) (2005) *Revisiting Nationalism: Theories and Processes*. London: Hurst.

Fettweis, C. (2003) War as Catalyst: Moving World War II to the Centre of Holocaust Scholarship. *Journal of Genocide Research* 5 (2), 225–36.

Ghobarah, H., Huth, P., and Russett, B. (2003) Civil Wars Kill and Maim People – Long After the Shooting Stops. *American Political Science Review* 97 (2), 189–202.

Hatzfeld, J. (2005) *A Time for Machetes: The Rwandan Genocide: The Killers Speak*. London: Serpent's Tail.

Hovannisian, R. (1988) The Armenian Genocide. In I. Charny (ed.) *Genocide: A Critical Bibliographic Review*, vol. 1. New York: Facts on File, pp. 89–115.

Kaligian, D. (2008) A Prelude to Genocide: CUP Population Policies and Provincial Insecurity, 1908–14. *Journal of Genocide Research* 10 (1), 77–94.

Jones, A. (2003) The Anfal Campaign (Iraqi Kurdistan), 1988, in W. Hewitt (ed.) *Defining the Horrific: Readings on Genocide and Holocaust in the Twentieth Century*. New York: Prentice-Hall, pp. 320–28.

Kaye, J., and Strath, B. (eds.) (2000) *Enlightenment and Genocide: Contradictions of Modernity*. Brussels: Presses Interuniversitaires Européennes.

Klein, J. (2007) Kurdish Nationalists and Non-nationalist Kurdists: Rethinking Minority Nationalism and the Dissolution of the

Ottoman Empire, 1908–1909. *Nations and Nationalism* 13 (1), 135–53.

Kriwaczek, P. (2005) *Yiddish Civilization: The Rise and Fall of a Forgotten Nation*. London: Weidenfeld and Nicolson.

Langenbacher, E. (2004) The Allies in World War Two: The Anglo-American Bombardment of German Cities. In A. Jones (ed.) *Genocide, War Crimes and the West: History and Complicity*. London: Zed Books.

Lemkin, Raphael. (1944). *Axis Rule in Occupied Europe* (Washington, D.C.: Carnegie Endowment for International Peace.

Levene, M., and Roberts, P. (eds.) (1999a) *The Massacre in History*. Oxford: Berghahn.

Lieberman, B. (2006) *Terrible Fate: Ethnic Cleansing in the Making of Modern Europe*. Chicago: Ivan R. Dee.

Levene, M. (2005) *Genocide in the Age of Nation State*, vol. 2: *The Rise of the West and the Coming of Genocide*. London: I.B. Tauris.

Mann, M. (2005) *The Dark Side of Democracy: Explaining Ethnic Cleansing*. Cambridge: Cambridge University Press.

Melson, R. (1992) *Revolution and Genocide: On the Origins of the Armenian Genocide and the Holocaust*. Chicago: University of Chicago Press.

Melson, R. (1996) The Armenian Genocide as Precursor and Prototype of Twentieth Century Genocide. In A.S. Rosenbaum (ed.) *Is the Holocaust Unique?* Boulder: Westview, pp. 87–100.

Naimark, N. (2001) *Fires of Hatred: Ethnic Cleansing in Twentieth-Century Europe*. Cambridge: Harvard University Press.

Owen, T., and Kiernan, B. (2006) Bombs over Cambodia. *The Walrus* (Canada), (Oct.), 62–9.

Porter, B. (2000) *When Nationalism Began to Hate: Imagining Modern Politics in Nineteenth-Century Poland*. Oxford: Oxford University Press.

Power, S. (2003) *A Problem from Hell: America and the Age of Genocide*. London: Flamingo.

Schaller, D., and Zimmerer, J. (2008) Late Ottoman Genocides: The Dissolution of the Ottoman Empire and Young Turkish Population and Extermination Policies – Introduction. *Journal of Genocide Research* 10 (1), 7–14.

Sengoopta, C. (2003) *Imprint of the Raj: How Fingerprinting Was Born in Colonial India*. Basingstoke, UK: Macmillan.

Shaw, M. (2003) *War and Genocide: Organized Killing in Modern Society*. Cambridge: Polity.

Shenfield, S. (1999) The Circassians: A Forgotten Genocide? In M. Levene and P. Roberts (eds.) *The Massacre in History*. Oxford: Berghahn, pp. 149–83.F

Üngor, U. (2006) When Persecution Bleeds into Mass Murder: The Processive Nature of Genocide. *Genocide Studies and Prevention* 1 (2) (Sept.), 173–96.

Walston, J. (1997) History and Memory of the Italian Concentration Camps. *Historical Journal* 40 (1) (Mar.), 169–83.

Weitz, E. (2003) *A Century of Genocide: Utopias of Race and Nation*. Princeton: Princeton University Press.

Winter, J. (2003) Under the Cover of War: The Armenian Genocide in the Context of Total War. In R. Gellately and B. Kiernan (eds.) *The Specter of Genocide: Mass Murder in Historical Perspective*. Cambridge: Cambridge University Press.

Annexture I: The 795th meeting of the AU Peace and Security Council on the African Standby Force (ASF)

Last Updated on Wednesday 03 October 2018

The Peace and Security Council (PSC) of the African Union (AU), at its 795th meeting held on 20 September 2018, in Addis Ababa, adopted the following decision on the African Standby Force (ASF).

Council:

1. Takes note of the briefing made by the Acting Director of the Peace and Security Department, Dr. Admore Mupoki Kambudzi, on behalf of the Commissioner for Peace and Security, Amb. Smail Chergui, on the harmonization of the African Capacity for Immediate Response to Crises (ACIRC) activities within the African Standby Force (ASF);

2. Recalls its previous communiques and press statements on the ASF, particularly, Press Statement [PSC/PR/BR. (DCLVII)] adopted at its 657th meeting held on 9 February 2017, Communique [PSC/PR/COMM. (DCCV)] adopted at its 705th Meeting held on 25 April 2017, and Communique PSC/PR/COMM. (DCCLXVII) adopted at 767th meeting held on 25 April 2018, on the ASF and the ACIRC. Council also recalls Assembly Decision [Assembly/AU/Dec.679(XXX)], which called on all stakeholders to support the realization of the full operationalization of the ASF, and harmonization of the activities of ACIRC with the Framework of the ASF and enhance cooperation with all ad-hoc coalitions namely, the Multinational Joint Task Force (MNJTF) against Boko Haram terrorist group, Group of Five Sahel Joint Force and the Regional Cooperation Initiative against the Lord's Resistance Army (RCI-LRA), and requested the Commission to submit a plan on the harmonization of ACIRC into ASF, including steps to be taken by the AU and the Regional Economic Communities/Regional Mechanisms for Conflict Prevention (RECs/RMs) to coordinate ad-hoc coalitions, within the context of Articles 13 and 16 of the Protocol Relating to the Establishment of the Peace and Security Council of the African Union;

3. Further recalls Assembly Decision [Assembly/AU/Dec.589 (XXVI)], in which the Assembly commended the progress made by the East African Standby Force (EASF), the Economic Community of Central

African States (ECCAS), the Economic Community of West African States (ECOWAS) and the Southern African Development Community (SADC) in operationalizing their respective standby forces and acknowledged the efforts of the North Africa Regional Capability (NARC) towards operationalizing its standby force;

4. Emphasizes, once again, the need for the Commission to expedite the process of harmonization of ACIRC within the ASF, in full compliance with the letter and spirit of Assembly Decisions 679 and 695. In this respect, Council stresses the imperative for the Commission to exclusively devote all available resources for ASF to activities of ASF and those aimed at expediting the harmonization process. In this respect, Council reiterates the importance for the RECs/RMs to fully participate in this exercise, taking into account the successful deployment, within the Framework of ASF, in Lesotho (SAPMIL) by the SADC, in the Gambia (ECOMIG) and in Guinea Bissau (ECOMIB) by the ECOWAS.

5. Decides that, in order to accelerate the harmonization process, the Commission should urgently organize a meeting of the PSC Military Staff Committee, with the facilitation of the Peace and Security Department, to identify and propose ways and means of fully implementing Assembly Decisions 679 and 695 and to make appropriate recommendations, including timelines and roadmap, to guide the PSC on how to overcome the challenges facing the harmonization of the ACIRC within the ASF;

6. Decides to remain actively seized of the matter.

Annexture II: *Case study of the life of Gustavus Vassa*

A good way of understanding the slave trade is to read the first-hand or eyewitness accounts written by actual slaves, after some were freed and taught to read and write in European languages. One of the most famous of these was written by Olaudah Equiano, who was captured as a young boy in southern Nigeria and sold into slavery in Europe. The Life of Gustavus Vassa (his slave name) was the first-ever slave autobiography. Here is an extract from his autobiography, a primary historical source:

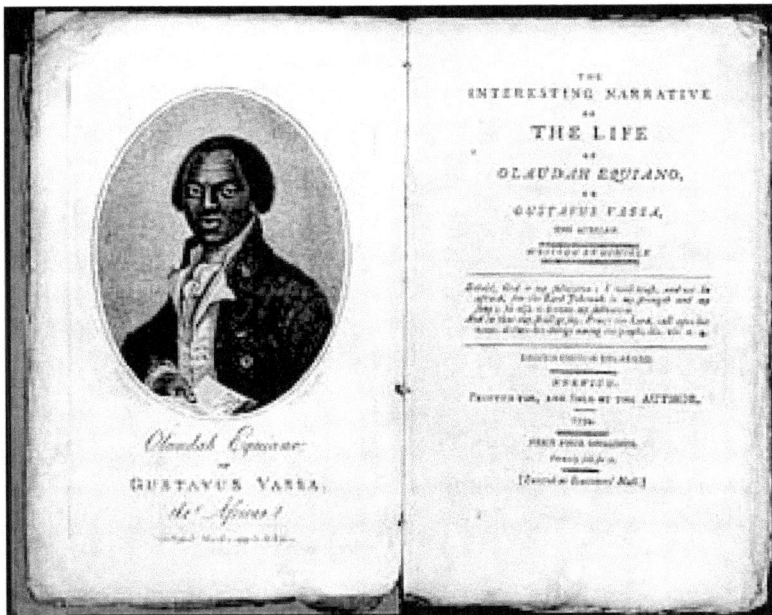

Vassa's autobiography (above) was funded by abolitionists and helped to further the anti-slavery cause. Source: memory.loc.gov

The first object which saluted my eyes when I arrived on the coast, was the sea, and a slave ship, which was then riding at anchor, and waiting for its cargo. These filled me with astonishment, which was soon converted into terror, when I was carried on board. I was immediately handled, and tossed up to see if I were sound, by some of the crew; and I was now persuaded that I had gotten into a world of bad spirits, and that they were going to kill me. Their complexions, too, differing so much from ours, their long hair, and the language they spoke (which was very different from any I had ever heard) united to confirm me in this belief. Indeed, such were the horrors of my views and fears at the

279

moment, that, if ten thousand worlds had been my own, I would have freely parted with them all to have exchanged my condition with that of the meanest slave in my own country. When I looked round the ship too, and saw a large furnace of copper boiling, and a multitude of black people of every description chained together, every one of their countenances expressing dejection and sorrow, I no longer doubted my fate; and, quite overpowered with horror and anguish, I fell motionless on the deck and fainted. When I recovered a little, I found some black people about me, who I believed were some of those who had brought me on board, and had been receiving their pay; they talked to me in order to cheer me, but all in vain. I asked them if we were not to be eaten by those white men with horrible looks, red faces, and long hair. They told me I was not: and one of the crew brought me a small portion of spirituous liquor in a wine glass, but, being afraid of him, I would not take it out of his hand. One of the blacks, therefore, took it from him and gave it to me, and I took a little down my palate, which, instead of reviving me, as they thought it would, threw me into the greatest consternation at the strange feeling it produced, having never tasted any such liquor before. Soon after this, the blacks who brought me on board went off, and left me abandoned to despair.

[later] We were conducted immediately to the merchant's yard, where we were all pent up together, like so many sheep in a fold, without regard to sex or age. As every object was new to me, everything I saw filled me with surprise. What struck me first, was, that the houses were built with bricks and stones, and in every other respect different from those I had seen in Africa; but I was still more astonished on seeing people on horseback. I did not know what this could mean; and, indeed, I thought these people were full of nothing but magical arts. While I was in this astonishment, one of my fellow-prisoners spoke to a countryman of his, about the horses, who said they were the same kind they had in their country. I understood them, though they were from a distant part of Africa; and I thought it odd I had not seen any horses there; but afterwards, when I came to converse with different Africans, I found they had many horses amongst them, and much larger than those I then saw.

We were not many days in the merchant's custody, before we were sold after their usual manner, which is this: On a signal given, (as the beat of a drum) the buyers rush at once into the yard where the slaves are confined, and make choice of that parcel they like best. The noise and clamour with which this is attended, and the eagerness visible in the countenances of the buyers, serve not a little to increase the apprehension of terrified Africans, who may well be supposed to consider them as the ministers of that destruction to which they think themselves devoted. In this manner, without scruple, are relations and friends separated, most of them never to see each other again. I remember, in the vessel in which I was brought over, in the men's apartment, there were several brothers, who, in the sale, were sold in different lots; and it was very moving on this occasion, to see and *hear their cries at parting. O, ye nominal Christians! Learned you this from your God, who says unto you, Do unto all men as you would men should do unto you? Is it not enough that we are torn from our country and friends, to toil for your luxury and lust of gain? Must every tender feeling be likewise sacrificed to your avarice? Are the dearest friends and relations, now rendered more dear by their separation from their kindred, still to be parted from each other, and thus prevented from cheering the gloom of slavery, with the small comfort of being together; and mingling their sufferings and sorrows? Why are parents to lose their children, brothers their sisters, husbands their wives? Surely, this is a new refinement in cruelty, which, while it has no advantage to atone for it, thus aggravates distress; and adds fresh horrors even to the wretchedness of slavery.*

- Source: *The Life of Gustavus Vassa*
by Olaudah Equiana,
London, 1789

Annexure III: Slavery's Roots-War and Economic Domination

- **6800 B.C.** The world's first city-state emerges in Mesopotamia. Land ownership and the early stages of technology bring war—in which enemies are captured and forced to work: slavery.
- **2575 B.C.** Temple art celebrates the capture of slaves in battle. Egyptians capture slaves by sending special expeditions up the Nile River.
- **550 B.C.** The city-state of Athens uses as many as 30,000 slaves in its silver mines.
- **120 A.D.** Roman military campaigns capture slaves by the thousands. Some estimate the population of Rome is more than half slave.
- **500** Anglo-Saxons enslave the native Britons after invading England.
- **1000** Slavery is a normal practice in England's rural, agricultural economy, as destitute workers place themselves and their families in a form of debt bondage to landowners.
- **1380** In the aftermath of the Black Plague, Europe's slave trade thrives in response to a labour shortage. Slaves pour in from all over the continent, the Middle East, and North Africa.
- **1444** Portuguese traders bring the first large cargo of slaves from West Africa to Europe by sea—establishing the Atlantic slave trade.
- **1526** Spanish explorers bring the first African slaves to settlements in what would become the United States. These first African-Americans stage the first known slave revolt in the Americas.
- **1550** Slaves are depicted as objects of conspicuous consumption in much Renaissance art.
- **1641** Massachusetts becomes the first British colony to legalize slavery.

The Age of Abolition
- **1781** Holy Roman Emperor Joseph II abolishes serfdom in the Austrian Habsburg dominions.
- **1787** The Society for the Abolition of the Slave Trade is founded in Britain.
- **1789** During the French Revolution, the National Assembly adopts the Declaration of the Rights of Man, one of the fundamental charters of

human liberties. The first of 17 articles states: "Men are born and remain free and equal in rights."

- **1803** Denmark-Norway becomes the first country in Europe to ban the African slave trade, forbidding trading in slaves and ending the importation of slaves into Danish dominions.

- **1807** The British Parliament makes it illegal for British ships to transport slaves and for British colonies to import them. U.S. President Thomas Jefferson signs into law the Act Prohibiting Importation of Slaves, forbidding the importation of African slaves into the United States.

- **1811-1867** Operating off the Atlantic coast of Africa, the British Navy's Anti-Slavery Squadron liberates 160,000 slaves.

- **1813** Sweden, a nation that never authorized slave traffic, consents to ban the African slave trade.

- **1814** The king of the Netherlands officially terminates Dutch participation in the African slave trade. At the Congress of Vienna, the assembled powers proclaim that the slave trade should be abolished as soon as possible but do not stipulate an actual effective date for abolition.

- **1820** The government of Spain abolishes the slave trade south of the Equator—but it continues in Cuba until 1888.

- **1833** The Factory Act in Britain establishes a working day in textile manufacture, provides for government inspection of working conditions, bans the employment of children under age 9, and limits the workday of children between 13 and 18 years of age to 12 hours.

- **1834** The Abolition Act abolishes slavery throughout the British Empire, including British colonies in North America. The bill emancipates slaves in all British colonies and appropriates nearly $100 million in today's money to compensate slave owners for their losses.

- **1840** The new British and Foreign Anti-Slavery Society calls the first World Anti-Slavery Convention in London to mobilize reformers and assist post-emancipation efforts throughout the world. A group of U.S. abolitionists attends, but Elizabeth Cady Stanton and Lucretia Mott, as well as several male supporters, leave the meeting in protest when women are excluded from seating on the convention floor.

- **1845** The British Navy assigns 36 ships to its Anti-Slavery Squadron, making it one of the largest fleets in the world.

- **1848** The government of France abolishes slavery in all French colonies.

- **1850** The government of Brazil ends the country's participation in the slave trade and declares slave traffic to be a form of piracy.
- **1861** Alexander II emancipates all Russian serfs, numbering about 50 million. His decree begins the Great Reform in Russia and earns him the title "Czar Liberator."
- **1863** President Abraham Lincoln issues The Emancipation Proclamation, freeing all U.S. slaves in states that had seceded from the Union, except for those in Confederate areas already controlled by the Union army.
- **1863** The government of the Netherlands takes official action to abolish slavery in all Dutch colonies.
- **1865** Congress gives final passage to, and a sufficient number of states ratify, the 13th Amendment to the U.S. Constitution to outlaw slavery. The amendment reads: "Neither slavery nor involuntary servitude, except as a punishment for crime whereof the party shall have been duly convicted, shall exist within the United States, or any place subject to their jurisdiction."
- **1888** The *Lei Aurea*, or Golden Law, ends slavery in South America when the legislature of Brazil frees the country's 725,000 slaves.
- **1865-1920** Following the American Civil War, hundreds of thousands of African Americans are re-enslaved in an abusive manipulation of the legal system called "peonage." Across the Deep South, African-American men and women are falsely arrested and convicted of crimes, then "leased" to coal and iron mines, brick factories, plantations, and other dangerous workplaces. The system slows down after World War I but doesn't fully end until the 1940s.

Abolition Spreads Worldwide
- **1909** The Congo Reform Association, founded in Britain, ends forced labour in the Congo Free State, today the Democratic Republic of the Congo. After years of anti-slavery activism, the association's Red Rubber Campaign stops the brutal system of Belgium's King Leopold II, whose officials forced local people to produce rubber for sale in Europe and terrorized those who refused, cutting off their hands and burning down their houses.

- **1910** The International Convention for the Suppression of the White Slave Trade, signed in Paris, is the first of its kind, obligating parties to punish anyone who recruits a woman or girl under age into prostitution, even if she consents.

- **1913** After a public outcry galvanized by media reports and subsequent peoples' petition, the British Parliament shuts down the Peruvian Amazon Company, a British entity that was torturing and exploiting indigenous Indians in Peru.

- **1915** The colonial government of Malaya officially abolishes slavery.

- **1918** The British governor of Hong Kong estimates that the majority of households that could afford it keep a young child as a household slave.

- **1919** The International Labour Organization (ILO) is founded to establish a code of global labour standards. Headquartered in Geneva, the ILO unites government, labour, and management to make recommendations concerning pay, working conditions, trade union rights, safety, woman and child labour, and social security.

- **1923** The British colonial government in Hong Kong bans the selling of little girls as domestic slaves.

- **1926** The League of Nations approves the Slavery Convention, which defines slavery as "status or condition of a person over whom any or all of the powers attaching to the right of ownership are exercised." More than 30 governments sign the document, which charges all member nations to work to suppress all forms of slavery.

- **1926** Burma abolishes legal slavery.

- **1927** Slavery is legally abolished in Sierra Leone, a country founded as a colony by the British in the 18th century to serve as a homeland for freed slaves.

- **1930** The U.S. Tariff Act prohibits the importation of products made with "forced or indentured labour." (In 1997, the Sanders Amendment clarified that this applies to products made with "forced or indentured child labour.")

- **1936** The King of Saudi Arabia issues a decree that ends the importation of new slaves, regulates the conditions of existing slaves, and provides for manumission—the act of slave owners freeing their slaves—under some conditions.

- **1938** The Japanese military establishes "comfort stations"—actually brothels—for Japanese troops. Thousands of Korean and Chinese women are forced into sex slavery during World War II as military "comfort women."
- **1939-1945** The German Nazi government uses widespread slave labour in farming and industry. Up to nine million people are forced to work to absolute exhaustion—then they are sent to concentration camps.
- **1941** The Adoption of Children Ordinance Law in Ceylon, now Sri Lanka, requires the registration of all children who are adopted and regular inspections to prevent adopted children from working as slaves.
- **1948** The Universal Declaration of Human Rights, created by the United Nations, provides: "No one shall be held in slavery or servitude; slavery and the slave trade shall be prohibited in all their forms."
- **1949** The Convention for the Suppression of the Traffic in Persons and Exploitation of the Prostitution of Others prohibits any person from procuring, enticing, or leading away another person for the purposes of prostitution, even with the other person's consent. This forms the legal basis for international protections against traffic in people still used today.

Abolition in Recent Times

- **1950-1989** International anti-slavery work slows during the Cold War, as the Soviet Block argues that slavery can only exist in capitalist societies, and the Western Block argues that all people living under communism are slaves. Both new and traditional forms of slavery in the developing world receive little attention.
- **1954** China passes the State Regulation on Reform through Labour, allowing prisoners to be used for labour in the *laogai* prison camps.
- **1956** The Supplementary Convention on the Abolition of Slavery regulates practices involving serfdom, debt bondage, the sale of wives, and child servitude.
- **1962** Slavery is abolished in Saudi Arabia and Yemen.
- **1964** The sixth World Muslim Congress, the world's oldest Muslim organization, pledges global support for all anti-slavery movements.
- **1973** The U.N. General Assembly adopts the International Convention on the Suppression and Punishment of the Crime of Apartheid, which outlaws a number of inhuman acts, including forced labour, committed for the purposes of establishing and maintaining domination by one racial group over another.

- **1974** Mauritania's emancipated slaves form the El Hor ("freedom") movement to oppose slavery, which continues to this day. El Hor leaders insist that emancipation is impossible without realistic means of enforcing anti-slavery laws and giving former slaves the means of achieving economic independence. El Hor demands land reform and encourages the formation of agricultural cooperatives.

- **1975** The U.N. Working Group on Contemporary Forms of Slavery is founded to collect information and make recommendations on slavery and slavery-like practices around the world.

- **1976** India passes a law banning bonded labour.

- **1980** Slavery is abolished for the fourth time in the Islamic republic of Mauritania, but the situation is not fundamentally changed. Although the law decrees that "slavery" no longer exists, the ban does not address how masters are to be compensated or how slaves are to gain property.

- **1989** The National Islamic Front takes over the government of Sudan and begins to arm Baggara tribesmen to fight the Dinka and Nuer tribes in the south. These new militias raid villages, capturing and enslaving inhabitants.

- **1989** The U.N. Convention on the Rights of the Child promotes basic health care, education, and protection for the young from abuse, exploitation, or neglect at home, at work, and in armed conflicts. All countries ratify it except Somalia and the United States.

- **1990** After adoption by 54 countries in the 1980s, the 19th Conference of Foreign Ministers of the Organization of the Islamic Conference formally adopts the Cairo Declaration on Human Rights in Islam, which states that "human beings are born free, and no one has the right to enslave, humiliate, oppress, or exploit them."

- **1992** The Pakistan National Assembly enacts the Bonded Labour Act, which abolishes indentured servitude and the *peshgi*, or bonded money, system. However, the government fails to provide for the implementation and enforcement of the law's provisions.

- **1995** The U.S. government issues the Model Business Principles, which urges all businesses to adopt and implement voluntary codes of conduct, including the avoidance of child and forced labour, as well as discrimination based on race, gender, national origin, or religious beliefs.

- **1995** Christian Solidarity International, a Swiss-based charity, begins to liberate slaves in Southern Sudan by buying them back. The policy ignites widespread controversy—many international agencies argue that

288

buying back slaves supports the market in human beings and feeds resources to slaveholders.

- **1996** The RugMark campaign is established in Germany to ensure that handwoven rugs are not made with slave or child labour. In 2010, RugMark changes its name to GoodWeave.
- **1996** The World Congress Against Commercial Sexual Exploitation of Children is held.
- **1997** The U.N. establishes a commission of inquiry to investigate reports of the widespread enslavement of people by the Burmese government.
- **1997** The United States bans imported goods made by child-bonded labour.
- **1998** The Global March against Child Labour is established to coordinate worldwide demonstrations against child labour and to call for a U.N. Convention on the Worst Forms of Child Labour.
- **1999** Despite being barred from entering Burma, the U.N. collects sufficient evidence to publicly condemn government-sponsored slavery, including unpaid forced labour and a brutal political system built on the use of force and intimidation to deny democracy and the rule of law.
- **1999** The ILO passes the Convention Against the Worst Forms of Child Labour, which establishes widely recognized international standards protecting children against forced or indentured labour, child prostitution and pornography, their use in drug trafficking, and other harmful work.
- **1999** The first global analysis of modern slavery and its role in the global economy, *Disposable People: New Slavery in the Global Economy*, estimates that there are 27 million people in slavery worldwide.

Abolition in the 21st Century
- **2000** Free the Slaves is formed, originally as the sister organization of Anti-Slavery International in the U.K. Today Free the Slaves is an independent organization.
- **2000** The government of Nepal bans all forms of debt bondage after a lengthy campaign by human rights organizations and freed labourers.
- **2000** The U.S. Congress passes the Trafficking Victims Protection Act to combat the trafficking of persons as a form of modern slavery. The legislation increases penalties for traffickers, provides social services for trafficking victims, and helps victims remain in the country.

- **2000** The U.N. passes the Protocol to Prevent, Suppress, and Punish Trafficking in Persons as part of the Convention against Transnational Organized Crime. The trafficking protocol is the first global legally binding instrument with an internationally agreed-upon definition on trafficking in persons.

- **2001** *Slavery: A Global Investigation*—the first major documentary film about modern slavery—is released in the U.S. and Europe. The film tells the story of slavery and forced child labour in the cocoa and chocolate industry and wins a Peabody Award and two Emmy Awards.

- **2002** The countries of the Economic Community of Western African States agree on an action plan to confront slavery and human trafficking in the region.

- **2002** The International Cocoa Initiative is established as a joint effort of anti-slavery groups and major chocolate companies—marking the first time an entire industry has banded together to address slavery in its supply chain.

- **2004** Brazil launches the National Pact for the Eradication of Slave Labour, which combines the efforts of civil organizations, businesses, and the government to get companies to commit to the prevention and eradication of forced labour within their supply chains, as well as to be monitored and placed on a "dirty list" if the products they sell are tainted by slavery.

- **2004** The U.N. appoints a Special Rapporteur (Reporter) on Human Trafficking.

- **2005** The U.N. International Labour Organization's first Global Report on Forced Labour puts the number of slaves worldwide at 12.3 million. The organization's 2012 update increases the number to 20.9 million people.

- **2007** *Ending Slavery: How We Free Today's Slaves* is published. Written by Free the Slaves co-founder Kevin Bales, it is the first plan for the global eradication of modern slavery, estimating the total cost of worldwide abolition at $10.8 billion over 25 years. President Bill Clinton highlights the plan at the Clinton Global Initiative. The book receives the 2011 University of Louisville Grawemeyer Award for Ideas Improving World Order.

- **2008** The Special Court for Sierra Leone judges forced marriage "a crime against humanity" and convicts three officers in the Revolutionary United Front of forced marriage—the first convictions of their kind within an international criminal tribunal.

- **2008** The U.N. International Labour Organization estimates that annual profits generated from trafficking in human beings are as high as $32 billion. In 2014 the organization increases that estimate to $150 billion in the report *Profits and Poverty: The Economics of Forced Labour.*

- **2010** Free the Slaves publishes *Slavery*, featuring images of slaves and survivors taken by humanitarian photographer Lisa Kristine and a foreword by South African Archbishop Emeritus Desmond Tutu. Kristine receives a 2013 Humanitarian Photographer of the Year Award from the Lucie foundation based in large part on her work with Free the Slaves.

- **2011** California enacts the California Transparency in Supply Chains Act, requiring major manufacturing and retail firms to publicly disclose what efforts, if any, they are taking to eliminate forced labour and human trafficking from their product supply chains.

- **2012** The U.S. Securities and Exchange Commission passes the Conflict Minerals Rule, requiring major publicly-held corporations to disclose if their products contain certain metals mined in the eastern Congo or an adjoining country and if payment for these minerals supports armed conflict in the region. The rule was required as part of the 2010 Dodd-Frank Wall Street Reform and Consumer Protection Act. Free the Slaves has documented that slavery is widespread at mining sites covered by this corporate disclosure requirement.

- **2013** The first Walk Free Global Slavery Index is released with country-by-country estimates for slavery worldwide. The research team estimates that 29.8 million people are enslaved today. The 2014 index increases that estimate to 35.8 million. The 2016 index increases that estimate to 45.8 million.

- **2015** Free the Slaves marks its 15th birthday by announcing that the organization has reached a historic benchmark—liberating more than 10,000 people from slavery.

- **2015** The U.N. adopts 17 Sustainable Development Goals, with 169 targets that include an end to slavery: "Take immediate and effective measures to eradicate forced labour, end modern slavery and human trafficking and secure the prohibition and elimination of the worst forms of child labour, including recruitment and use of child soldiers, and by 2025 end child labour in all its forms."

- **2017** A research consortium including the U.N. International Labour Organization, the group Walk Free, and the U.N. International Organization for Migration release a combined global study indicating that

40 million people are trapped in modern forms of slavery worldwide: 50 percent in forced labour in agriculture, manufacturing, construction, mining, fishing and other physical-labour industries; 12.5 percent in sex slavery, and 37.5 percent in forced marriage slavery.

Many historical timeline entries are adapted from New Slavery: A Reference Handbook *by Kevin Bales, Second Edition, Santa Barbara: ABC-CLIO, 2004, pp. 55-68.*

www.ingramcontent.com/pod-product-compliance
Lightning Source LLC
Chambersburg PA
CBHW071412290326
41932CB00047B/2591

9789956550579